PROMISES
KEPT

SPIEGEL & GRAU TRADE PAPERBACKS
NEW YORK

PROMISES KEPT

Raising Black Boys
to Succeed in School
and in Life

**Joe Brewster, M.D., and
Michèle Stephenson**

with Hilary Beard

A Spiegel & Grau Trade Paperback Original

Published in the United States by Spiegel & Grau, an imprint of Random House, a division of Random House LLC, a Penguin Random House Company, New York.

SPIEGEL & GRAU and the HOUSE colophon are registered trademarks of Random House LLC.

Library of Congress Cataloging-in-Publication Data
Brewster, Joe (Psychiatrist)
  Promises kept : raising Black boys to succeed in school and in life / Joe Brewster, M.D., Michèle Stephenson, Hilary Beard.
      pages cm
  Includes bibliographical references and index.
  ISBN 978-0-8129-8489-7 (alk. paper)—ISBN 978-0-8129-9449-0 (ebook : alk. paper)
1. African American boys—Education. 2. African American boys—Conduct of life. 3. African American boys—Social conditions. 4. Academic achievement—United States. 5. Educational equalization—United States. 6. Parenting—United States. I. Title.
  LC2731.B73 2013
  371.829'96073—dc23   2013015343

Printed in the United States of America on acid-free paper

www.spiegelandgrau.com

987654321

First Edition

Book design by Karin Batten

To our black and brown sons, brothers,
fathers, and friends, who by accident of birth
were born into a society that often cannot see them.

"The truth is the light and the light is the truth."

RALPH ELLISON, *Invisible Man*

CONTENTS

5 HUG HIM AND TELL HIM YOU LOVE HIM: How to Use Parenting Styles that Work

6 YOU BROUGHT HIM INTO THIS WORLD, DON'T LET OTHER FOLKS TAKE HIM OUT: How to Discipline Our Sons for Best Results

7 PROTECT HIM FROM TIME BANDITS: How to Teach Our Sons to Manage Their Time

8 EDUCATION TO MATCH HIS NEEDS: How to Understand Our Sons' Learning Styles and Special Needs

9 WORKING HARD WILL MAKE HIM SMARTER: How to Teach Our Sons to Combat Stereotype Threat and Develop Persistence

10 **MAKE YOUR PRESENCE FELT IN HIS SCHOOL: How to Participate in Our Sons' Formal School and Advocate for Change**

INTRODUCTION

The year was 1998—when Google was founded, impeachment hearings against Bill Clinton began, Lauryn Hill sang about "miseducation," and Jay Z rhymed about the "Hard Knock Life." We were a young black family in Brooklyn trying to figure out how to get our soon-to-be-four-year-old son the education he deserved—one that would help him evade the pitfalls and limitations that tripped up so many black boys. One that would allow him to fulfill his potential.

We lived in the Clinton Hill/Fort Greene section of Brooklyn, New York, before gentrification—back when the community was more racially and socioeconomically diverse and bustling with artists: writers, actors, visual artists, and filmmakers like us. We had purchased a fixer-upper across the street from what would have been our neighborhood elementary school. Unfortunately, it was the sort of public school that is all too common in New York and other big cities: no one who had any other options would ever send their child there. So we began to explore our options for Idris, our firstborn son, who was then three years old.

Both of us had grown up in low-income families. Joe is from South Central Los Angeles, and Michèle was born in Haiti (she is of Haitian and Panamanian descent). Michèle had attended predominately white public schools in Canada, where she had been teased for being different, called a nigger. She wanted Idris to attend a good public school, but one where he could have a multicultural experience and not be subjected to the racial isolation and teasing that she'd been through.

Joe had gone to Crenshaw High in Los Angeles, which was public and predominately black and Asian. In college—at Stanford—he'd had to play catch-up academically. But at Stanford he was also exposed to exceptionally bright black students who arrived much better prepared than he was: He remembered a kid called Milwaukee, who could write an eighty-page term paper on the night before it was due, and another one who smoked weed but would still score highly on math exams. Joe envisioned Idris as Milwaukee meets math geek—preferably minus the marijuana.

Both Milwaukee and math geek had gotten a college preparatory, or prep school, education. Prep schools operate independently from local school systems and receive their funding from a combination of tuition and donations, primarily from alumni. They typically offer more rigorous academics and smaller class sizes—*Forbes* lists some as having student-to-teacher ratios as low as 5 to 1—than you'll find in even the best public schools.[1] Many cost around $15,000 per year, but the most prestigious private schools now fall in the $30,000–$35,000 range. If they are boarding schools, throw in another ten grand for your kid to live on campus. Needless to say, prep schools mostly educate the elite. For parents, the tuition is a steep investment, but the return for their kids is a superior education, a social network of elites, and average SAT scores north of 2000 on a 2400-point scale. Most prep school graduates go on to attend the top tier of colleges and universities.

That's what we wanted for Idris. His test scores—in the top 3 percent—were high enough for a gifted and talented (G&T) program, but we were shocked to discover that New York City's public G&T programs are almost exclusively composed of white and Asian, middle-class and affluent children. If we were going to put Idris in a predominately white, privileged environment, we figured we might as well go all the way and get the full range of benefits a prep school promised. Unfortunately, we didn't have private-school money. Someone directed us to Early Steps, a program that helps families of color with grade school–aged children connect with prep schools. When we asked the woman from Early Steps what schools were offering financial aid, she said, "Your son is a Dalton boy."

The Dalton School educates the children of New York City's elite, from the scions of the city's old-money families to the children of artists and others who have risen to the forefront of their fields. The school is also an academic powerhouse: Today, the *average* SAT score there is 2200 out of a possible 2400; the *bottom half* of the high school's graduating class has higher SAT scores than the *top twenty-five students* in most other schools around the country.

Joe went on a Dalton School parents' tour and came home insisting that Michèle visit right away. Michèle had been warned away from Dalton by a Jewish coworker who had gone there fifteen years earlier and had found it too elite and cliquish. But when Michèle went on the school tour, she was completely blown away by the school's commitment to fostering children's social and emotional growth, building self-esteem, and creating "passionate lifelong learners." Babby Krentz, the headmistress (a fancy name for a principal), told us that Dalton was also newly committed to making its demographics match those of Manhattan itself, which is roughly 50 percent non-white. When the school admitted Idris and offered us great financial aid, there was no way that we could turn the opportunity down. We had Milwaukee, math geek, multicultural—and now money!

Idris was admitted to Dalton's third class under this new diversity initiative. It appeared that almost 25 percent of his class consisted of African Americans, Caribbean blacks, Latinos, and/or children of Asian descent. And the icing on the cake? His friend, Oluwaseun ("Seun," pronounced "shay-on") Summers, had also gotten in. Seun's parents, Tony and Stacey, were as excited and hopeful as we were. Our sons would have an experience available only to a privileged few—one that we dreamed would allow this black boy to bypass racism and achieve his human potential. Since he would be something of a pioneer, we were sure that our son would encounter racial prejudice, issues related to socioeconomic class, and other difference-related challenges. But we had overcome those issues, and Idris could too. We would help him. We promised.

THE PRICE OF ADMISSION

In addition to being excited as parents, our inner filmmaker was thrilled, too. Wouldn't it be fascinating to film a documentary about diversity in this elite, historically white environment? we thought. It could be a longitudinal film similar to the *Up* series, which had checked in with fourteen British children every seven years beginning in 1964 (the most recent film in the series was *56 Up,* which was released in the United States in 2013). Perhaps we could follow a diverse group of kids through their twelve-year journey at Dalton.

We asked Seun's parents Tony and Stacey as well as the parents of two other students of diverse backgrounds—a white girl and a mixed Latina-Greek girl—and the school leadership at Dalton if they would be involved. They all agreed. We started filming at school, in our homes, and at various events in each student's life (recitals, birthday parties, and the like) for a few days each month. We had high hopes that our film would capture the possibilities that diversity and a great education offered. But had we known then what we would document, we might never have picked up a camera.

Everything at Dalton started off well. In the beginning we shot the footage ourselves, which meant that we were in the classroom relatively often (the older the boys became, the more they resisted having us behind the camera). We were excited to see Dalton's imaginative approach and access to resources on display in the early grades, like when Idris learned about reproduction in kindergarten by studying, incubating, and raising baby chicks in the classroom. But it didn't take long for us to have some concerns. Just two weeks into first grade, Idris's teacher claimed that he was behind in his reading. The school wanted him to participate in special supportive reading sessions that would pull him out of the classroom. We were shocked! They had decided this based on observing him and without getting to know anything about Idris or his abilities. He had come in reading at a very high level and had continued reading at a high level. We thought they were awfully quick and just a little too comfortable in reaching that conclusion—especially when they offered nothing concrete as evidence. When we pushed back, they told us that we had not quite understood—if this had been public school Idris would be fine, but at Dalton his skills wouldn't cut it.

Excuse you!

It is still painful to remember how humiliating and poorly managed those early conversations were—and how naive we were in our belief that Dalton was prepared to educate *our* son. Coming from humble beginnings, neither of us were (or are) quick to throw our credentials around, but did the teacher know that we both were Ivy League graduates with graduate degrees? (In addition to being filmmakers, Joe is a Harvard-educated psychiatrist; Michèle is a Columbia-educated lawyer.) Did the school realize how much time we spent with our son? Did they know how much we read to him? Did they see how verbal Idris was (and is)? What if he had just not been feeling well on the day the observation was made? The reading support had begun right away, but we insisted to the head of the lower school that he not be removed from the classroom. We also asked that they reconsider their assessment. They realized that he didn't need reading support after all. This was one of several early incidents that were all somewhat ambiguous—we didn't yet understand their common roots in racial bias—but created enough of a pattern to make us feel defensive.

As if these sorts of incidents weren't bothersome enough, Idris and Seun were becoming unsettled emotionally. Some of Idris's classmates had interrogated him about whether his parents were rich or poor, which made him very uncomfortable. He decided that he didn't like the name Idris and wanted to change it to John or Tom. Apparently Seun had begun criticizing things at home that related to black people. One night he had brushed his gums until they bled—he wanted pink gums like the white kids' gums, not brown gums like his own. Add academic stresses on top of that. The level of rigor and learning was tremendous. Our sons were competing with the children of millionaires. On one occasion Seun vomited when the teacher called him to the front of the class. In second grade Seun and in third grade Idris began to struggle scholastically. Both sets of parents were surprised, since the boys' test scores up to that point had been very high. Idris now had trouble focusing. He would forget to bring home his homework; when he did his homework, he would forget to turn it in, or he would do well on his homework but get low grades on his tests. None of this made sense, given how hard he was trying. The school suggested that we have him tested for ADD. We didn't buy it. We were convinced that he was going through normal "boy stuff." We had heard many white parents talking about boys forgetting, getting distracted, or struggling with being organized—the same issues we were experiencing with Idris. We worried that he was getting picked on because he was black. In the end, it turned out to be more complicated than that—but we'll get to that story later.

Our concerns about Dalton's ability to handle the needs of a black boy continued to mount. When Idris was in fourth grade, the school had suspended him for two days for hitting another student, a boy who had also hit Idris but had not been punished. Adding insult to injury, the school had suspended our son for an additional day for allegedly lying about not hitting the boy. Idris insisted that he was telling the truth, and knowing a lot about how our son behaved when he lied, we believed him. Was Idris suspended because he was black and the other boy was white? Because the other kid's parents were among Dalton's benefactors and we weren't? For some other reason? There was no way to know. But our Spidey senses were tingling.

By sixth grade Dalton was sending us warnings that Idris was not performing up to the standard the school expected at his grade level. Our constant interventions—from homework help to assisting him to stay organized—helped him keep up, barely. Seun fell behind and was put on academic watch. The school suggested that Seun and Idris take advantage of tutoring that they offered to students on financial aid, which we did. Only later did we learn that the only two kids in the sixth grade seeing the tutor also happened to be the only two black boys. At first we were insulted. But then the school told us that they offered the free tutoring to help level the playing field—apparently our sons' classmates had been getting private tutoring all along; we just hadn't known about it. And not only had they been getting tutored for years, they had been getting tutored to the tune of *$20,000 to $30,000 a year.*

We were flabbergasted! Were they really telling us that a $25,000-a-year education wasn't enough?! No wonder our sons couldn't keep up! We had stumbled across the inner workings of the Educational-Industrial Complex, a world where private tutors and test-prep classes help middle-class and (especially) affluent families customize their children's educational experiences, increase their children's study time, and maximize their children's academic capacities. Back then people were paying $250 an hour for some of these private tutors. We couldn't afford that. (Today, we understand, the range is between $400 and $500 an hour. Imagine . . .) Ultimately these tutoring sessions weren't enough, though. Both Idris and Seun needed more.

The emotional wear and tear on the boys was extremely hard to stomach. Idris was scoring in the 97th percentile nationally on sixth grade tests, but when he went to school, he felt like a failure. Seun hated school.

Idris was also struggling with identity issues. From time to time he would question us about how he fit into the stereotypes that our society spins about black males—that they are dumb, criminal, violent, dangerous, and naturally gifted athletes and performers. It shocked us to learn that at times even Idris felt more capable of playing in the NBA than being a scientist, the latter of which was far more likely. As he moved back and forth between his predominately white educational environment and his predominately black community at home, we watched him struggle to *code-switch*—change his speech patterns and dialect as he navigated back and forth across cultures. One of his white basketball teammates at Dalton was picking on him, but so were some of the kids on the mostly black team he played with on weekends, who had been bullying him and telling him he talked "white."

Culturally, emotionally, and socially, Idris was struggling, and it was starting to look as though his spirit might break. We'd known that Dalton would exact an emotional price, but we were starting to think maybe that price was too high. Of course, we could always have pulled him out of Dalton, but we hoped not to have to do that. We had gotten him into this mess, and it was our responsibility to help him figure it out. In the meantime, one by one the families in our diversity film had dropped out of the project, except the Summerses. But Tony and Stacey were concerned about exposing Seun's difficulties. We kept filming even though we no longer knew what our film would be about. Increasingly, the cameras were capturing the struggles, tears, frustration, and yelling that were becoming more common in our homes—and the less picture-perfect side of Dalton.

MIND THE GAP

We vowed to figure out how to help our son. We decided that we would start by talking to some psychiatrists about why so many black boys struggle during middle school. We also wanted advice on how to support Idris emotionally and academically: we wanted to help him get test scores that would reflect his level of effort, resist the very limiting and negative images of black males that the media was bombarding him with, and develop a healthy sense of himself that would allow him to navigate different environments and cultures.

Joe arranged a meeting with his mentor, the acclaimed black child development pioneer, Dr. Alvin Poussaint, who is also a psychiatry professor at Harvard Medical School. We went with two goals in mind. First, we wanted to show Dr. Poussaint some of the footage we had gotten with Idris's behavior—for instance, his efforts to try to fit in as he moved between middle-class and low-income black communities and then again between those black communities and the wealthy whites at Dalton—in the hopes that he could give us some advice on how to handle it. We also wanted to film the conversation with Dr. Poussaint. Our documentary was morphing into something that we couldn't quite wrap our heads around, but we knew it would involve black boys. We had a feeling that Dr. Poussaint might end up being a part of it.

During the meeting, Dr. Poussaint described how stages of childhood development play out differently for black boys because of the unique challenges that they face. He made some parenting suggestions based on the footage—about fitting in, for instance. He suggested that obstacles we faced were temporary and commonplace. Dr. Poussaint supported us and encouraged us to persevere. He also directed us toward a network of leading authorities on black boys, black families, and multicultural education. Among the experts we would eventually connect with were urban sociologist Pedro Noguera, a professor at New York University and an expert in education, black boys, and *achievement gaps*, the academic performance deficits that impact almost all black boys; Joshua Aronson, an associate professor at NYU known for his research on *stereotype threat*, a type of performance anxiety that can cause black boys in particular to test very poorly; Jelani Mandara, a professor at Northwestern University and an expert in black families and parenting styles; Ron Ferguson, the economics professor who heads Harvard University's Achievement Gap Initiative, which focuses on narrowing these types of academic gaps; and Sonia Nieto, a professor at the University of Massachusetts at Amherst, and an expert on teacher training and multicultural education. We already knew Ivory Toldson, an author, Howard University counseling psychology professor, and a senior researcher for the Congressional Black Caucus Foundation before being appointed in 2013 deputy director of the White House's Initiative on Historically Black Colleges and Universities. Since we were making a film, Dr. Poussaint recommended that we also write a book to extend the conversation. He told us that nothing about black boys had been published for a long time. But a book was the last thing on our minds. We were just hell-bent on saving our son.

Between the time Idris was twelve and the time he turned seventeen, we picked the brains of some of our nation's top minds in a wide variety of disciplines that relate to black boys. Some were blown away that we had captured on videotape several of the developmental and racial dynamics they had been researching and writing about for years. They suggested that the video we had compiled would be priceless in advancing the conversation about black boys. In fact, most let us videotape them sharing their expertise about black boys, even though we were still figuring out what our film would become. They also introduced us to some long-standing advocates in education and black male development—from the Black Alliance for Educational Options (BAEO) and the Center for Urban Families to the Coalition of Schools Educating Boys of Color (COSEBOC).

These experts helped us understand the magnitude of the problem. For example, they taught us that educational achievement gaps are not exclusive to race: they exist between rich and poor children, boys and girls, blacks and whites, whites and Asians, whites and Latinos, and American children and their international peers. In fact, the gap between low-income and affluent children of all races is growing exponentially, as wealthier parents invest in their children in ways that other families cannot compete with. We were particularly interested in the black/white gap, which was most visible in the often inexplicably low GPAs and test scores that black children tend to earn compared to their white peers. The gaps affecting black boys are particularly disturbing. We were shocked to learn the following things:

- On the 2011 National Assessment of Educational Progress test (also called the Nation's Report Card), only 10 percent of black eighth grade males were reading on an eighth grade level, as compared to 16 percent of Latino males and 35 percent of white males.[2] (Notice that even white boys are performing poorly.)
- In a study of more than 7,100 students attending 95 high-performing suburban high schools, 50 percent of whites and Asians had an A or A- grade point average, whereas only 15 percent of blacks and 21 percent of Hispanics did; 35 percent of black and 26 percent of Hispanic students had a C+ to C- average, but only 12 percent of whites and Asians did.[3]
- Black children are three times more likely to be suspended or expelled from school than their white peers—causing them to miss valuable classroom learning time, depressing their academic performance, and increasing the risk that they'll repeat a grade and eventually drop out of school. They are often suspended or expelled for minor or discretionary offenses like being tardy or using their cell phones.[4] Black kids represent 18 percent of all students, but 35 percent of students suspended once, 46 percent of those suspended multiple times, and 39 percent of all students

expelled.[5] Black boys comprise 9 percent of students but 24 percent of students who received out-of-school suspensions and 26 percent of students who were expelled, pushing them into what is known as the school-to-prison pipeline.[6] Not only do black students tend to get punished more often for the same offenses that white children commit, but when they do get punished they also tend to be punished more harshly.[7]

- Even though giftedness is evenly distributed through the population, black boys are 2.5 times less likely to be enrolled in G&T programs, even if their prior achievement demonstrates their ability to succeed. Once students are "locked out" of these programs and tracked into lower-level coursework in elementary school, they tend to remain there for the duration of their academic years. A strong correlation exists that links race, gender, class, and academic-track placement.[8]

- Black boys are no more likely than other children to be diagnosed with a learning disability but are almost 40 percent more likely to be placed in special education. Many black boys in special education *don't have a disability*.

- Black boys are 2.5 times more likely to be classified as mentally retarded. Black male students comprise 9 percent of the student population but 20 percent of all students classified as mentally retarded.[9]

- Only 52 percent of black male students graduate high school within four years, as compared to 58 percent of Latino males, and 78 percent of white males. This, however, reflects an increase of ten percentage points over the 42 percent four-year graduation rate in 2002.[10] Eighty percent of black males have completed high school or have gone on to obtain a GED.[11] Eleven percent of black males drop out, leaving more than two million black men in America without a high school education.[12]

- Black males disproportionately lack the resources and support to complete college. In 2008, 4.6 million black males attended college, but only half actually graduated. Nationally, only 11 percent of black males complete a bachelor's degree.[13] However, both the number and percentage of black males with college degrees are increasing.

We know that people often blame the victim when they see this kind of information and that some will wrongly interpret these facts as "proof" of black male inferiority. But institutional racism, entrenched institutional practices that create a concrete ceiling on opportunity for students of color, and structural and systemic obstacles—primarily poverty and underfunded schools—make it impossible for many black boys to get the education that will allow them to fulfill their potential. As the Schott Foundation for Public Education stated in its 2012 report: "[We] firmly believe these data are not indicative of a character flaw in black boys and men, but rather they are evidence of an unconscionable level of willful neglect and disparate resource allocation by federal, state, and local entities and a level of indifference by too many community leaders." Amen. These statistics reflect gaps in outcomes, but underneath them lie the many structural, systemic, cultural, and personal gaps—and failures—that our society seems not to want to discuss. There are gaps in wealth and income, gaps in the enforcement of drug laws and administration of criminal justice, gaps in employment, gaps in health, gaps in nutrition, gaps in school and neighborhood segregation, gaps in funding (particularly of urban schools in neighborhoods of color), gaps in teacher quality and experience level, gaps in the rigor of course offerings in certain schools, and gaps in media portrayals. There are gaps in the number of parents in homes; gaps in parents' education levels; gaps in social and cultural capital; gaps in the number of books in homes; gaps in the hours of television watched; gaps in the expectations black parents have of their sons as opposed to their daughters; and gaps in levels of school involvement. And beyond that, there are gaps in educators' knowledge of the lives of black and brown children; gaps in know-how about how to teach black boys effectively; gaps in educators' expectations of black, brown, and poor children; gaps in society's understanding of black children's strengths and how to leverage them; and gaps in knowledge of how to parent or co-parent a black boy in a society that vilifies him. Uncomfortable, unconscionable gaps that we are all a part of and that compound over the course of children's lives.

IT'S BIGGER THAN US

Since poverty contributes to some of these shortfalls, we assumed that neither the traditional achievement gaps nor the gaps behind the gaps affected middle- and higher-income black boys. Boy, were we wrong. Ron Ferguson, the head of Harvard University's Achievement Gap Initiative, hipped us to the fact that black middle-class and upper-income boys generally don't achieve to their academic ability either.

"One of the patterns in the data that people find most surprising is that the gaps in test scores tend to be largest among the children of the most educated parents," Dr. Ferguson told us. "In the National Assessment of Educational Progress (NAEP), if we compare the test scores of the children of whites whose parents are college-educated with blacks whose parents are college-educated, there's a bigger gap than if you compare the test scores of children whose parents have less education."

You could have picked us up off the floor. But the truth is we knew that even with Idris's relatively privileged background, he was struggling compared to his white peers and so were his friends. It was something of a relief to know the challenges we were experiencing were bigger than us. It was also distressing. Professor Aronson talked to us about how to help our son perform better on tests but he also told us not to be surprised if Idris still scored 100 points lower than his peers on each of the three portions of the SAT. We protested, but Dr. Aronson turned out to be right. Idris scored well, especially compared to the national average of 1500.[14] But he didn't reach 2200—the average Dalton score. The distance between those two scores is enough to keep a child from attending the college of his dreams. The question we still had to answer was *why*?

We learned more about the special social and emotional stresses faced by black boys in predominately white settings that are, at best,

ambivalent about their presence. These stressors include feeling insecure, developing self-esteem issues related to whether they belong or
are accepted, having to code-switch, experiencing implicit and explicit bias from their peers and teachers, and suffering from stereotype threat (don't worry if you're not familiar with all of these terms,
we'll break them down later in the book). Both Idris and Seun were
having these types of troubles. In fact, one of our most heartbreaking
moments as parents was listening to Idris talk about being invited to
bar mitzvahs at the time when many of his Jewish classmates were
having them. He told us that he enjoyed them—except for the part
when you have to dance with a girl. His female classmates wouldn't
dance with him. This confused and hurt him deeply—he suspected
that his race was the problem, which made him wonder aloud to us
whether he would be better off if he had been born white.

CANARIES IN THE MINE

But black boys' academic and emotional struggles don't occur in isolation. Education in the United States is in crisis—for all students.
Students in Australia, Canada, Finland, Hong Kong, Shanghai
(China), Singapore, and other countries have far surpassed American
kids,[15] who now earn only average scores in reading and science and
below-average scores in math on tests of student achievement interna-
tionally.[16] And the problems are especially acute among boys. Beginning in early elementary school and continuing through their college
years, girls are earning higher scores than boys and surpass their male
classmates in graduating high school and college.[17]

There's an African American folk adage: "When white folks
sneeze, black folks catch a cold." At a 2010 conference about black
males convened by the Educational Testing Service (ETS), Oscar Barbarin, Ph.D., the head of Tulane University's psychology department,
characterized black males as being like a "finely tuned barometer," a
"canary in the mines," or an "early warning signal that things are not
right" in American society. We were surprised to discover that conversations both about achievement gaps and about reducing the prej-

udice directed at black boys are taking place not only at Harvard and the Educational Testing Service but also at major foundations, in educational nonprofits, in schools, and across other diverse sectors of American society, public and private. Our leaders know that the nation's future depends increasingly upon children of color, that achievement gaps are undermining our competitiveness, and that creating an environment in which all children can excel is vital to our nation's success in a global economy. But while a lot of people have been talking *about* black boys, we think that more conversations should take place *with* black parents as well as educators. We didn't know about these gaps, or the gaps within gaps, or how to close them, and we were betting that many other parents—and a lot of our sons' teachers—didn't know either.

As we began to talk to various educational experts, we began to think that our film—which had evolved into an educational coming-of-age story called *American Promise* that would chronicle Idris's and Seun's educational journeys—could help spark a greater conversation about the barriers that all of our sons face and how to remove them. We envisioned viewers leaving the theater with concrete takeaways to implement in their homes, extended families, schools, churches, and communities. If a lot of people were willing to make one small change, we imagined, maybe the collective impact would transform the environment surrounding our sons.

That's when we remembered Dr. Poussaint's suggestion to write a book. It would be criminal to hoard the information that so many experts had generously shared or to pretend that we had navigated our tough times on our own. Other black parents deserve to have the same information that we did. Imagine the possibilities! As one African proverb states: If you want to go fast, go alone; if you want to go far, go together.

ABOUT THIS BOOK

In this book we will share what we learned along our journey that helped us to support our son in fulfilling his promise. We also reached out to more than sixty of the most accomplished researchers in the nation, experts who are performing cutting-edge studies on a wide variety of issues that impact the intellectual, social, and emotional well-being of black boys. Indeed, a lot is known about how to create an environment in which black males will succeed. Within these pages we set forth ten parenting and educational strategies that researchers have discovered can assist parents, educators, and other members of their proverbial "Village"—aunties, uncles, neighbors, coaches, youth leaders, faith leaders, and others—in helping black boys become the happy, healthy, well-educated, well-developed people they are capable of being. These ideas are intended to address both the achievement gaps captured by official government assessments such as the Nation's Report Card and No Child Left Behind (NCLB) but also some of the gaps that lie beneath these gaps.

We share these strategies through the lens of our personal experiences raising Idris and Miles and through the stories of other black parents and boys from many different backgrounds, including Tony, Stacey, and Seun. To protect their privacy, we have masked the identifying characteristics of most of these parents and children, except in the final chapter, where some activists and advocates asked us to use their real names. For similar reasons we do not include the names of the educators who have shared the joys, challenges, and heartbreaks they've experienced while teaching and co-parenting our sons. We do, however, credit the many academic and medical experts whose research and ideas have informed the strategies. Importantly, although they strongly impact the outcomes of black children's lives, we will not delve into the social, political, economic, or historical factors that have resulted in unearned privilege for some and unearned disadvantage for others, including depressed black male achievement. Experts ranging from Michelle Alexander, to Lisa Delpit, to Asa Hilliard III, to Jonathan Kozol, to Carter Woodson and some of the scholars we've interviewed can do a far better job of shedding light on these topics than we can. We encourage you to educate yourself.

To our surprise, even before we finished writing *Promises Kept,* we started to receive feedback about it. A lot of folks wanted to swap horror stories, but three concerns surfaced repeatedly:

- Why were we writing a book about black boys when black girls are struggling also?
- Why were we writing a book only about black boys when boys of all races and backgrounds are in crisis?
- And why were we airing black people's and Dalton's "dirty laundry" in an era when our nation has elected a black male as president—not once but twice—and the school has been so progressive?

In response, we say that we hope that *Promises Kept* helps improve the lives of all children, but in our household we are raising black males. The questions we asked, the information we gathered, and the advocacy in which we engaged pertains directly to our sons. That said, many of the ideas we share transcend race, gender, and color. We encourage you to apply whatever seems relevant to your own experience, no matter the background of the child you are parenting or teaching. When possible, we include information about black girls (whose well-being is closely intertwined with that of their brothers) and Latinos, who often face challenges similar to black boys' (also, through Michèle's ancestry, Idris and Miles have Panamanian heritage). In the few instances where data include mixed-race children, we report it, although children of many backgrounds can be classified as mixed-race. And while we don't buy into the stereotype of Asians as a "model minority," in certain areas Asian children set the performance standard. When it makes sense and the data are available we include them in the statistics.

What about the question of dirty laundry? The Dalton School has provided our son with an amazing education, has been a forerunner in providing a diverse independent-school education—today the number of students of color at the school has significantly increased since Idris started kindergarten—and were very generous to allow us to film at the school, although as with everyone else, there were times they backed out. No institution is perfect, and Dalton, with its tremendous resources and emphasis on critical thinking, has a great capacity to absorb, benefit, and grow from the critique they receive from us. In fact, Dalton still has a lot of growing to do. While it is

critical—especially as the nation's racial demographics are changing—
that independent schools increase the number of diverse students they
educate, that is only the first step.

Particularly in elite schools such as Dalton, but also in our public
schools, deeper conversations need to occur with parents of all backgrounds, not just the parents of color whose children are entering
predominately white environments. White parents need to understand that diversity is not a one-way street; diversity benefits their
children as well. And schools need to advance beyond entry-level activities such as celebrating our respective heritages. School leaders
should be encouraging critical thinking and the unpacking of issues
such as white privilege, the impact that stereotypes and racial bias
have on children of all backgrounds, and the important role that af-
firmative action plays (especially come college application time)—and
not just with the students, but with parents and faculty also. These
are difficult conversations, but are an integral part of reducing the
racial achievement gap for students who go this route.

At the same time, more than a few middle-class and affluent black
parents have worried aloud to us that drawing connections between
their sons and lower-income black boys may cause their sons to experience more stigma than they already face. Indeed, we have encountered a surprising amount of resistance from middle-class black
parents, many of whom hope or believe that their socioeconomic status, education, good job, great schools, and nice neighborhood can
insulate their sons from the structural and systemic difficulties plagu-
ing other black males. And they are probably right to a certain degree,
but as we discovered firsthand—and as the experts that we cite
throughout the book attest—this is largely wishful thinking.

"It's not just poor black boys who are having problems, it's black
boys," says developmental psychologist Aisha Ray, senior vice president for academic affairs and dean of the faculty at the Erikson Institute, a graduate school in child development located in Chicago.

In fact, we've concluded that parental denial is one of the greatest
risk factors facing middle-class and affluent black boys—and we
admit that we suffered from it.

"It's a horrible head game we're playing," Atlanta-based sociologist Adria Welcher put it. "There are not enough markers that you can possess that will make a predominately white, affluent community welcoming of too many of you, even if you're the highest of the high income."

Well said.

And the truth is, Barack Obama may be in the White House, but most black middle-class parents we talk to eventually confess to being worried about something that's going on with their boy. As one suburban Atlanta father told us: "Our daughters are doing well in school, going on to college, and being successful in their lives. But black DeKalb County's secret lament is, 'What's happening to our sons?'"

Even though they are still children with immature and still-developing intellectual, emotional, and social selves our sons are not merely the victims that we may want to portray; they are active participants in life who make choices. At one point or another, some do behave in ways that Dr. Noguera says can "make them complicit in their own failure." For instance, Dr. Welcher told us about black boys who had grown up in suburban McMansions but had internalized a criminal identity from the media—and were breaking into their neighbors' homes.

We hope that by making ourselves vulnerable and by being transparent, we will spark a fresh, frank, and thoughtful conversation about race and gender that doesn't cast aspersions, play the "race card," manipulate (or avoid) guilty feelings, recycle played-out platitudes, or conform to worn-out social conventions. Some of the ideas we share may feel unfamiliar to people who aren't black or of color; people who may not engage in such discussions often; folks who may not even see themselves as a member of a racial group; or those who may not have realized that they experience racial, cultural, or skin-color privilege, for instance. Still, enough nonblack educators have told us that they want to become more effective in educating diverse children. So we feel very optimistic about the prospects honest dialogue holds.

As one white school psychologist told us, "At my school we are just starting to talk about these types of things. We have more diverse students than we have had in the past, and I haven't always known how to handle the issues that come up. I want to do a better job."

We believe that she speaks for many.

EMBRACING CHANGE

Joe's training as a psychiatrist taught us that if we talk about uncomfortable topics, step outside our comfort zones, quit worrying about what others will think about us, and use guilt to motivate ourselves rather than paralyze ourselves, we can grow and overcome being stuck. On many different occasions, the truths that we have had to face about ourselves, our sons, our family, our approach to parenting, our educational system, our community, American society, and our world have made us very uncomfortable. But we're learning and growing from them in a way that helps us to advocate not just for our own black boys but for other people's children as well.

Knowing how much we have grown makes us feel very optimistic about the amount of change that we can achieve collectively. Change is extremely difficult, of course, and it is best undertaken as the maxim describes: one bite at a time. We should expect to encounter resistance—you may resist, your son will definitely resist, his Village will resist, society will resist. Resistance, opposition, and even haters are all part of the change process. Human beings are wired to embrace ideas that feel comfortable and familiar and resist those that require change or extra effort. However, that we live under the gravitational pull of a certain worldview doesn't mean that we shouldn't jump from time to time or attempt to build an airplane, space shuttle, or create some new way of catapulting ourselves into a universe of undiscovered ideas, possibilities, and solutions.

At the ETS conference, Dr. Barbarin informed the audience that although "black boys respond more negatively and have greater deficits when environments are poor and deficient, when those environments improve they show the greatest gains. If we improve things for them we improve them for everyone."

Consistent with this, we think that it's time to stop thinking of black males as a problem and instead start seeing them as solutions to many of the challenges America faces. Rather than only seeing them as being "at risk," we think we need to see more of their promise.

We hope that you learn something in *Promises Kept* that helps you enhance a black boy's environment, whether you are a parent, a grandparent, a teacher, a school superintendent, a coach, a faith leader, a tutor, the head of a nonprofit, a social service provider, or the president of a corporation. Together we can improve the life trajectories of many children and help them unleash their potential to transform our world.

PROMISES KEPT

1

CLOSE THE GAP BEFORE IT OPENS

How to Make the Right Choices for Your Son—Before He's Even Born

It was an accident, but understanding how things work, maybe it wasn't really an accident. I could have been more careful. I took a "morning after" test but was torn about my desire to become a mom. I already had one abortion back in my twenties. I'm thirty-five now; I want to get married and have a family. But my biological clock is ticking, and I haven't met the right man. I can work on myself, but I can't manufacture a partner.

Some of my friends who are my age and a little bit older are starting to have problems conceiving and are starting in vitro fertilization. One of my girlfriends is forty-three and just devastated about her inability to conceive. That scares the crap out of me. I don't want to be that woman. When my boyfriend and I didn't use a condom a couple of times, I figured we both knew what could happen. Even though I have to admit I didn't think I would really get pregnant because my doctor had told me some things during my twenties that made me doubt if I was even fertile. When I found out that I was actually pregnant, I panicked.

When I told my boyfriend, he basically told me that I was on my own; he didn't want me to have his baby. We weren't exactly in a committed relationship, and he already has a child. That's what happens to a lot of my girlfriends—they get pregnant and the guy gets scared because he has kids or doesn't have enough money or doesn't want the commitment. Dudes run. That's what they do. I'm choosing not to judge or blame myself or demonize him. There wasn't any animosity between us before I told him I was pregnant. Maybe he'll change his mind sometime in the future. In the meantime I'm having the baby. My family has already told me that they'll support me.

—Janelle, age 35

A TIME OF HOPE, A TIME OF ANXIETY

We know that for many couples—women, in particular—pregnancy is a time of great anticipation but also of fear. No one can protect the unborn fetus from every risk factor, but there are choices that both expectant mothers and fathers can make to reduce some of the biggest risks.

In this chapter we will share information that will help black mothers- and fathers-to-be make lifestyle choices before conception and during pregnancy that lay the foundation for a strong and stable brain:

- We'll talk about the important role that mom and dad's health play in determining the quality of egg and sperm.
- You'll learn how nutrition builds a fetus's brain and learn about foods that support brain development.
- We'll also talk about the important role men play before, during, and after pregnancy in determining the strength of a baby's brain.
- We also hope to shine a light on some challenging topics in the hopes of sparking fresh dialogue—kitchen table conversations in which partners, family members, babysitters, childcare providers, caregivers, and others can roll up our sleeves and work together to create new solutions that help our sons get a head start on the achievement gap before it gets ahead of them.

> **Promise your son that you will set him up for success by getting healthy before you conceive, taking parenting classes, obtaining early prenatal care, preparing to breast-feed, and otherwise making lifestyle choices that increase the odds that his life will get off to the start he deserves.**

A SIGN OF THE TIMES

He loves to play peek-a-boo, pull himself up in front of the entertainment center, and jabber with you as though he's making a point. Although nine-month-old children can't yet tell us what's on their mind, if you test their cognitive abilities—which at that age include their ability to explore, make sounds, gesture, and solve problems—children of all races and backgrounds tend to perform pretty similarly.

"Around the age of one, there aren't many differences," says Ronald Ferguson, head of the Achievement Gap Initiative at Harvard University's Graduate School of Education.

But when child development experts test their skills at age two, developmental differences begin to clearly emerge. Smaller percentages of black, Hispanic, and Native American children than white and Asian children are proficient in communicating, understanding what they're told, discriminating between different objects, and knowing their counting words and quantities. So even before black boys have been potty-trained, we see early indications of an achievement gap.

Surprisingly, these differences span the socioeconomic spectrum.

"It doesn't matter whether they're high-income or low-income," said applied developmental psychologist Iheoma Iruka, of the Frank Porter Graham Child Development Center at the University of North Carolina, Chapel Hill, while speaking at a conference on black boys and the achievement gap convened by ETS.[1]

The gap widens by preschool, when experts can test early language, literacy, math, and numeracy (the ability to understand and work with numbers) skills. By the time black boys are between ages three and five, they lag behind white children by "about half a grade," said Dr. Iruka.

"By age two, the differences start to become apparent, and we think it has to do with early-childhood parenting and early-childhood experiences more generally," Dr. Ferguson says.

The experts are quick to admit that they don't have all the answers, and the answers that they do have don't apply to every child—although, as you'll learn, these statistics apply to more children than you might think. What they do know is that a child's experience as a fetus and during his first months as a newborn, when his brain is developing at an explosive rate, sets the stage for his physical health, ability to think and learn, and emotional well-being for the rest of his life.

THE GREATEST WONDER

Of course, our brains all begin in the same truly wondrous way. During the first hours following conception—long before women have any idea they're pregnant—their baby's brain and spinal cord have already started growing, and an intricately choreographed dance of cells forming, neurons firing, and structures forming has started to unfold.

During the first few weeks after conception takes place, the neural tube—the precursor to the brain and spinal cord—begins to form. Shortly after it closes, at the four-week mark, immature brain cells begin to proliferate. At this point the mother may still not know that she's pregnant.

Next, a phase of rapid cell migration occurs as immature cells differentiate themselves and travel to their designated locations, where they take on their preprogrammed roles.

"Think of it as cells taking the subway to a stop," says Charles Nelson III, chair of pediatric developmental medicine research at Boston Children's Hospital and professor of pediatrics and neuroscience at Harvard Medical School. Once a cell reaches its destination, "then the cell matures, which means it starts to be capable of forming connections with other cells—synapses," he adds.

The cortex—the wrinkly outer covering—of a baby's brain begins to form between the sixth and twenty-fourth weeks. The first synapses begin to appear a little after week twenty. And if a fetus survives to the twenty-fourth week, it reaches what's called the age of viability. If a fetus survives for this long, the chances are good he will live. At this point most doctors will intervene to save a fetus's life if something goes awry.

The next phase of brain development occurs during weeks twenty-five through forty (the third trimester), as synapses proliferate and *myelination*, the process of coating certain neurons (nerve cells that send and receive messages) with an electrically insulating substance, takes place.

Synapses continue to form, and myelination occurs even after a baby is born and into late adolescence.

"When you insulate these circuits, the efficiency gain is a factor of one hundred," says David Grissmer, research professor at the Center for Advanced Study of Teaching and Learning at the University of Virginia. "But if you don't build the circuits and get them myelinated, they're inefficient when you use them later."

The *cerebral cortex* and *cerebellum* explode during the final twelve to sixteen weeks. The cerebral cortex is responsible for thinking, feeling, conscious experiences, voluntary actions, and memory. The cerebellum processes movement, balance, posture, coordination, muscle tone, and some cognitive functions. Both are vital to our ability to learn, think, process, talk, and apply information to things we've already learned—or our *cognitive abilities*.

Cognitive abilities refer to our ability to learn, think, process, talk, and apply information to things we've already learned. The **cerebral cortex** and **cerebellum** are two parts of our brain that are critical to our cognitive functions.

Just between the end of the second trimester and full term, a baby's brain weight triples, from about 100 grams to about 300 grams. Eventually it will reach approximately 1,500 grams, or about 3.3 pounds.[2]

These mind-boggling processes almost always go right. As a result most U.S. babies (including black babies) arrive healthy, with brains perfectly positioned for sensing, learning, and carrying them through life. A child's brain doesn't finish developing until he's well into his twenties. Yet most of his brain's foundational architecture is in place at the time he is born. The challenge of this extremely rapid development process is that the brain remains extraordinarily impressionable. Anything that impacts an immature brain—whether a fetus's or a young child's—will have a disproportionate effect on the rest of his life, for better or worse.

A DIFFERENT WORLD

One factor that can greatly impact a child's development is being born *prematurely*, or earlier than thirty-seven full weeks after conception.

There was a time when people didn't worry about babies being born even two or three weeks early, but some evidence exists that even being born at thirty-six weeks can impact development.

"As you drop below thirty-four weeks, then to thirty weeks, then to twenty-five, the risk increases exponentially," Dr. Nelson says. "The brain is now developing in a completely different environment than it expected—outside of the uterus instead of inside the uterus. The nutritional world, the auditory world, the sensory world generally are all dramatically different outside of the womb than in the womb. The brain was expecting to be in this protective environment."

The baby's brain continues to develop; however, outside of the uterus it develops differently.

Typically, premature and *low–birth weight* babies—those weighing less than five pounds, eight ounces—experience difficulties with their hearing, vision, and other senses, and have learning disabilities, as well as respiratory illnesses such as asthma.[3] All of these can affect the child's ability to attend school and learn. A smaller percentage of preterm babies experience serious complications, such as bleeding in the brain or even death.

Learning problems "increase exponentially" the earlier a baby is born, Dr. Nelson says. How prematurely they're born can have the potential to impact their learning, although he notes that he's taught students at Harvard who were born at thirty weeks and were brilliant anyway.

Although his IQ may still fall within a normal range, a premature baby will tend to score about ten points lower on an IQ test than a child born at full term. For reference, an IQ score of 100 is considered average intelligence and roughly correlates with graduating from high school in the middle of the pack and going to college for a year or two; a score of 115 correlates with graduating college and becoming a professional or a fairly high-ranking business manager; and a score of 85 places a person at the bottom of the normal range and often correlates with dropping out of high school and working as a laborer.[4]

Children who were born preterm are 50 percent more likely to be enrolled in special education services once they attend school.[5] And babies born at thirty weeks or less have a greater risk of attention deficit-hyperactivity disorder (ADHD).

"Many children who are born early end up being developmentally delayed in terms of reaching all types of milestones—their ability to reach out and grasp, their ability to crawl, to stand, to walk, to talk," says pediatrician Michelle Gourdine, clinical assistant professor at the University of Maryland School of Medicine. "Those developmental milestones are met either late or sometimes not at all. Typically, development is very, very delayed in these small babies."

In general, the earlier a baby is born, the less he or she weighs. And approximately half of low–birth weight babies have damage to their cerebrum.[6]

"We're only now beginning to understand all the problems that premature infants have," says Mary Beth Hatten, a developmental neurobiologist at Rockefeller University. "Many face substantive developmental deficits, only some of which babies can 'grow out of.'"[7]

Although even a woman who does all the "right" things during pregnancy can have a premature baby, some known risk factors exist, including: having already had a preterm baby; carrying more than one baby; problems with the uterus or cervix; chronic health problems with the mother such as high blood pressure, diabetes, and blood clotting disorders; and smoking cigarettes, drinking alcohol, and using illegal drugs during pregnancy.[8]

CUTTING ACROSS CLASS

Although most black women deliver their babies at full term, a disproportionate percentage of black children are born prematurely and at a low birth weight.

In 2010, 17 percent of black babies were delivered preterm, as compared to 10 percent of white babies—the lowest prematurity rate reported for black babies since 1989. Approximately 14 percent of black babies were born with a *low birth weight,* or weighing five pounds, eight ounces or below, versus about 7 percent of babies overall. Three percent of black babies are born with a very low birth weight, less than three pounds, four ounces—the highest risk category—almost three times the rate of white newborns.[9]

This means that approximately one in six African American children arrives before his brain, heart, lungs, and other organs are optimally developed.

"The preterm delivery rate is two to three times higher among black women, although in general today, even when a woman delivers a baby at six months the baby can be saved," says ob-gyn M. Natalie Achong, a board-certified obstetrician-gynecologist at the Department of Obstetrics, Gynecology and Reproductive Sciences at Yale University School of Medicine and a Fellow of the American College of Obstetricians and Gynecologists (FACOG). "But a certain proportion of those babies may ultimately have issues in terms of their lungs, their brain development, and their psychological development."

Experts don't fully understand why so many black women have problems during their pregnancies. They do know that money doesn't shield them from this risk. Surprisingly, college-educated black women with health insurance face as many challenges with conception, pregnancy, and childbirth as non-college-educated, unemployed, and uninsured white women.[10]

"Among women of color—and black women in particular—the higher preterm delivery rate cuts across all lines of education, economics, and insurance status, and we don't know exactly why," says Dr. Achong.

A connection exists between rising Cesarean section and preterm birth rates. Only 17 percent of women warrant invasive pregnancy care—a category that includes C-sections, for sure, but also induced labor, fetal monitoring, epidurals, the placement of pressure on a woman's belly to push the baby out, and so on.[11] But in 2009—despite recommendations from the federal government, the American College of Obstetricians and Gynecologists, and other medical and women's health groups discouraging their overuse—about 33 percent of American women and 36 percent of black women had Cesarean sections. Insurance companies pay hospitals and doctors about 50 percent more for C-sections than they do for vaginal deliveries.[12] Perhaps it isn't so surprising that it has become the most common surgery in the United States.[13]

About 90 percent of C-sections deliver babies prematurely. For some women and babies, a C-section is a vital, even lifesaving, procedure. But many experts worry that C-sections and other maternity practices originally intended to address medical problems are now being used too liberally—and causing unexpected adverse effects. C-sections, for example, can adversely affect later pregnancies, and they increase the risks of preterm birth, low birth weight, small size for gestational age, hysterectomy, and problems with the placenta and also lead to lower breastfeeding rates.[14] Although sometimes C-sections happen in situations that don't allow for much discussion—when women have their feet up and in the stirrups in full-on labor—women and families should, if at all possible, always question the need for pregnancy interventions, including induced labor and C-sections that are scheduled for nonmedical reasons such as fear of going through labor. C-sections also increase the risk of maternal death. Women who have delivered a previous preterm baby should talk to the ob-gyn about whether they are candidates to receive an injection of an FDA-approved progesterone medication called Makena (17-hydroxyprogesterone caproate), which may reduce the risk of preterm delivery in pregnant women who have a history of delivering early.[15]

Some experts speculate that black mothers and fathers may be in worse health and more poorly nourished both when they conceive and during pregnancy, black people's higher rates of unplanned pregnancies and sexually transmitted infections magnify this risk, or that elevated levels of stress—including stress caused by racism—can add another perilous factor to black women's pregnancies.

Fortunately, both mothers and fathers can prevent many of these risk factors and increase the likelihood that their child will be born healthy, fully developed, and at his optimal weight. We will lay out some of these strategies later in this chapter.

DO YOU KANGAROO?

Even when a child is born early or at a low birth weight, we can protect his health and assist his development.

If we know we are going to deliver a baby prematurely, we can ask what measures the team in the neonatal intensive care unit, also called the NICU, takes to protect baby from sensory overload. Many nurseries protect babies from light and sound, time caregiving and medical care to minimize stress, provide bedding that provides a baby with physical boundaries, and so on. However, not all of them provide these services.

We can also make it known to the medical team that we want the parents' bodies to be the child's first natural habitat; this is called *kangaroo care*. Some evidence suggests that when premature infants snuggle skin-to-skin between their mother's breasts or on their father's bare chest, the parents' mature physiological rhythms help stabilize the baby's fragile physiology. The parent's body helps to organize the baby's sleep patterns, helps him use oxygen and regulate his temperature better, and develop more positive attachment relationships later on. And even though some babies on ventilators may experience adverse reactions to being moved to the mother's chest, the benefits to both mother and baby seem to outweigh them.

> **Kangaroo care** refers to skin-to-skin contact between a newborn infant, often premature, and his mother or father's chest. Research suggests kangaroo care offers many immediate and long-term physical and emotional benefits to the child.

Research shows that mothers who kangaroo their babies produce more milk and experience less physiological and psychological stress. In fact, while kangaroo care is especially good for preemies, parents of full-term babies can let the staff know that they, too, want to kangaroo their baby.[16]

Talk to your doctor about caring for your "preemie" during his first two years of life. He or she may recommend that your son take vitamins, iron, and, if he is bottle-fed, a special formula. As we describe below, if you are able to breastfeed a premature baby, it's best to do so.[17]

A parent's Village and employers can assist by doing as much as they can to free the parents to be at the hospital to provide kangaroo care and to restore bonds with their baby that have been disrupted by hospital procedures. Some hospitals have volunteers hold babies when their parents can't be there to hold them.

OOPS! I'VE DONE IT AGAIN

Before we even get to that point, there are things that can be done to lower the risk of having a premature or low–birth weight baby. One way to prevent having a premature or low–birth weight baby is for both men and women to begin to plan for pregnancy—and that includes starting your planning before you try to conceive.

About half the time when American couples get pregnant, one or both partners view the pregnancy as unexpected.[18] When the parents don't plan a baby, or when he's unwanted, the baby's risks of being born prematurely or at a low birth weight increase. For starters, a woman who becomes pregnant by accident is more likely to smoke or drink while with child and less likely to receive early prenatal care—all of which increase his chances of being born early, at a low weight, or with some other health or developmental problem. If the child's father was not planning to conceive a child, he may not have been making lifestyle choices that would help him contribute the quality of sperm that leads to the best pregnancy outcomes.

According to a study of 1,800 young adults of all races and ethnicities published by the National Campaign to Prevent Teen and Unplanned Pregnancy in 2009, women in their twenties get pregnant by accident more often than any other demographic group—and that includes teenagers. They slip up at more than twice the national rate, often throwing their lives off course.[19]

More than 85 percent of twentysomethings who are currently in a sexual relationship report that they don't want to get pregnant. Yet 19 percent used no contraception at all within the previous month, and 24 percent used it inconsistently. Other research shows that millennials are also undoing the connection that traditionally existed between childbirth and marriage. In 2010, 41 percent of babies in the United States were born to women who weren't married.[20]

Both these trends apply to black millennials, for whom 73 percent of pregnancies and about a third of babies are unplanned.[21] In the study, 26 percent of black twentysomethings reported that they do not use contraception at all, and 18 percent use it inconsistently. Fifty percent of black unmarried young adults say that they have already had an unplanned pregnancy, and 83 percent say that many of their friends have. Black women, on average, begin childbearing at twenty-three (as compared to twenty-six for white women)—five years before the average age that they marry.[22]

"My former boyfriend and I had discussed how one day we both wanted to be married and have children. So when we started slipping with the condoms, I just assumed that he would be okay with it if I ended up pregnant," says Tara, 29, a sales rep who's taking night classes to get her MBA. "When I found out that I was pregnant, I was ecstatic—until he told me he didn't want it. I was shocked and just sick to my stomach! When I told him that I wanted to have our baby, he accused me of tricking him. Excuse me? How did I trick you? I had told you that I wanted children. And you did have sex without a condom, dude. What the hell did you think could happen?"

So why are so many young adults getting caught out there? In a nutshell, what the National Campaign to Prevent Teen and Unplanned Pregnancy discovered is that young adults of all backgrounds are poorly educated about sexual and reproductive health and harbor a shocking number of myths and misconceptions about contraception and pregnancy. In fact, urban legends about contraception and reproductive health abound.

"My doctor told me that I could pregnant while I was nursing, but my girlfriend told me that she didn't think I could. I was stupid and listened to her—and here I am pregnant again," says Ayana, 26, a married mother with her second child on the way. Ayana and her husband welcome their new addition, but the pregnancy comes at a time when you can hear the breeze blowing through their bank account.

Researchers found the disconnect between what twentysome-things say they want and the way they behave is so profound and widespread that they labeled the twenties the "fog zone," a time when fear, misperceptions, and uncertainty about contraception and pregnancy reign.

> "Many young adults between the ages of eighteen and twenty-nine exhibit what we call 'magical thinking' as well as ambivalence about pregnancy and planning for pregnancy. The majority of folks in their twenties are fertile. Of course, if you're not doing something to prevent pregnancy, yet you're being sexually active, then you are going to have an unplanned pregnancy—eventually, it is going to happen."
>
> —Vanessa Cullins, vice president for external affairs for Planned Parenthood Federation of America

One of the biggest misconceptions that young adults harbored was the belief that they were infertile. Approximately 22 percent of black young women and 8 percent of black young men thought that they couldn't have children, as opposed to actual infertility rates of 8 percent among young adults. Shockingly, 25 percent of black women based their beliefs on information they had received from a doctor, as Janelle experienced.

Perhaps the high level of confusion about sexual and reproductive health issues among this generation of young adults shouldn't surprise us, given the inconsistent, confusing, and often inaccurate sexual health information that passed for truth in sex ed class—if they had one—during the abstinence-only era—from the early 1980s through the George W. Bush administration. It has left young adults poorly prepared to plan their childbearing—yet shockingly overconfident, the study found, that they know how to protect themselves.

When black women move out of the "fog zone" and into their thirties, they are generally more prepared to become parents as far as their education and finances are concerned, but they walk smack into the double trouble of a demographic gender imbalance and declining fertility.

"A lot of young black women are despondent because they have no one to date. A lot of the depression I see is, 'I'm getting these skills, but for what? Am I ever going to have kids?'" says Philadelphia therapist Pamela Freeman. "They know that it's really hard being on your own and raising a child in a healthy way, and they don't want to have a baby and not give it time and healthy attention. So many middle-class women in their late twenties and early thirties are struggling with this."

"There are fewer marriageable men available, and black women who want to have children and may not have a husband are getting older and saying, 'I want to have a baby and I'll have it with whomever.' This is rampant," says Jermane Bond, a research associate for the Health Policy Institute of the Joint Center for Political and Economic Studies, a Washington, D.C.–based think tank focused on black people.

Some women resolve this conflict by choosing to have a baby and raise their child on their own. Others get pregnant with their fingers crossed that the baby will cement the relationship.

"Yes, okay, so I did that," says Carmen, 31, of her pregnancy at 26. "It was wishful thinking, but I was in love even though our relationship was kind of crazy. I just felt these mad urges to have a baby and was praying that everything would work out. But it didn't, and everyone's saying, 'I told you so.' And here I am now. It's greasy."

"The existence of the child tends not to cause someone to stay in a relationship. It places stressors on the relationships," says Dr. Cullins.

TWO TO TANGO

One of the most important things that black men and women can do to prevent unplanned pregnancies, preterm births, low–birth weight babies, and other pregnancy-related problems that can interfere both with a child's health and his ability to learn is to engage in preconception planning throughout the reproductive years, starting long before we start thinking about becoming parents.

Experts have long known that a mother can reduce the risks to herself and her baby by getting *prenatal care* as early during the first trimester of her pregnancy as possible. Nearly one-third of women experience some sort of complication during pregnancy. Prenatal care during the first trimester provides the greatest opportunity either to prevent them or to get a jump on them before they get out of hand. Yet in 2008 only 59 percent of black women received first-trimester care, as compared to 76 percent of white women.[23] Remember: You have to know, first, that you're pregnant and, second, that you want to keep the baby before you seek prenatal care. So unexpected pregnancies, where the mother is either unsure that she's pregenant or uncertain that she wants to have a baby, can cause women to obtain care late. This is not a judgment, just a reality.

It's particularly important for black couples to get ahead of the game, since we are more likely than others to be overweight and even to have pre-hypertension or hypertension, or pre-diabetes or diabetes, even at a young age. Such health challenges not only complicate the current pregnancy, they can also set women up to experience more difficult pregnancies later.

"If diabetes is well controlled, then there's much less of a risk, if any, to the offspring," says Dr. Nelson. "But if the mother's diabetes is poorly controlled, then the risk to the offspring is considerable."

Psychological and social challenges, such as feeling stressed out, being depressed, and not having enough support, can also make pregnancy more difficult.

The father also has an important prenatal role. A father who actively supports the mom while she's pregnant lightens her (extra-heavy) load by allowing her to rest, for example, which is good for mom, but also protects the growing fetus.

"The moms who have the dads involved," says Roland Warren, executive director of the National Fatherhood Initiative, a fatherhood advocacy organization, "are more likely to seek prenatal care, less likely to have low–birth weight babies, more likely to breastfeed, and have a lesser chance that their infant will die."

A study conducted on 101 pregnant, well-educated (62 percent had college degrees), black Atlanta-area women ages twenty through forty-two found that even middle-class women experience the high levels of stress particular to black women. Many of the women reported experiencing feeling overloaded in their roles as caregivers and nurturers—expectations they said that others had of them but that they also had of themselves. Some worried about the world that their son would enter; others described family members, partners, and friends who got ghost during their pregnancy; still others shared that they took care of others even while pregnant, yet no one took care of them. Perhaps not surprisingly, almost 25 percent of the women in the study experienced depression—almost twice the 13 percent rate experienced by women overall.[24]

"Evidence suggests that stress may be associated with an increased risk of attention deficit disorder in the child. There is some evidence, although incomplete, that stress during pregnancy leads to lower IQs in children. There's also evidence that it increases children's risk of depression," says Dr. Gourdine, who is the author of *Reclaiming Our Health: A Guide to African American Wellness*. "And stress during pregnancy tends to have a more adverse effect on African American pregnant women than on white pregnant women. We're still trying to figure out why."

Women who were married or partnered experienced depression less.[25]

"Our hypothesis is that paternal involvement is the missing link in improving pregnancy outcomes," says Dr. Bond, who also directed the Commission on Paternal Involvement in Pregnancy Outcomes.

A low level of stress isn't likely to negatively impact your pregnancy. And though we can't eliminate all stress, we may be able to take steps to keep it toward the lower end of the scale. Having an active partner in the pregnancy can help.

But to be an active partner requires preparation. During preconception black men can prepare themselves for the many hats they will need to don during preconception, pregnancy, at birth, and throughout their child's life. Among the most important? Supporting mommy through pregnancy and encouraging her to breastfeed.

"The motivation to be an involved father is tied to having the skills," says Warren. The National Fatherhood Initiative (NFI) surveyed men whose children were eighteen or younger to learn how ready men were for fatherhood when their children were born. "Nearly half the fathers responded that they weren't prepared. They didn't have skills," Warren says. "And then we asked, 'To what degree do you feel you're replaceable by mom or some other guy?' Over half of the fathers felt that they were replaceable."

"None of my friends knew how to be a father and neither did I," says Jason, 43, a Houston information-technology professional. "We used to talk about it sometimes. None of us had our dads around, so none of us really knew quite what to do. It was ironic. Here we were with bachelors degrees, MBAs, law degrees, and all these skills for the world of work—but none of the skills that really mattered for raising our sons."

PRECONCEPTION HEALTH FOR FUTURE MOMS AND DADS

Just as a woman who wants to get pregnant may need to switch her favorite drink from a Bahama Mama to a Shirley Temple, her partner may need to make lifestyle adjustments as well—from eating fewer cheese steaks and more black-eyed peas and reducing his exposure to toxic chemicals at work to making moves that will put a bigger knot in his pocket.

"Early prenatal care is too late, given what we know now about preterm birth, low birth weight, and infant mortality for African Americans," says Dr. Bond. "What we are focusing on now is preconception health and care—mostly for women but also for young men and boys."

Preconception health care involves protecting your reproductive health and preparing for parenthood with the specific intention of safeguarding your unborn children. But rather than waiting until you have a bun in the oven, you can take charge before you even conceive. Books like *Mama Glow: Your Guide to a Fabulous Abundant Pregnancy* by Latham Thomas and *The Mocha Manual to a Fabulous Pregnancy* by Kimberly Seals-Allers can help you lay the groundwork for a healthy baby. *Health First: The Black Woman's Wellness Guide* can help you understand how to take care of yourself across the life cycle, including during your reproductive years.

Until recently conversations about preconception care have focused entirely on women. But today more experts are beginning to understand that a man's sperm plays a role in his baby's health.

"When people think of the father's preconception health, most times they think about low sperm count or violence, but the father also needs a balanced, nutritious, healthy diet and to drink enough water," says nutritionist Goulda Downer, an assistant professor at the Howard University College of Medicine. "If we're not eating healthily, we're not laying a good foundation for the building material that will be required to build a healthy egg, make healthy sperm, make a healthy zygote, make a healthy baby. If we're not, it's just not there."

Preconception Care for Men

Although preconception care guidelines exist for women, no clear standards exist for men. Nor are medical practitioners trained to support men through the process.[26] But don't let their lack of knowledge stop you—this merely means that you need to take charge of your own health. We strongly encourage both men and women to print out the preconception checklists that the Centers for Disease Control and Prevention publishes and to use them to guide their self-care activities (http://www.cdc.gov/preconception/index.html).

We realize that many black men will need to reconnect with the healthcare system, since they may not have been to a physician since they played in Pop Warner football league. Women can help their partner research doctors. Assist him in overcoming his anxiety by emphasizing that the doctor will help him stay strong rather than merely look for what's wrong and by offering to go with him to his appointment. For tips, we suggest that you check out *The Black Woman's Guide to Black Men's Health* by Andrea King Collier and Willarda V. Edwards.

The self-care strategies below can help you head off some of the risks specific to black people before conception and during pregnancy that can jeopardize your unborn child's development. From well-woman visits to gestational diabetes screenings to STI testing and counseling to breastfeeding support to screening for intimate-partner violence—women's health services are free under the Affordable Care Act. Visit http://www.hrsa.gov/womensguidelines/ for more information.[27]

Create a Reproductive Life Plan

Whether or not you're already a parent, you've probably fantasized about your ideal family. However, few people go so far as to write down their vision or share it with their friends, sexual partners, or doctors. Formal preconception includes dreaming about when you'd like to have a family and thinking about what that family would look like. Will you have two children or three? Do you plan to marry? To adopt? Just let your mind wander and then jot down your thoughts. Your plan can be as simple as this:

I really want to have children, but not until I get my degree and get a good job with enough benefits. That will probably take three more years. But after that I'd like to get married and have two children back-to-back so that they grow up together. Between now and then I need to find a form of contraception that has a very low failure rate. But I also want to use condoms so I don't jeopardize my fertility by getting a sexually transmitted infection.

Or this:

We already have one child and we're both working full time and finishing school. I don't want us to have any more babies until after we both graduate; otherwise, it's too much pressure. After that we're going to get an apartment, and I want us to settle down. But I don't want to wait too long after that to start trying again.

"We don't commonly have conversations about this," says Planned Parenthood's Dr. Cullins. "The dialogue acknowledging that 'Yes, I am a sexually active being and I want to begin to start having a family at this age, or this income level, or within this particular set of circumstances'—and the 'what-if' scenarios that come with that—is an exercise that should be done mentally for sure. But it's best if you can do it with other people, such as close friends and potential partners."

That so many young adults live at home into their mid-twenties or longer presents a prime opportunity for their parents and older extended-family members to help them to make good decisions about becoming parents. Ask them questions like: Are you aware of all of your contraceptive options? Do you want to get pregnant, and if so, when? What can I help you think about so you can plan it?

"For some, preconception doesn't come up until after their first child," says Dr. Bond, making the period after a pregnancy an optimal time for men who are already fathers to think through a reproductive life plan.

Get a Checkup

Seeing a healthcare provider can help you identify any steps you need to take to ensure that you're in shape once you're ready to have a baby. If you don't already have a doctor, Dr. Bond suggests finding a *family practitioner,* or *family doctor,* a healthcare practitioner trained to help care for a person's mental, physical, and emotional health as well as that of their family. Not only can both parents get a handle on any health conditions that may impact a fetus, they both can take steps to improve the health of their eggs and sperm.

"We used to think that women were born with all the eggs they'll ever have," says Carol Cheatham, Ph.D., a developmental cognitive neuroscientist who studies the impact of nutrition on brain development at the Nutrition Research Institute at the University of North Carolina. "It turns out that that's not true. They've found stem cells in the ovaries, so the female body is likely making eggs throughout her lifetime. The newer eggs would be influenced by everything she's done in her lifetime."

"We want to make sure that mentally and physically everything is doing well," says Dr. Downer. "If we don't eat balanced nutritious meals and drink enough water, it's just not there. We can make an embryo but it's not the healthiest embryo."

Men create new sperm every forty-two to seventy-six days. So not only can they take dramatic steps to help improve their own fertility, they can reduce the chances that nicotine, alcohol, drugs (including steroids), caffeine, low-nutrient foods, toxins, and other factors will damage the DNA that they pass to their child.

"Most of the time when men think about preconception and health, they think about the woman and believe that it has nothing to do with them," says Dr. Downer. "But what men eat and drink determines the quality of the cells that make the sperm that contribute 50 percent of the DNA of their child. So I ask men to think about what they are doing—about the child who will carry their name to the next generation."

"At the moment of conception, dad is providing one-half of what it takes to create a baby," says Dr. Cheatham. "Dad makes sperm all day long. It could be affected acutely if he was drinking or taking some sort of prescription drug when the sperm were created. I think that sperm are more of a wild card than we once thought they were."

When we've talked to dads and future dads about this, the response is usually a variation on what we heard from a young man named Kelvin. "Wow, I didn't know that. I always thought that when a baby has problems, it was the woman's fault. I didn't think that I played a part in the process, but I guess it makes sense now that I think about it."

Also be sure to discuss these topics as part of your preconception planning with your partner or physician.

Emotional health. An increasing body of evidence suggests that high levels of stress can cause preterm births, particularly among black women. Be honest with your doctor about your troubles and ask to be checked for depression if you ever feel blue. Depressed parents have a harder time interacting with an infant in the ways that will help his brain develop.

Sexually transmitted infections. An STI epidemic exists among American young adults in general and among black folks in particular. For example, among black women the rate of the most common STI, chlamydia, is six times that of white women and the rate among black men is nine times that of white men. Rates of gonorrhea and syphilis rates are also disproportionately high.[28] For a variety of different reasons—poverty, the lack of health insurance, and the fact that STIs travel in social sexual networks among them—STIs are so widespread in black communities that even having unprotected sex once or twice can put you at risk.[29] Many STIs increase the risk of preterm and low-birth weight deliveries and cause other problems. But despite the stigma that people who have STIs are "nasty," you don't have to be "out there" to get a sexually transmitted infection "down there" (or in your throat). The most common STIs don't have any symptoms—many times people don't know that they have them. But some doctors are too embarrassed to bring STIs up or don't want to risk offending their patients. Tell your doctor if you're having unprotected sex. Even married people should get tested for STIs regularly.

Vaccines. The chicken pox, the flu, and the measles—any of them can jeopardize the health of your fetus. Get vaccinated before you conceive.

Violence or abuse history. Women between the ages of twenty and twenty-four are at the greatest risk of intimate-partner violence (IPV). According to a U.S. Justice Department study, nearly 30 percent of black women have experienced IPV at least once.[30]

Nutrition

One of the most important ways you can protect your baby before he is born—or even conceived—is to eat as healthily as you're able to.

The quality of a woman's diet during pregnancy, in particular, influences the growth of her baby's brain, which is most sensitive to nutrition between mid-pregnancy—the time when the synapses begin to develop and myelination begins—and two years of age.[31]

"Eat a well-balanced diet that includes fruit, vegetables, low-fat milk and other dairy products, breads, grains and cereals, and low-fat poultry and meat," says Dr. Downer.

Women during their reproductive years should take 400 to 600 micrograms of folate each day—the amount available in most over-the-counter vitamins.

"Neural-tube defects occur in the first weeks of life," says Charles Nelson III, chair of pediatric developmental medicine research at Boston Children's Hospital and professor of pediatrics and neuroscience at Harvard Medical School. "That's when the neural tube forms. So someone who is two months pregnant taking folic acid has missed that window of opportunity—it's too late."

Nevertheless, if you're not already taking a prenatal vitamin containing folate, start as soon as you discover you're pregnant. Today scientists know that all B vitamins play an essential role and that *choline* may actually be as important as folate, if not more important. (Folate can be found in beef liver, chicken, eggs, milk, tofu, and other foods; choline is found in eggs, beef, chicken, pork, turkey, and salmon.) Also make sure you are consuming enough iron as well as iodine, which reduces the risk of stillbirths, miscarriage, preterm delivery, and birth defects and can be found in dairy products and meats.

In some of Dr. Cheatham's research on the fatty acid DHA—an omega-3 fatty acid that supports the development of a baby's brain, eyes, and nervous system—she was surprised to discover evidence of the mother's prenatal nutrition in the brains of sixteen- to twenty-month-old toddlers, some of whom hadn't even been breastfed.

But even if you don't achieve your nutrition goals during pregnancy—or you adopt a baby and don't know how well his mother took care of herself while she was pregnant—you can take steps to compensate once he's born.

"It's possible that the brain is so plastic when the baby's born that what happens after birth can make up for some of what happened in utero," says Dr. Cheatham. "Say mom didn't get good prenatal care and didn't eat very well. That's not a lost baby. The brain is very plastic."

Prepare to Breastfeed Your Baby

One of the most important steps you can take nutritionally is to breastfeed your newborn within an hour of his arrival.[32] Breast milk was designed to be a baby's first food and offers the best combination of nutrients to help his brain grow and to prepare him for learning.

"We know how beneficial breastfeeding is not just to the mother but also to the child," says Dr. Downer. "It reduces incidence of obesity, certain viruses, allergies, respiratory illnesses, ear infection, meningitis, the list goes on."

Breast milk can save the lives and improve the health of babies who arrive sick or prematurely and helps inoculate preemies against infections of the gut and respiratory tract, systemic infections, and meningitis. It also helps a baby's immune system, vision, hearing, and skin (less eczema) and reduces diarrhea and stinky poop.

"And there's a demonstrated connection between breastfeeding and cognitive development—intelligence," says Dr. Downer.

Indeed, breastfeeding is associated with higher scores on developmental tests.[33] Recent research indicates that it can even raise a child's IQ by seven points, and some studies suggest that breast milk can raise an IQ even higher.[34]

"When you breastfeed a baby, his brain cells are still developing. His ability to breathe, to suckle, for his eyes to track your finger, for him to look at his environment, to express discomfort—all that involves cognition, learning, and connecting to their world," says Dr. Downer.

Even though many of us are forced to rely on it, the fact is, from a nutritional perspective, infant formula can't carry breast milk's diaper bag. For that reason the American Academy of Pediatrics recommends that women breastfeed exclusively for the first six months and ideally for twelve months or longer.

"African American women are least likely of all ethnic groups to initiate breastfeeding, breastfeed after six months—lowest—and after twelve months—lowest," says Dr. Downer. This difference extends across socioeconomic groups, with even college-educated black women breastfeeding less often than whites.

Slightly over half of black women breastfeed their newborn at all, as compared to 75 percent of American women overall. Studies show that 18 percent of black women are still breastfeeding at the six-month mark versus 44 percent of all women, and 12 percent of black women are still breastfeeding at a year versus 24 percent overall.[35]

While these are significantly higher than our historical (very low) rates, if we want to best prepare our kids, emotionally and cognitively, we need to breastfeed for much longer.

A wide variety of factors contribute to black women's low rates of breastfeeding—from efforts by formula companies to discourage it in previous generations to hospital practices that disrupt early bonding and encourage formula use, to a lack of knowledge about the benefits of breastfeeding, to perceptions that linger within many black communities that breast milk is inferior to formula, to a lack of support from our mates and families, to real-world realities that force us to go back to work, to the inability to pump on the job.[36]

Mama Glow author Latham Thomas recounts that even though her mother breastfed her, when Thomas breastfed her own son, her grandmother "had a discouraging tone about how breastfeeding almost wasn't ladylike, clean, or esteemed," she recalls. "She was not proposing that I stop, but she was almost passively saying, 'Why are you going through the effort?' I talked to my mother and said, 'I'm not stopping, I'm just not going to talk to her about it.'"

By contrast, Thomas's mother helped and supported her during the first week after she gave birth to her son. This included helping her nurse and hiring a lactation consultant. "She helped me have everything at my fingertips to be successful," Thomas recalls.

Thomas says you can set yourself up for success before your child even arrives.

"Find lactation support groups such as La Leche League, Facebook groups, plus meetups to talk to elders in your community and people who are going through it who can share breastfeeding stories that help you do it successfully. That will help you increase your sense of competency and capacity to do it," she says, including dealing with issues involving breastfeeding and work.

"The Affordable Care Act is so important because workplace barriers are being torn down," says Dr. Downer. "The ACA requires that most employers provide unpaid time for mothers to express milk in a clean space. This is wonderful news! Express the milk, and take it home to your baby."

Breastfeeding is exceedingly difficult, if not impossible, for some women and infants. Thomas reminds women that if they're not producing enough milk, it could be because they're stressed out, not eating enough, or not well hydrated. Importantly, don't forget that the Affordable Care Act covers the cost of lactation support and counseling offered by a trained expert during pregnancy or the postpartum period and the costs of renting breastfeeding equipment.[37]

Take Parenting Classes

The preconception period is also a great time to get the 411 about child development and to prepare to road test your parenting skills.

"There's a great need for parenting education for everybody—it's vital," says Alvin Poussaint. "You have to know what to do with the baby before it comes out of the womb: how to take care of its health and avoid stress, for instance."

"Even middle-class black women don't know what they need to about child development," says one parenting educator. "They tend to rely a lot on physical punishment because it was used on them."

Sharpen Your Relationship Skills

With all the pressures on black relationships and children (and family life sure to bring more), preconception can be a great time to strengthen relationship skills through individual or couple's counseling or family therapy, which increasing numbers of black men and women embrace these days.

"A healthy relationship involves give-and-take. You come to the relationship as equals with different areas of skill or expertise and you try to work together as a team," says Dr. Cullins. "You're being re-spected, what you say is being respected, and you also respect what you're hearing from the other person. You are never going to agree on everything 100 percent, so at a certain point you have to either kind of walk away from the issue, agree to disagree, or decide that the issue is so important that you will walk away from the actual relationship. The relationship is not one of property and control. I don't own you; you don't own me."

It's also a good idea before children arrive for us to make up our minds that, no matter how our relationship with our child's mother or father goes, we will interact in a way that will allow us to co-parent until our son becomes an adult.

Protect Yourself from Toxins

A wide variety of chemicals can impact a baby's developing brain, but four types of toxins can be particularly damaging to the brain of an embryo, fetus, or newborn child: heavy metals, certain pesticides, rec-reational drugs, and certain prescription medications. The risks that chemicals pose to embryos, fetuses, and developing children are expo-nentially greater than they are to adults. Pound for pound, a baby takes on more toxins than an adult does; his biological systems—especially his brain—are developing, and he's not able to flush toxins out yet. Even small doses can cause tremendous harm, particularly during *sensitive periods* when cells are migrating in order to build new structures, or information is traveling through the brain.[38] You can't live in a bubble, of course, but you should concentrate on avoid-ing these chemicals.

Heavy Metals
Lead. High levels of lead in a pregnant woman's body can cause her to miscarry or to deliver prematurely or at a low birth weight.[39] Lead poisoning can also cause developmental challenges—from behavioral and attention difficulties, to hearing and kidney problems, to slow growth.[40] Experts argue about whether low levels of lead exposure lower a child's IQ and, if so, by how much.

One of the most common sources of lead today is in the chips and dust (dust resulting from stripping or sanding) from paint in houses built before 1978. More than one-fifth of black children who live in housing built before 1946 have high levels of lead in their blood.[41]

Also, exercise caution when giving your son old toys, buying him paint and art supplies (read labels), and letting him handle rechargeable batteries, fishing sinkers, or (do we really need to say this?) bullets.[42]

To learn more about lead or the symptoms of lead exposure, visit http://www.epa.gov/lead or contact the National Lead Information Center at (800) 424-5323. If you suspect you may have lead paint in your house, get advice on how to remove it safely by calling the Department of Housing and Urban Development (HUD) at 800-RID-LEAD or the National Information Center at 800-LEAD-FYI.

Mercury. During pregnancy, exposure to high levels of mercury can cause developmental delays in a fetus or young child. Even low levels of exposure may make it more likely that a child will develop behaviors related to ADHD.[43] Your body needs fish while you're pregnant, but limit your choices to salmon, flounder, tilapia, trout, pollock, and catfish. Although tuna may fit into your budget, while you are pregnant and lactating don't eat more than six ounces per week, always choosing light over "white" (albacore) tuna. Avoid shark, swordfish, tilefish, and king mackerel like the plague.[44]

Organophosphate Pesticides

Several studies have reported that pregnant women with higher levels of exposure to pesticides had children whose IQ scores were seven points lower when they started school than children with the lowest levels of exposure.[45] The women in the study were farm workers, so you're likely at much lower risk. However, the same chemicals can be found in sprays used to eradicate mosquitoes, fight West Nile virus, and kill roaches in apartments and workplaces. (See if caulking cracks along baseboards helps fix your roach problem.)

Pesticides are also found as residue on conventionally grown foods. During pregnancy and the first year of your child's life, you may want to consider purchasing organic fruits and vegetables (if you can afford them), washing conventionally grown produce very carefully, and avoiding the Environmental Working Group's "Dirty Dozen" fruits and vegetables that typically contain the most pesticide: apples, celery, sweet bell peppers, peaches, strawberries, imported nectarines, grapes, spinach, lettuce, cucumbers, domestic blueberries, and potatoes.[46]

To go organic on a budget, shop at farmer's markets late in the day, when many farmers will sell produce at a discount to avoid hauling it home. Latham Thomas notes that many farmers who farm organically can't afford to obtain the official organic designation, so if you ask the farmers about their farming methods, you may be able to obtain organic for less than you pay in the store.

Endocrine Disruptors

While you're pregnant, try to avoid two types of plastics: bisphenol A (BPA), which makes plastics hard and clear and keeps them from shattering, and phthalates, which make them soft and pliable and help perfumes and makeup hang on to their fragrance. In animals, male offspring exposed to BPA during gestation develop abnormalities in their masculinity. In humans, boys exposed to toxic levels of phthalates can end up with the opening to their urethra in the wrong place.

Many manufacturers have removed BPA from baby products, but read product labels just to be safe. Also scour your kitchen for products with recycling codes 3, 6, and 7 on the bottom of the container— then get rid of them. The government has banned phthalates from children's toys, but they're present in many other products—from hairspray to cosmetics to perfumes to lotions. However, their presence may not be noted on the label. Hairdressers in particular should avoid hairspray while pregnant.[47]

Prescription Drugs

You might assume that a prescription medication that's safe for you is also safe during pregnancy and when you're breastfeeding. It's not necessarily the case. Among the ones to avoid: the anticonvulsant drug *valproate,* which can cause cognitive deficits, including mental retardation, and impaired emotional control; *acne medicines* (and the nutritional supplement vitamin A), whose interference with the development of the embryo or fetus can cause a wide range of impairments; and *methylphenidate* (the trademarked product is Ritalin), which, taken during pregnancy, can impair fetal functioning.[48]

Recreational Drugs

Alcohol. That glass of wine you want? It's not worth the risk. No amount of alcohol has been proven safe during pregnancy.[49] Drinking alcohol during pregnancy can cause premature delivery; low birth weight; heart, brain, or other organ defects; vision or hearing problems; learning disabilities; problems with sleeping and sucking; delays in speech and language development; and behavioral problems.[50]

"Within one month of conception the spinal cord closes, and most women don't even know that they're pregnant during this time," says Dr. Downer, the former executive director of the National Organization on Fetal Alcohol Syndrome. She recommends that women avoid alcoholic beverages completely if there's any chance that they may be pregnant or become pregnant. "If the cells are migrating to make the arm or the heart or the eyes, alcohol can interfere with that, causing the cells to do any number of things that result in a deformity," Dr. Downer says.

She believes that even one glass of wine or mimosa involves taking a risk.

"There are alcohol-related neurological diseases and birth defects. *Fetal alcohol syndrome* is at the end of that spectrum, the most advanced form of the disease," says Dr. Downer. "But a lot of people are walking around with fetal alcohol *effects* and don't even know it. With fetal alcohol *syndrome,* you can see facial effects, abnormalities, and growth deficiencies, but when you have central nervous system dysfunction—say, the child who is hyperactive—you can't see anything physical, there's just their behavior, but you may not associate it with alcohol."

Illegal drugs. If you're reading this book, you probably don't do them, but we'd be remiss if we didn't mention that about 8 percent of black women use illegal drugs—almost twice the percentage of white (4.4 percent) and Hispanic (3.1 percent) women.[51] If you do use it, stop or seek help.

Nicotine. People often look down their nose at folks who smoke while they're pregnant. No wonder a lot of smokers hide their habit when they're expecting. Although black women (14 percent) and Hispanic (7 percent) women are less likely than white women (22 percent) to smoke during pregnancy, research shows that black women are more likely to hide their habit.[52]

Smoking increases the risk of low birth weight, premature delivery, lifelong learning disabilities, and birth defects. Quitting early in your pregnancy can benefit your baby tremendously.

Keeping the Promise

1. **Plan to conceive.** Not every pregnancy is a planned one, but if you're in a relationship that might lead to a pregnancy, preconception planning is vital.

2. **Preconception and prenatal planning involves both parents.** Fathers and mothers should both engage in preconception planning—from health and nutrition issues to emotional and practical ones.

3. **Eat right and keep your bodies free from toxins.** Good nutrition is a must, for mother and father, but so is avoiding chemical toxins, alcohol, and smoking. All of these things lead to long-term negative outcomes for our sons, and put them at risk of falling into the gap.

2

BUILD YOUR SON'S BRAIN

Using Brain Science (and Common Sense) to Develop Our Sons Throughout Early Childhood

For years I dreamed about opening an urban boarding school for inner-city boys. But the more I peeled back the onion on what it would take and the impact it would have, the more I realized that by middle school, much of the trajectory of a child's life has already been set. If I wanted to maximize my impact, I needed to touch them when they were young. I also know that to impact the kids, you have to impact the parents as well—it has to be a package deal.

We're located in an inner-city neighborhood but attract kids from all walks of life. Our parents are very interested in investing in their child educationally. We teach Spanish, Mandarin, and sign language, for instance. So I've been surprised to realize how much parenting education everybody needs. For example, regardless of their socioeconomic status, almost all the parents walk in with their cell phones to their ear. They drop their children off while they're talking. Very little communication is happening—so little that we now ask parents not to use their phones in the center. We feed the children a nutritious breakfast, but a lot of children walk in with a donut in their hand, including some middle-class kids.

One of the biggest things I notice is the lack of hugs— how many parents drop their children off and don't hug them goodbye, the number of kids who come in crying and there's no hug for that. We had a situation where a two-year-old was acting up in the classroom and no one could comfort him. Eventually I got involved. I got down on his level and gave him a hug. He hugged me tight and just sat in my arms on the floor. Then he was cool for the rest of the day. That made me wonder if maybe my teachers needed hugs. So I stopped in each classroom and gave each teacher a hug. When we discussed it in our staff meeting, we realized that everyone needed a hug.

It may sound simplistic, but the foundation for raising a child has to be love. A lot of children are being neglected for one reason or another, no matter their race or socioeconomic class. If the child is a burden or an inconvenience, that's a problem. Unfortunately a lot of children become that.

—*Marty, father of four and owner of several daycare centers*

FIRST IMPRESSIONS LAST

Nothing determines our son's intellectual, emotional, and behavioral trajectory more than the quality of caregiving he receives and the environments that we expose him to throughout his first five years of life. During this time his brain is undergoing a process of extremely rapid development so miraculous that researchers are only beginning to comprehend it. Recently, new information from fields as far flung as genetics, brain science, molecular biology, and the behavioral and social sciences has deepened researchers' knowledge about how the brain develops during infancy and early childhood. We now know, for instance, that the degree of attentiveness that a baby's caregivers demonstrate toward him plays a far more important role in helping his brain develop than researchers ever understood before. Positive and enriching experiences help to wire his brain as well. This combination of nurturing caregivers and enriching experiences during early childhood helps to position our young ones to excel in school, behave well as a teen, and thrive during adulthood. Brain games and iPad apps can't come close to making that happen.

But a baby's immature brain is also more vulnerable to negative experiences than experts ever knew. And changes that interrupt his relationships with his first caregivers create stress that doesn't merely upset him emotionally but can also change the layout of his brain in ways that alter his life trajectory forever.

In this chapter we will share some of the latest brain science and relate it to black children, particularly black boys:

- We'll discuss the essential role that you, your family, and other caregivers and Village members can play in helping your son's brain build itself in ways that optimize his ability to learn.
- We'll also take on a few controversial issues, which we will warn you ahead of time may hit close to home. For example, we'll suggest that some of the time-honored child-rearing advice passed down for generations in some

African American families may be ready for a retirement party.

- We'll also examine some of American culture and our community's contemporary assumptions about child-rearing that, if we're not careful, could increase the risk that some of the roots of a black boy's struggles exist in our own home. But we don't want to guilt anybody—children are resilient even in the midst of life's difficulties but especially when they have appropriate support. The new research also implies that significant upside opportunities exist for parents, extended families, friends, educators, schools, churches, ministries, neighborhoods, communities, fraternities and sororities, social and civic organizations, allies of other races, and policymakers to implement fresh strategies that support and protect children and families during this time of early brain development.

> **Promise your son that you will intentionally and proactively interact with him in ways that build his brain and that you will protect him from threats to his brain's development, by any means necessary, for his entire life but especially until he is five years old.**

LAYING A FIRM FOUNDATION

Almost every child has the potential to grow, learn, and thrive. The nature of the relationships he has with his closest caregivers and the experiences he has when he's in their care strongly determine how much of his potential he actually achieves. In fact, science now tells us that a child's brain develops not only because cells replicate and synapses spark on their own but also because the interactions he has with his caregivers and the environments he's in help to construct and shape it. Consider, for example, the fact that babies are born into different geographies, climates, cultures, language groups, families, and so on. Your child's brain shapes itself to the needs of his environment as he encounters these and other factors.

> "During the first days, weeks, and months of life, babies are building their very earliest relationships with parents and loved ones. Their brains are the most impressionable that they will ever be. Likewise, because of this heightened time in brain development, they are the most vulnerable and susceptible to negative experiences in relationships."
>
> —*Rashanda Perryman, senior policy associate for the Children's Defense Fund at the 2011 "A Strong Start" Conference, about the achievement gap and black boys convened by ETS.*

Since a brain looks about as organized as a pile of dirty laundry, we may not think of it as having specific architecture—yet it does. From the brain stem to the limbic system to the cerebellum, the brain's structures and circuits construct themselves in a precise and intricate manner, laying the foundations first, then building increasingly complex structures and circuits on top of them. When your son is born, for example, his brain stem and spinal cord are already up and running, managing vital functions like his heartbeat, breathing, circulation, sleep, sucking, swallowing, and so on. Over time, the parts of his brain that help him babble, laugh, point, crawl, stand, regulate his emotions, read, think, and solve problems will develop. But he can't master higher functions unless the structures that underlie them exist and are stable.

Our relationship with our child helps his brain construct itself properly.

"Early relationships and the experiences that come from these relationships affect the quality of brain architecture by establishing either a sturdy foundation or fragile foundation for everything that is to follow: learning, behavior, and health—both mental and physical," says Rashanda Perryman, senior policy associate for the Children's Defense Fund.

Indeed, almost all of an infant's experiences occur with, through, or because of the people who take care of him. The family members and friends who raise and care for a child become his gateway to the world and help to shape who he will become. A youngster whose caregivers attend to his needs and who lives in surroundings that are safe, stable, predictable, nourishing, and orderly stands an excellent chance of having a strong and stable brain. Conversely, the brain (and body) of a child thrust into a setting with poverty, an insecure family life, poor nourishment, violent surroundings, and other traumatic factors will be tested. Fortunately, the human brain is tremendously malleable and the spirit indomitable, so a child born into a "hard knock life" can do well in spite of it, as long as just a few members of his Village shower him with love and attention.

So our charge, as parents, as a child's Village, and as a larger community, is to create a protective environment that lasts for *no less than five years* so that his brain can lay a strong and stable foundation on which his personality, interests, gifts, and talents can safely and robustly emerge.

PROMPTLY, WARMLY, SENSITIVELY

Our foremost goal for our newborn child doesn't involve decorating his nursery, buying a stylish diaper bag, or getting the cutest baby booties. Instead, focus on creating an environment of stable relationships around him, particularly with his primary caregiver. This caregiver—typically his mother, although it could be his father, grandparent, adoptive parent, or another loved one—should focus on creating a *secure attachment* with him, a nonverbal emotional relationship that tells him he's safe and loved and that his needs will be met. A baby is capable of having a secure attachment with one—and only one—primary caregiver. It develops when that caregiver responds to his coos, cries, gestures, and facial expressions and then matches the caregiving to his needs, whether for food, a clean diaper, a nap, or some cuddling. Seems simple, right? But it's actually very profound. Responding to a baby's needs very attentively helps his brain to organize itself. A securely attached infant is well on his way to a successful life because the attachment lays the groundwork that will help him communicate clearly, interact effectively, and have successful relationships as he grows and develops.

> A **secure attachment** refers to a nonverbal emotional relationship we have with our son that tells him he's safe and loved, and that his needs will be met. Developing a secure attachment with our new child is of primary importance.

But establishing a secure attachment doesn't happen automatically just because you're the baby's parent—it takes effort. The most effective way to develop the attachment is to use a *contingent responsive*, or *serve-and-return*, approach to interacting with him, a three-step process of sensing and responding to his needs. Step One takes place when your son *signals* by babbling, crying, gesturing, or looking at you in that heart-melting way that indicates he wants you to respond. But wait, what did that babbling actually *mean*? At first, you'll have to follow your intuition (or guess) until you learn instinctively what each signal means.

"We don't always interpret the signals correctly, but that's okay," says educational researcher Ursula Johnson. "We just continue to try until we get it right. Kids will let you know."

Step Two involves responding to your son so that he knows that you understand (or are trying to understand) what he's communicating. "Respond promptly, warmly, and sensitively," says Dr. Johnson. "Pay attention to your tone; if you're doing something fun, then your tone should match that. If you're trying to soothe or cajole, your tone should be softer and slower."

Once you respond, he'll engage in Step Three—answering your response to him by signaling again.

Over time, your attentiveness will teach your son that you love and understand him and are there to meet all his needs. Before long he will feel safe enough in his relationship with you to scoot, crawl, or wander off, knowing that you will provide a safe haven no matter what happens. Teach all of his caregivers to interact with him in this manner—whether his siblings, daycare providers, your niece who watches him for you, babysitters you hire, or your nanny. And even though you (or they) may be stretched between the stove and the washing machine, remember to place your son where he can see you. Securely attached babies are likely to grow into self-reliant children and ambitious adults, able to have productive relationships, try new things, solve problems easily, and manage stress effectively.

As simple as this process sounds, it's easier said than done.

Different people have different natural abilities. This has nothing to do with their formal education or even their best intentions. For example, even though Michèle's mother doesn't have much formal education, she was able to smile and coo at her grandbabies for hours at a time. But others—who may understand the importance of this kind of attachment in an academic sense—may struggle, perhaps because that wasn't how they themselves were raised. If you don't have a natural knack, you need to cultivate the skill.

Also, these days many parents have a hard time de-stressing, especially in the presence of a needful baby making cryptic sounds. But when we're stressed, our vocal tone becomes unpleasant, and it's hard for us to slow our words down to a pace a young child can relate to.

> "Pay attention to your rate of speech. Sometimes we talk too fast and our kids can't catch up to what we're trying to tell them. And keep an eye on your facial expressions. We may be in a good mood but look angry, and our kids pick up on that."
>
> —Ursula Johnson, education researcher

Our daycare operator Marty noticed how many parents are distracted by their cell phones and pay less attention to their children's needs than is optimal. This could also be true when we use other types of electronic devices.

Even if you're not the child's primary caretaker, you still play an important role in expressing your love and making your presence felt. In our family, even though Joe isn't a coo-at-the-baby type, he communicated his love for his baby sons by spending long hours with them.

But this serve-and-return approach to interacting with babies may bump heads with the child-rearing conventions of some African American families, among them the belief that you shouldn't comfort your baby too much when he fusses or you risk spoiling him and the idea that to raise a tough boy, you shouldn't cuddle or hold him a lot. We do not know definitively where these beliefs come from. Some experts believe that our elders adopted these practices as coping mechanisms during slavery, Reconstruction, and the segregation of Jim Crow. Back then, black children were often wrenched away from or otherwise separated from their parents—particularly their mothers, who were often required to attend to the needs of white children. So a black child who was so attached to his parents that he couldn't survive apart from them was at risk. And parents taught their sons to limit their emotional expressiveness, lest a relaxed moment get them whipped or strung up from a tree.

These and other legacy parenting practices helped many a black boy live to see another day. But early-parenting practices inherited from the days of slavery and Jim Crow will not create a black child who can thrive in the Information Age. In fact, using these techniques today will likely lead to an *insecure attachment*. Insecurely attached babies grow to become children who avoid people, have a difficult time forming successful relationships, stress out easily, and demonstrate excessive levels of anger, anxiety, and fear. Today's world rewards males who can relate to others effectively, thrive under stress, and express a wide range of emotions—except anger, which mainstream society does not tolerate from black males of any age. Research shows that fewer black (53 percent) and Hispanic (57 percent) children form a secure emotional attachment to their mother than do white (65 percent) and Asian (61 percent) children.

So although we may need to approach early parenting a little differently than Big Mama may have, how wonderful to know that one of the most important keys to a black boy's ability to develop these qualities can be found as close as our own families and extended community—it's something we can do simply by following and cultivating our natural urge to love them! And it is available to us free of charge. We can even educate our Village about serve-and-return nurturing, starting with the people who attend our bridal or baby shower—perhaps even in the form of a game at the shower itself!—so that when we interact with and care for each other's children, we do so in ways that help them grow and develop.

EXECUTIVE EDUCATION

Using a serve-and-return parenting style also gives a black boy a head start on developing his higher cognitive functions.

"We know that high-quality, warm, responsive caregiving in the early years really supports optimal brain development, which is critical to achievement," says Dr. Aisha Ray. "This development takes place in the prefrontal cortex of the brain, where executive functioning—that is, higher-order thinking, figuring out ambiguities, and handling emotional and intellectual complexities—is situated. . . . That's all wrapped up in caregiving."

The prefrontal cortex is essential to learning, problem solving, and particularly abstract problem solving.

Children with strong executive function can process a lot of information coming at them at once, make better decisions, recognize and correct mistakes, plan for the future, and manage their frustrations. They also tend to exhibit *soft skills*—the ability to focus, sit still, control their behavior, manage their emotions, and build relationships— that they need to succeed in other areas of life, from the classroom and their Cub Scout troop to their basketball team and, later, the world of work.

It is particularly important for parents of black boys to cultivate their sons' executive function. When all black children are preschoolers, they begin to experience racial *micro-aggressions,* brief but frequent indignities that others may or may not intend or even realize they committed. Learning to handle these situations in a controlled manner is crucial. These acts of aggression can come from other kids. For example, Wren's experience with her son is not unusual:

"My four-year-old son used to love to go to daycare, but after a while he didn't want to go to school," she says. "We had made a choice to send him to an almost all-white program because we wanted the education. But one day he told us that a kid had told him that he was dirty. We pulled him out of there right away and put him in the daycare at a black church. He has to be able to be comfortable—literally—in his own skin. He needed a more nurturing environment."

But these kinds of situations are not unique to kids. Because the media portrays—and people throughout society internalize and act upon—very distorted and devastating images and stereotypes of black boys as being violent, dangerous, hypersexual, and otherwise incorrigible, black boys, starting in the very early years, begin to experience a shocking amount of inappropriate behavior and even hostility from adults.

"When I ask people what grade they think a black kid is most likely to be expelled at, most people assume middle school because that's when pubertal changes kick in. But it's actually pre-K," says clinical psychologist Howard Stevenson, a professor in the applied psychology and human development division of the Graduate School of Education at the University of Pennsylvania and an expert in black children and families. "The research shows that black males are two to four times more likely to be expelled even though they're not behaving any differently compared to other kids. When black boys are emotional, disruptive, or distractible in a classroom, it's often looked at as a behavioral-management issue rather than through the lens of normal child development." (We'll explore negative media images in greater depth in Chapter 4, and the racial gap in discipline in Chapter 6.)

A child whose brain is developing closer to its greatest capacity will be better able to handle micro-insults. He'll be more adept at sidestepping negativity coming from others and managing his own emotions than a child whose brain is less robustly developed.

But let's not fool ourselves—it's also true that some children are really out of hand.

"I had a two-year-old pick up a chair above his head and throw it across the room. His grandmother had bought him the movie *Child's Play 1–4,* and he was watching it before coming to school," says Charlotte, the director of a nursery school. "The family followed my directions to get him some help, but then they ran into the quagmire of trying to access it. It took two months to get an appointment and another two to three months to get services. That's five months that I have to deal with a kid throwing chairs, but I'm liable once he does it the second time. Another parent could say: 'Didn't you know he does this? Why didn't you do something to protect my child?' I had to ask the family to leave my program. Needless to say, the mother cussed me out. That's when I knew, there's nothing I can do with this kid."

We know that these kinds of situations exist. Not every child (or parent) has received what Big Mama used to call "good home training."

"The prefrontal cortex can help children handle the stressful situations, micro-aggressions, and environmental cues that they experience from a very early age that tell them that the larger society evaluates them differently and may think that something is wrong with them because they are black males," says Dr. Ray.

A well-developed prefrontal cortex can also help black children deal with life situations whose complexity lies far beyond their child development stage, situations that many black kids are forced to deal with, like needing to help with siblings and manage household responsibilities at a young age.

The prefrontal cortex can also help black children process the high degree of ambiguity that they encounter. For example, they not only have to distinguish between a capital O and a zero, as other children do, they also need to discern between, say, the color black and the racial/sociopolitical designation black.

But this part of the brain, so crucial to learning, "is very substantially affected by short-term stress and almost surely by long-term stress as well," says University of Michigan social psychologist Richard Nisbett, author of *Intelligence and How to Get It: Why Schools and Cultures Count,* at a 2011 conference hosted by Harvard University's Achievement Gap Initiative. "If you look at an inner-city neighborhood in the weeks following a murder in that neighborhood, IQ scores are ten points lower. It's an absolutely massive short-term effect."

Of course, IQ tests measure only one out of the many different types of intelligence, but remember, a score of 100 designates average intelligence and roughly correlates with a person's ability to earn an associate's degree, and 85 lies at the bottom of the normal range and often correlates with becoming a high school dropout.[1] So a ten-point drop can have life-altering consequences. Far too many of our children live in neighborhoods where murder and other forms of violence—not to mention other stressors—are common.

"We're beginning to get evidence that long-term stress, which is far more common with lower-SES [socioeconomic status] kids, may do permanent damage to the prefrontal cortex," Dr. Nisbett says. "So attempts to reduce stress are surely important in the short term and surely have an effect on learning in the short term and may have very important long-term effects as well."[2]

HANDLE WITH CARE

Unfortunately, many black children are born into circumstances that make it exceedingly difficult for their loved ones to provide the type of childcare that allows their prefrontal cortex to develop optimally.

For example, almost 40 percent of black children grow up in poverty, which threatens a child's physical, mental, emotional, and even spiritual well-being, even though many children overcome it and go on to live successful and productive lives.[3]

Many factors beyond a child's control increase the odds that he will grow up in a low-income family—from his parents' health and educational level to the zip code he lives in. One factor that dramatically increases those chances is being born to unmarried parents. In 2011, more than 70 percent of black children were born to single mothers, and almost 70 percent of black children lived in single-parent families.[4]

Many people associate single parenting with low levels of education and low socioeconomic status. That's not always the case. In

2009, 32 percent of black children were born to single women who had a college degree, according to *The New York Times*.[5] But no matter what your socioeconomic position, let's face it: It's a lot harder to make ends meet and to parent the way you'd really like to when you're carrying the entire load by yourself.

For example, children who live with two married parents (67 percent) are far more likely to be read to every day than children who live with only one (43 percent) or with two unmarried parents (24 percent). (The reason for the difference between one- and two-parent unmarried households is unclear—but perhaps it just means that single parents really do work harder.)[6]

Frankly, we are not big believers in marriage. Not only is it a relatively new institution for humankind, the marriage itself is less important than the partners' ability to sustain long-term intimate relationships. Put another way, to have a healthy long-term intimate relationship, a person has to be able to trust his or her mate, have strong self-esteem, and possess mature *defensive coping skills*—the capacity to transform uncomfortable thoughts and feelings into more comfortable ones rather than shoving them aside as though they aren't there, only to have them surface in other ways. A person could be—and many are—married, but the relationship may not have these healthy characteristics. In fact, depending on the situation, the child might be better off if the couple weren't married. The point being, if you have those skills, you can have a stable relationship even if you're not married.

We had been living together for two years when Idris was born, for eight years when we had Miles. When we finally married, it was not because of religious or moral reasons (although for years Michèle's mother had been making it very clear that she didn't like our choice); we got married because Michèle needed health insurance. By then Miles was nine months old and Idris was already seven. So we are the last people who thought we'd ever be talking about the downside of having children outside of marriage.

But having said that, we don't want to ignore the data, for they challenge us to think creatively and plan proactively around how we can come together as couples, extended families, and Villages and in other configurations we possibly haven't thought of yet to create environments where our children's brains can develop optimally and to protect their prefrontal cortexes from stress. This is not a conversation about morality; it's a conversation about protecting our son's prefrontal cortex so he can learn, manage his emotions, and regulate his behavior.

Generally, children who live with two married biological or adoptive parents have better health and access to health care and fewer emotional and behavioral problems. When they live with two parents in a marriage without a lot of conflict in it, they tend to do better across the board than do children who grow up with stepparents. In fact, young people who grow up with stepparents often perform similarly to children who live in single-parent homes. Kids whose parents are divorced tend not to do as well in school, socially or psychologically, as children living with married parents.[7]

Children whose parents are married are more than twice as likely to live in a family whose income falls in the top third of U.S. households (more than $89,000) than children in the lowest third (less than $42,000). Kids who grow up with both their folks in the home are more likely to move to a higher socioeconomic group than children who don't.[8] From a financial standpoint, cohabitating families tend to fall between married families and single-parent families. Children who live with a mother and a grandparent sometimes do better and sometimes do worse than those who live just with their mom.[9]

In a world in which more affluent parents have a tremendous advantage in helping their children take music lessons, attend specialized summer camps, go on vacations, and otherwise participate in experiences that develop their intelligence and critical-thinking skills, having a higher income can give a child a leg up.

This doesn't mean that a single parent can't raise a very successful son. Can you say President Barack Obama, Dr. Ben Carson, Malcolm X, LeBron James, and Shawn Carter (Jay Z), for example?

"There's a bias that says that black boys aren't going to grow up quite well enough if their mothers raise them. But there's a lot of contradictory evidence that suggests that single parents, whether male or female, can successfully raise children. There are a lot of black boys whose mamas raised them, and they're doing just fine. What determines whether an adult can successfully rear a boy is not gender, but the love and deep caring that the adult gives the boy."

—*Dr. Aisha Ray*

But raising a child is a whole lot easier when someone else is there to help—assuming that your marriage or long-term co-parenting relationship is healthy. And let's be real: two incomes are better than one, especially during an era in which we can no longer count on the existence of a social safety net.

"Instability and complexity affect children's well-being," says Oscar Barbarin III, chair of the psychology department at Tulane University and an expert in the psychology of black males. "There's more asthma, more obesity, more depression and anxiety, more aggressive behavior—particularly among boys—and more attention problems. These are related causally to the instability and complexity of the family."[10]

And research shows that rocky relationships—particularly break-ups—destabilize boys more than they destabilize girls.

"We have found that boys in general are more sensitive and seem to react more than girls to family instability; that is, changes in partnerships," says sociologist and public affairs professor Sara McLanahan, director of Princeton University's Center for Research on Child Well-being, whose work focuses on families with children under age ten.

"My son was a toddler when his mom and I split up. He's sixteen now and doesn't remember us being together," says Bernard. "Some of the most painful memories I have are of leaving him and his incredible emotional dramatic response every time."

Research by Dr. McLanahan and others shows that families

headed by black unmarried parents tend to be significantly less stable, and the parents' relationships less likely to endure, than the unmarried partnerships among people of other backgrounds. In fact, studies show that if a black boy's parents weren't married when he was born, the chances that they will have gotten married or will be living together by the time he turns five are very low—9 percent and 13 percent, respectively. Another 6 percent will still be seeing each other romantically but not living together.[11] More than 20 percent of black couples who had been living together when their son was born, 28 percent of those who were dating, and 44 percent of those who weren't romantically involved will no longer be a couple by the time of their son's fifth birthday.[12]

The facts are painful: Racism as well as factors such as failing schools, the high unemployment rate, the so-called war on drugs, the demographic imbalance created by the mass incarceration of black men, social service policies that pull black families apart, and other factors continue to challenge black family stability. It isn't right, but it's true. Black couples, extended families, and Villages need to be strategic about maximizing our resources and optimizing whatever family construct and environment we live in so that our sons can fulfill their potential.

KEEPING DAD IN THE PICTURE

But finances aren't the only factor in this equation. Breakups increase the likelihood that the boy will become estranged from his father, a relationship that is tremendously important to his well-being.

"Men serve as teachers and role models for their sons and the first safe male relationship or 'beau' for their daughters," says Margaret Beale Spencer, a professor of human development and urban education at the University of Chicago. "Fathers must teach and model for boys what it means to be a responsible and psychologically healthy man, so boys and young men don't have to engage in hypermasculine [excessively macho] behavior to reaffirm their manhood because they know what authentic manhood looks like."

Boys whose fathers are highly involved in their lives—meaning that they consistently eat with them, play with them, work on projects together, read to them, help with homework, go to their activities, have private conversations, and go on outings with them—do better in life than boys whose fathers are not involved. An elementary school–aged boy with an actively engaged dad is more likely to be sociable, have greater initiative, and achieve As in school, and he is less likely to have behavioral problems or repeat a grade than a boy whose pop doesn't hang out with him much. The same is true during adolescence, when a young man whose dad is involved in his life is more likely to enjoy school and get mostly As and less likely to get suspended or expelled. In fact, having an active dad predicts whether a boy will get mostly As in school more accurately than having an amazing mom.[13]

The benefits extend to kids whose dads don't live in their home.

"Research shows that the children of dads who were not residential fathers on average were better if their dad was involved," says Roland Warren, executive director of the National Fatherhood Initiative.

A father's presence is particularly important for black boys, who can be especially vulnerable in their communities—urban, suburban, and otherwise—and whose fathers can help shield them from some of the risks they face.

Despite the negative media portrayals of black men as deadbeats—and our personal knowledge of a dad (and mom) or two whom we wish would be more involved—several studies show that black non-resident fathers are more engaged with their children than fathers of other races and ethnicities are. They tend to have better co-parenting relationships with the mother of the boy.[14]

In fact, one study found that nonresident black fathers are more likely to visit their children than white or Hispanic counterparts. Another study found that they are more likely to participate in decisions around child-raising.[15] These are strengths that couples, families, and communities can build on in the interest of cultivating the child's developing brain and helping him become socially well adjusted and emotionally stable.

"Good fathers do three things: they provide, they nurture, and they guide," says Warren. "The 'provide' part most guys get, but it's not just about *presents,* it's about *presence.* The most valuable commodity that anyone has is their time. Kids are wired to understand that the most important thing you can give is your time and your love."

Deemphasizing the traditional provider role and increasing emphasis on the nurturing and guiding aspects of fatherhood may be particularly important during these times of high un- and underemployment and economic uncertainty.

Still, many fathers are not involved enough—often because of relationship strain. For example, many nonresident fathers of all races become less involved with their existing children when they move on to new relationships and have children with new partners. And some custodial mothers restrict access to the couple's children based on how well she's getting along with the father or whether he's paying his child support.

"The most important thing is for fathers to make sure they have a good relationship with the mother of their children," Warren says. "It provides an on-ramp for having access to your kids in a non-conflict way. And when you can affirm her, you're actually affirming your child, because your child loves her. But if you have not developed an ability to turn mom from a gatekeeper to a gateway, all this other stuff is moot."

"Fathers have to get beyond the relationship with the mother," says Rev. Dr. Alyn E. Waller, senior pastor of the Enon Tabernacle Baptist Church in Philadelphia, whose training is in marriage and family counseling. "A lot of times the relationship with the mother is the determining factor of whether the father will get adequate time with their child. As soon as something goes wrong with the mother, the father wants nothing to do with the child. We've got to help men understand that in spite of your relationship with the woman, you have to raise your child if you want to change what is happening in your family life."

Breakups tend to result in more complex families, which typically create a less stable environment for a child. In Dr. McLanahan's study, almost 25 percent of black unmarried moms bore at least one child by a different partner within the first five years of their son's life, as compared to 18 percent of all women and 17 percent of Hispanic women.[16] (The study authors didn't measure the percentage of fathers having children by additional partners; we would guess that it's high.) Dad's relationship with any additional children and family he has can detract from time with his other children.

Remember, the first five years are a particularly critical time for strong brain development, and family instability has a greater impact on boys. A couple's ability to co-parent cooperatively and provide their son with stability during these years—whether they are together as a couple or not—may give him the edge he needs to excel academically, experience emotional stability, and exhibit balanced behavior so that he can fulfill his potential.

NEW CONVERSATIONS

But how do we create the stable marriages, unions, and relationships that are so important for our children's development during this period when centuries' worth of systemic and structural forces—from slavery, the difficult migration to the North, government social welfare policies, high unemployment, the crack epidemic, and now mass incarceration—pull black relationships and families apart even when parents love each other and want to be together?

We don't profess to have all—or even many—of the answers. But we believe that by laying out the relationships between what a child needs for his brain to develop optimally and the conditions that are required for that to happen, we can spur novel conversations about how we can approach these issues collectively. Some couples, for example, may decide to get married, or commit themselves to staying together or at least to developing strong co-parenting relationships until their son graduates kindergarten. Elders may decide to play a more proactive and supportive role in helping young couples work out their difficulties in ways that promote healthy relationships.

"Back in the day, parents would tell you that they stayed together for the sake of the kids," says Roberta, a mother of four and grand-mom of ten.

Single women may decide not to bear children solo or to get more support from their extended families than they originally envisioned.

"I never imagined that at thirty-two I'd move back to my home-town and live with my parents, but that may be the best thing to do, so I can take some time off to take care of my son like I want to," says Jana.

Perhaps we need to live in more intergenerational households—ones with low stress and high cooperation.

The 97 Percent

Only 3 percent of single moms across all races and eth-nicities **do not** change partners at all during the first five years of the life of the child.

There's certainly a role for the Village to play in reimagining the types of support services they provide to children and young families. For example, perhaps more churches will offer parenting classes and others will develop ministries whose specific goal is to support young parents. Maybe biological and "play" aunties, uncles, and grandpar-ents can provide a cocoon of loving relationships that will nurture a young child. Social service organizations could certainly provide ser-vices that support young children. And policies that help people access high-quality daycare, earn a living wage, reduce mass incarceration, and so on will help stabilize families and communities.

Nonblack educators and allies of other races can remember that some children endure significant challenges at home. Be patient, re-member that they're children, and show them that you love them.

And if you have children whom you've already raised differently, or are a single parent and "it is what it is," so to speak, take heart.

"It would be nice in this world if every child had two loving, caring parents. But every kid doesn't have those folks," says Dr. Ray. "What really matters is the degree to which whoever is rearing you loves the hell out of you and is able to show you that in a way that helps you learn how to be a loving, mature, and caring person."

Keeping the Promise

1. **Create a secure attachment with your child.** Combine your natural urge to love your child with deliberate techniques to express it effectively.

2. **Develop his executive functions.** Higher level brain functions can be cultivated early in life and will help your young son excel in any environment and cope with difficulties when they arise.

3. **Maximize resources.** Whether married or not, or if both parents are present or not, we must optimize whatever family construct we have to help our sons fulfill their potential.

3

BE HIS FIRST TEACHER

How to Begin Your Son's Education at Home

As a single parent I spent a lot of time in the car with my children, picking them up and taking them back. One evening we were on our way home, and it was one of those days that the sunset was spectacular, and I just made what I thought was a simple comment: "Wow, isn't that beautiful. Look at the sun going down. . . ." And I remember just as plain as day, my three-year-old son asking me, "Where is the sun going?"

Now, I wasn't concerned about teaching my children A-B-C, 1-2-3—anyone can do that; you can train a monkey to count. I was concerned about teaching them reasoning skills and to think critically about the world around them. And I knew the kind of mind my son would need to have in order to thrive as a black male. I also knew my own limitations and that I'd have to be resourceful to accomplish that. I don't have a lot of money to give my son things. But I knew I could ground him in a factual reasoning process.

So when my son asked that question, I felt like I was at a parental fork in the road. I could have told him some fairy-tale, make-believe stuff—you know, the sun goes to sleep like you go to sleep and it wakes up like you wake up. But I didn't want to stunt his growth. So I called down to a friend of mine who was a security guard at the science museum and told him what I was trying to do. The museum was closed, but he let us in after hours and turned on the lights to the planetarium. I had never been to the planetarium before, and I haven't been there since. But that night he and I sat there with my three-year-old son, looking at the solar system on the ceiling. We looked at the orbit of the sun and moon around the sky, and that the sun isn't going anywhere; it's the earth that's moving.

My three-year-old son engaged and processed the information. And that's when I learned what the capacity of a child is even at that young age. From that point on, it was a matter of nurturing what he clearly was already prepared for and capable of. But it easily could have been a missed opportunity that played itself out over a lifetime.

—*Louis, health educator*

SEARCHING UPSTREAM

Until recently, educators and experts have assumed that black boys' struggles began at eight or nine and escalate during their teens. But research suggests that black boys' academic and perhaps behavioral challenges tend to begin at a far earlier age.

"We're pulling drowning kids out of the water rather than seeing what upstream is pushing them in," says psychologist Oscar Barbarin of Tulane University.[1]

In this chapter we'll talk about early learning at home, including:

- Understanding your role as your son's first teacher.
- Discovering pre-reading and early math activities you and your child can engage in easily and inexpensively to build up abilities that will help him avoid the third grade slump.
- Figuring out how to take charge of closing at least some of the early gap by being much more aggressive in our approach to educating our children early.
- Understanding methods to teach our sons by playing and having fun with them, which allows us to de-stress.
- Identifying quality daycare so that your son's not getting "pushed in" while you're out makin' the bacon.

> **Promise your son that you will ignite his love of learning long before he starts preschool by talking to him constantly, using adult words, reading to him daily, exposing him to the world and explaining it to him, playing with him and encouraging physical activity, and leaving him with caregivers who stimulate his brain.**

The Gap by the Numbers

The Early Childhood Longitudinal Study, Birth Cohort (ECLS-B), tested a nationally representative group of fourteen thousand American children born in 2001 to assess their cognitive, social, emotional, and physical development when they were infants, toddlers, and preschoolers.[2] When the children were nine months old, few differences existed in cognitive abilities. But by the time children were two, smaller percentages of black and Hispanic children than white, Asian, or mixed-race children were proficient in all of the cognitive skills. Black children were more skillful at fine and gross motor skills.[3] When the children were retested at four, cognitive differences still existed: Fewer black (55 percent) and Hispanic (51 percent) children knew their numbers and shapes than white (73 percent), Asian (81 percent), and mixed-race (65 percent) children. By that age Asian, white, and mixed-race children had passed black children in fine motor skill development.[4] By *fine motor skills* we mean coordinating their eyes with their use of the small muscles of their fingers and hands—activities such as pinching, grabbing a cup, turning the pages of a book, and in time, drawing or playing with Legos. By *gross motor skills* we mean the ability to use his larger, stronger muscles to, say, hold up his head, sit, crawl, and eventually walk, run, and jump.

The good news is that these are the types of deficits that parents, caregivers, and other members of the Village can address—and some of us already are addressing it. In fact, in 2005 black parents were far more likely to read to their three- to five-year-old children (79 percent); teach them letters, words, or numbers (81 percent); or teach them songs or music (56 percent) than they were in 1993. Black parents had caught up with white parents in telling their children stories (54 percent) and had surpassed everyone, including Asians (61 percent), in teaching letters, words, or numbers (63 percent). They were also more likely than any parents but Hispanics (59 percent) to teach their children songs or music (56 percent). (Low-income families of all races made some of the greatest improvements during these years, although their children still lag considerably behind other children.)

We should celebrate our community's progress, but if black children are to catch up, individually and collectively, we need to redouble our efforts.[5] In spite of these improvements, black (35 percent) and Hispanic (37 percent) parents are far less likely to read to their young children every day than white (67 percent) and Asian (60 percent) parents are.[6] And as we'll explain in Chapter 7, our use of electronics is jeopardizing these gains.

A study of school readiness published in 2010 examined the learning experiences of a group of diverse students who entered kindergarten in 1998-1999 and tracked them through eighth grade, in 2007.[7] When the children entered kindergarten, researchers tested children's fine motor, executive function, and early comprehension abilities. At that very young age, *executive function* means their ability to focus, demonstrate self-control, stay on task, transition smoothly between activities, and not bother their neighbors while they work. And *early comprehension* means how well they understand basic facts about the world—say, knowing their colors and when the moon rises.[8] These are the precursors to early math and reading skills.

The data showed that when these black children started kindergarten, on average they were already testing nine months behind their white classmates in fine motor skills, ten months behind in executive function, and fifteen months behind in early comprehension, says the study's lead author, David Grissmer, a research professor at the Center for Advanced Study of Teaching and Learning at the University of Virginia, whose work includes researching how to close these pre-K gaps.

"Boys are worse than girls in building executive function and motor skills. So black boys are starting with a year or more of developmental delay in those skills when they start kindergarten," says Dr. Grissmer.

"If a child is behind at age five, the gap between where they are and where they should be does not decrease over time, it expands," says Oscar Barbarin III, a psychology professor at Tulane University.[9]

Indeed, the reading gap between black and white children increases dramatically between the first and third grades and grows through middle school. The math gap progressively widens from kindergarten through the eighth grade. By contrast, Hispanic children's reading gap levels off at third grade, and their math gap narrows between kindergarten and eighth grade.[10] By twelfth grade, the reading skills of the average black child, who scores 269, are years behind those of the average Asian student, who scores 298.[11] Significant differences in test scores exist in math, science, and writing skills as well; you can get quick snapshots at the Child Trends Data Bank (www.childtrends.org, under the tabs "our research education"). It's unclear to what extent test scores measure actual ability—this is a matter that even the leading authorities debate. Questions also exist about the degree to which tests are biased.

And experts tell us that this gap crosses socioeconomic lines. For example, the 2007 Nation's Report Card shows that black eighth grade children of all socioeconomic groups scored significantly worse in math than low-income whites.[12] And the black eighth-graders in the ECLS-K cohort and who are not from low-income backgrounds score similarly to low-income whites.

Before our sons reach that stage, we need to get ahead of these problems by dealing with them at the earliest points.

GIVE HIM A LEG UP

A young child's brain grows at an explosive rate—increasing from 25 percent of the weight of an adult's brain at birth to 80 percent by the age of three and to 90 percent by the age of five.

Between the ages of three and five, the areas that handle language, executive function, emotional development, and social skills develop faster than Usain Bolt can run the 100-meter dash.

"These are the cognitive parts of the brain you need to develop early in order to have high functioning later," says Dr. Grissmer. "If you don't build these brain circuits, it makes everything you do later with them inefficient."

In fact, beginning when their children are very young, highly educated parents give their children a leg up by intentionally investing time and resources to build these areas of their brain. Given the high stakes, parents of other backgrounds can no longer afford to leave their baby's brain development to chance or to wait until preschool or kindergarten to begin his formal education. Instead, it's important that we take charge of stimulating our son's brain at home not only so it is wired to learn when he begins school but so that he enjoys learning as well.

A parent's inclination to educate the child at home may be influenced by their own socioeconomic upbringing. Those of us who come from families whose members weren't highly educated may unknowingly take a less aggressive approach to starting our child's education than more affluent parents do. For example, we may tend to wait until preschool before beginning our son's formal education or believe that a professional educator can do a better job of teaching him than we can. Consistent with this, parents who have a bachelor's degree are more likely than parents who have some college education (but not a four-year degree) to tell researchers that upon entering kindergarten, their child can recognize all their letters (39 percent vs. 28 percent), count to 20 or higher (71 percent vs. 62 percent), write his name (68 percent vs. 60 percent), hold a pencil with his fingers (90 percent vs. 83 percent), speak clearly enough that a stranger can understand him (97 percent vs. 93 percent), and read words written in books (10 percent vs. 8 percent). (The average black parent's responses track somewhere in between these two groups.) As parents obtain more education (or have less), these differences widen.[13]

"As far as his education, I don't really know what I'm supposed to do," says Krystal, the high school–educated mother of a four-year-old son. "He has his toys and we read sometimes but as far as getting him flash cards and those educational games—I don't get into all that. His teachers at his preschool take care of what he is supposed to learn. We do the work that they send home."

"With working-class parents it's a reasonable decision to turn over responsibility to schools or doctors or other institutions," says sociologist Annette Lareau, author of *Unequal Childhoods: Class, Race, and Family Life*. "After all, the parents are high school dropouts or high school graduates. Why should they know how to educate their kids? They don't know. They have a notion of educators as experts. . . . Parents who have a college degree could have become a teacher; they simply chose not to. They are an equal with an educator. If anything they're a social superior. I think that provides an advantage," says Dr. Lareau.

Perhaps not surprisingly, given that many black families have only recently entered the middle class, the data suggest that the average black parent's beliefs about the role they play in educating their pre-kindergartner are very similar to the expectations of working-class (and low-income) parents. For example, fewer black parents than white parents believe that they need to prepare their children before kindergarten in the following ways: teaching him the alphabet (43 percent vs. 66 percent), to share (38 percent vs. 76 percent), to read (41 percent vs. 48 percent), to know his numbers (43 percent vs. 62 percent), or how to hold a pencil (34 percent vs. 47 percent). Interestingly, Asian and Latino parents' responses to these questions are very similar to black parents' answers. All are comparable to those of people with a high school diploma as well as to the responses of low-income parents. The average parent of all backgrounds reads to their child for about twenty-one minutes at a time.[14]

Yet both white (67 percent) and Asian (60 percent) parents are significantly more aggressive than black (35 percent) and Hispanic (37 percent) parents when it comes to reading to their son every day. Black parents (43 percent) are more likely to report reading to their son three or more times a week. The frequency with which black parents of all income groups read to their children is similar to the general subset of poor parents.[15]

But don't get down on black parents just yet.

Black children are just as likely to recognize all of the letters, count to 20 or higher, and hold a pencil with their fingers and are twice as likely to read written words in books as are white children before entering kindergarten.[16] And when black parents do read to their kids, they are significantly more likely to ask what is in a picture (63 percent vs. 59 percent Hispanic and 54 percent Asian), to stop reading to point out letters (41 percent vs. 37 percent Hispanic and 32 percent Asian), to ask him to read along with them (32 percent vs. 29 percent Asian and 26 percent Hispanic), and to talk about what happened in the story (68 percent vs. 58 percent Hispanic and 54 percent white) than are any other parents. In fact, our interactivity in these areas smokes even parents with a graduate or professional degree.[17] These facts make us feel excited and optimistic about the amount of progress our community will make once we connect these activities and combine our greater interactivity with a greater number of reading sessions each week.

However, in order to move forward, we will need to pull our children away from the TV. Black pre-kindergartners watch considerably more television and videos on weekdays (3.1 hours) and weekends (3.3 hours) than do Asian (2.2 and 2.5) and white (2.4 and 2.6) children, with Hispanic children falling somewhere in between. In fact, the average black preschooler spent more time watching TV than either poor children or the children of high school dropouts.[18]

Our children lag academically but lead in watching the boob tube. And as we will lay out in Chapter 7, as our children grow older, this disparity widens, particularly for black boys.

SET THE PATTERN AND THE TONE

But as these statistics suggest, you don't have to have a four-year degree or even much money to ignite your son's brain. The most important piece of information you need is the knowledge that parents play
a critical role in educating their children and that it's important to
start during their earliest years. No matter how much money or formal education we have, we can use food, the park, the sky, the library,
a museum, and even pots and pans or other common household objects to teach our son, to make learning fun, to help him look forward
to preschool and kindergarten, and to teach him about school's importance. It's essential that fathers and father figures play a part in
these early learning activities. And almost anything can be an opportunity for learning.

"Starting when my children were very young—like before kindergarten age—I started teaching them black history by talking to them
about music," says Edwin. "Whether it was Bill 'Bojangles' Robinson
or James Brown or Michael Jackson or whatever young boy was sam-
pling their music, there was always a lesson going on. When they got
older and my son was listening to hip-hop, I'd ask, 'Who wrote that
song, son?' and he'd say something like, 'Well, it couldn't have been
this artist because I heard James Brown sing it first.' That's right!"

When we take on the role of our son's first teachers, we help him
build strong brain circuits and essential skills, such as those required
for early literacy. We also level the playing field and reduce the power
differential that can exist between parents and educators. As we become expert about our baby or toddler's learning process, we position ourselves to partner with professional educators. So when he
starts preschool or kindergarten, we know his likes and dislikes, his
habits, his learning style, his pet peeves, and so on better than anyone
else. We can hip his teacher to them. But if we don't work out our
son's brain during early childhood, by the time he begins formal
schooling he will likely lag behind the children of parents who have
invested in early learning.

American children can begin kindergarten at a range of ages span-ning a total of eighteen months. What's more, children develop at different rates. Just because our child is four going on five or even five doesn't mean that he's ready for kindergarten.

"You can walk into a kindergarten room and tell who will be dropouts and who will not," says one educator. "Kids who don't know their primary colors, who can't count, who don't know the whole alphabet—there's no way that kindergarten teacher can catch those kids up. They stay behind all the way through the system."

"Some of the kindergarten students don't know their address, don't know how to spell their names," another educator told us.

Unfortunately, these children may be more likely to be black or Hispanic. Although 66 percent of Asian children and 64 percent of white children aged three to six who aren't in kindergarten yet know how to write their first name, only 58 percent of black children and 50 percent of Hispanic children do.[19]

These children represent one end of the school readiness spectrum. At the other end, many affluent parents give their sons (in particular) the upper hand by *redshirting* them—holding them back from starting kindergarten—until they are 6. Redshirting boys is *en vogue* in certain circles, as kindergarten becomes more academic and people become more aware that boys tend to develop certain skills later than girls do. As a matter of fact, back in 2007 almost 10 percent of white parents were planning to redshirt their children—a percentage we believe is rising.[20] At that age, a one-year head start—which could make him as much as two years older than the youngest children in his class—can provide a boy with a tremendous intellectual, emotional, and social advantage; however, the jury's out on the long-term impact of delaying a boy's start date. Still, some black parents may want to consider redshirting their son, particularly if he would be one of the youngest members of his class or if he is slow to develop literacy skills.

"I think black kids right now should probably all start a year later—they are that far behind," Dr. Grissmer says, although he notes that holding children back does not necessarily build their skills. He recommends that at-risk black children attend two years of preschool with a curriculum that cultivates their development skills, especially by engaging in music, the arts, and other play-based activities, as we discuss below.

> **Redshirting** refers to the practice of holding back your child so that he starts kindergarten at a later age to give him more time to develop basic skills.

Redshirting has obvious financial implications—a parent has to be able to pay for an additional year of preschool for every child they hold back. Parents who can't ensure that their son will receive some kind of reguar cognitive stimulation during the delay year are probably better off starting him in school. And it's important to consider that redshirting could exacerbate the achievement gap, because it places older children—often children from families with greater resources—in the same classroom or testing cohort with children who are significantly younger or less affluent.

If you're wondering whether your child is kindergarten-ready, you can have a *child assessment psychologist* test him while he's still in preschool. Traditionally, *early childhood testing* has determined which children need special education services; however, it can serve other purposes, such as determining school readiness.

"You take a kid to the doctor and he gets his blood tested, weight, height, and everything else," says Dr. Grissmer. "We ought to measure children's executive function, fine motor skills, early comprehension. These are fairly simple tests and they are as important, if not more important, than height and weight."

OPEN THE GATEWAY

But while kindergarten is becoming increasingly academic, the latest science tells us that flash cards and worksheets aren't the best way to prepare children to compete in a world in which math, science, and reading skills are increasingly important.

"You can build a child's skills in a playful manner—no worksheets or flash cards," even when it comes to math, says Susan Levine, co-director of the Center for Early Childhood Research and chair of the psychology department at the University of Chicago.

There is a growing body of new findings about factors that impact *school readiness*, the combination of physical and motor development, personal and social development, early literacy and math skills, knowledge of the world, and other abilities that promote a youngster's success in kindergarten and beyond. The new research suggests that in addition to the basic math and reading abilities that you might predict would affect a child's test scores later on, several surprising *precognitive* skills—that is, skills that seem to have little to do with thinking or reasoning but actually precede and undergird those abilities—help him do well in math, reading, and even science all the way until middle school.

Groundbreaking research has discovered that a child's executive function, fine motor, and early comprehension skills when he enters kindergarten strongly predict how highly he will score in math and reading as far out into the future as eighth grade.[21]

"We discovered that if you could equalize these three skill sets at kindergarten entrance, you could basically wipe out three-fourths of the gap in eighth grade reading without changing the schools" or solving other intractable problems such as poverty, according to Dr. Grissmer, the study's lead author. And when the researchers looked at early math and early reading skills as well as executive function, fine motor skills, and early comprehension, they could account for about 45 percent of the variance in eighth grade math scores.

"Most people thought that the environment was shaping children's habits and behavior," Dr. Grissmer says. "What this indicates to us is that all the things that parents do *and* the environment can build particular skills in kids."

Consistent with this new understanding, researchers now know that there are many activities that parents can engage in that will help develop the brain architecture children need to read and do math—but they don't involve reading and math at all.

"Kids don't just learn the skills they need in math through math instruction only," says Dr. Grissmer. "They need these early developmental skills, which are developed completely independent of math instruction"—knowledge of their world, concentration, and fine motor skills.

We can intentionally kick-start our children's precognitive development by developing the parts of the brain that are used for later cognitive work.

And we can recruit our son's grandparents, aunties and uncles, daycare providers, babysitters, and other members of his Village to be involved.

Early Comprehension

The 800-Pound Gorilla

Beginning when he's a baby and throughout the rest of his life, read to your son and encourage him to read as often as possible—not just so that he learns how to read but also because the more education he has, the more reading he'll have to do.

"Sometimes we view reading in isolation, but it affects your ability to do well in other subjects," says Stephen Jones, associate dean of students and strategic planning at Villanova University.

Children become aware of language and develop literacy skills long before they know how to read. By *literacy skills* we mean the abilities that undergird reading and writing—knowing how language sounds, being aware of print, understanding the relationship between letters and sounds, having a vocabulary, knowing how to spell, and being able to comprehend ideas. Developing such skills early in life helps them improve their school readiness and makes it easier for them to succeed academically.

When we read to children regularly, we help them develop a larger vocabulary, increase their awareness of the sounds of speech and the names of letters, and up their ability to decode letters. The greater a child's vocabulary, the greater their later academic success. In fact, experts can predict a child's reading comprehension at age ten by knowing how many vocabulary words they know at age three. And the number of vocabulary words a child knows in first grade predicts almost one-third of his reading comprehension scores when he reaches eleventh grade.

"Math has word problems, even science has word problems. So language is the 800-pound gorilla of schooling," says sociologist Annette Lareau, a professor at the University of Pennsylvania, in Philadelphia, and author of *Unequal Childhoods: Class, Race, and Family Life.* "I interviewed an African American mom whose teacher recommended that her kid repeat first grade. The mom was dumbfounded. She told me, 'Everything is fine; the teacher just had one little thing with his reading.' But you see, a teacher sees reading as an 800-pound gorilla. You can't advance in school if your reading skills aren't good. It's a major barrier. Major!"

"It's a critical skill for everything you do. The more you read and the more outside reading you do, the more you'll be able to handle the volume of work when you go to college or trade school," says Dr. Jones.

Our son's early comprehension relies on his brain's *hippocampus,* a structure that helps create, store, and organize memories. We use our hippocampus when we make connections between different ideas—Michael Jordan and air, Jay Z and Brooklyn, Don King's afro and, umm . . . a bird's nest.

Researchers were surprised to learn that early comprehension was one of the strongest predictors of later math and reading scores. In fact, a kindergartner's early comprehension skills predict his eighth grade reading and science scores more than any other ability. In fact, Dr. Grissmer's research shows that you can do a better job of predicting a child's eighth grade reading scores by looking at his first grade early comprehension skills than you can by looking at his first grade reading scores.[22]

One of the best ways to improve this general type of knowledge is by exposing your son to a wide variety of activities—from going to the park to visiting a petting zoo to taking him to hear live music.

Dr. Grissmer believes that many black children's early comprehension gap exists because they "lack exposure to the world and somebody to help them understand that exposure."

So whatever you do with your son, be sure to point things out to him and talk to him about his experiences.

It's also essential that we read to our sons.

"Reading to children is one of the best activities for developing early comprehension skills," Dr. Grissmer says. It will strengthen his brain in ways that specifically prepare him for a world in which children with strong reading skills possess a tremendous advantage that grows over time.

"I bought my children books before they were born and read to them from the moment they came out of my belly," says Kia, the mother of one middle-schooler and one elementary school–aged boy. "They have loved books since they were able to grasp them. Early on it was difficult to tell the difference between their eating books and reading them. I didn't care—as long as they liked them. At least once a week we went to the library and looked at books and went to the story hour. Even now we go to the library at least once a week. Today, they absolutely love to read. I have to yell at my oldest son, 'Put that book down!' He'll read in the dark; he'll read on the toilet; he'll try to read in the car when it's dark outside. My youngest son's school called to tell me that he knew how to read at age three. I told them that he had just memorized the story. They told me, No, he can read. I believe that's from cultivating an early love of reading."

What's more, the function of the hippocampus can easily be undermined by stress, deficient diets, and difficulties during pregnancy—risks we discussed during Chapters 1 and 2.[23]

This is yet another reason to minimize the stress he experiences during his early years.

Fine Motor Skills

Every movement our son makes requires his brain to process very complex information, even when he's only a baby trying to grab something or bat at the mobile over his head.

"The brain is controlling hundreds of muscles with millisecond precision," says Dr. Grissmer.

This continues once he begins to walk.

"When he's moving around the room, he's building a GPS in his head," Dr. Grissmer says. "Motor skills build a very complex set of skills in the mind. The mind's learning center is built when you're doing early motor skills."

It turns out that a child relies on a lot of those very same networks when he learns to read, do math, and other tasks later on.

"Academic skills and other skills pull up those same networks that are built doing motor skills," says Dr. Grissmer. He notes that the motor circuits "get myelinated at three, four, five, six, seven—when you start using them, basically."

Your cognitive behavior and performance are affected by the amount of energy available to help your brain do what you want it to do. If a child builds circuits and they get myelinated earlier, they operate more efficiently, giving him more energy to learn new things.

"For the brain to develop something new when it comes to reading or math, it has to build on the networks that evolution gave it," Dr. Grissmer says.

A child's gross motor skills form the basis for the development of his fine motor skills—his ability to use his hands, fingers, wrists, toes, lips, and tongue. Both sets of skills help a child develop the brain networks he will use later when he does cognitive work.

"But fine motor skills develop some different things than gross motor skills do," Dr. Grissmer says. "And copy-design tasks are the largest predictors of math scores."

Copy-design tasks involve fine motor skills, but what exactly is a copy-design task? "The ability to look at something, think about it, and use your muscles to duplicate it," Dr. Grissmer says. Drawing a picture from an object or an image. Fuse Beads, Wikki Stix, Legos, Tinker Toys—any toy that involves replicating an image or structure can help a child build this capacity. So can playing an instrument. "It's one of the best ways you can learn fine motor skills," Dr. Grissmer adds.

These same precognitive skills also underlie his ability to read and understand science.

Dr. Grissmer notes that Asian children often have superior fine motor skills.

Asian alphabets, he says, require "copy-design skills like crazy" and help children develop their fine motor and physio-spatial skills. "There's sort of an ingrained fine motor culture."

Executive Function

To build a child's executive function—which, remember, lies in the prefrontal cortex—engage him in tasks that require him to replicate things.

"It's the ability to look at something, put it through your head, and have it come out of your muscles and duplicate it," says Dr. Grissmer, whether your son is looking at an image on paper or a three-dimensional model of something.

Along with the activities above, Legos and the like, and games that stop and start—hopscotch, Red light/Green light, and Simon Says, for instance—can help.

"Exercise and play in general will help the prefrontal cortex, which is very much involved in fine motor skills," said John Ratey, the author of *Spark: The Revolutionary New Science of Exercise and the Brain,* at a 2011 conference hosted by Harvard University's Achievement Gap Initiative.[24] "When you have someone moving, their prefrontal cortex is turned on and it grows. In fit versus unfit kids, their hippocampi are bigger, their prefrontal cortexes are more engaged, and parts of it are enlarged compared to unfit kids."

As soon as your son is able to sit still, try teaching him how to meditate, a skill that will help him manage stress and become more self-aware when he's older. You don't have to teach him to stop his thoughts or chant some Buddhist mantra. Just turn on some peaceful music, have him sit or lie down, and deep breathe through his nose, as though he's stopping to smell the roses, and exhale through his mouth as though he's blowing out a birthday cake.

PLAY, NOT WORKSHEETS

Play and exercise are vital to human development, but in these days of increasing screen time and teaching to the test, that fact has been all but forgotten.

"We need parents to know that play and exercise are vital to the brain development of our children," said Dr. Ratey.[25] "Our brains evolved to help us be better movers. The front part of our brain grew when we were hunter-gatherers and needed to be more precise, more planful, more sequential, smarter. Our thinking brain is the internalization of our moving brain."

Research shows that play and exercise help prime the brain to learn.

"Exercise is sort of an essential nutrient," Dr. Ratey says. "[Children] you keep from playing have smaller brains, do less well on their SATs, have a harder time socially, and become bullies or bully."

We learned that Idris performed better and had a better attention span when he exercised before school, so we always had him go shoot some baskets.

Dr. Ratey says that schools that have their children move throughout the day—from doing physical education first thing in the morning to dancing down the halls between classes—see improvements in attendance and test scores and reductions in discipline problems—even schools with few resources and low-income students.

You can even use play to teach math and reading skills.

"Make math enjoyable," says Dr. Levine. "Relate to their curiosity to get them intrigued about math and the relationships of objects to each other."

And while you may want to focus your home life on education during the week, on weekends, over breaks, and during the summer, Dr. Grissmer suggests that we intentionally play games with our children.

Playing an instrument, engaging in art, free play, playing games, and physical education develop a child's pre-cognitive abilities, both effectively and enjoyably.

"Playing games is as important as reading books," says Dr. Grissmer.

TALK THAT TALK

Talk to the Hand

Not every parent will find it easy to talk more or use a larger vocabulary—or at least not very quickly. But experts have long known that gesturing when we talk—which, with toddlers, merely means pointing to the things we're talking about and holding them up for them to look at—causes children to gesture as well. For reasons researchers don't yet understand, gesturing causes a child to use more words.

But there's one area of gesturing that researchers don't recommend—the movements promoted as "baby sign language." They don't know if it works.

We can also prepare our sons to succeed in school and start to read by making sure that they understand the vocabulary words that their teachers and other adults use as well as the ones they encounter in books and hear in movies and on TV. How much his parents and caregivers talk to him determines how much—and how quickly—a child's vocabulary grows. And, remember, a child's vocabulary goes a long way toward determining how well he reads and uses language at nine or ten and how well he understands what he reads when he's ready to take the SAT.

Some parents define good babies as ones who don't make much noise. As the old adage goes, children are to be "seen and not heard." But a baby's babbles and shrieks are precursors to speaking—we should embrace them.

Other parents don't understand why we should talk to our baby before our baby can talk back. They don't realize that even talking to him is teaching him.

"The baby learns how to talk, then you teach the baby language," says Alvin Poussaint, a professor of psychiatry and associate dean at Harvard Medical School.

"Being a mother was always important to me. I was always the kid who babysat all my cousins," says Jelissa, the mother of two sons and a daughter. "I remember that two of our cousins spoke better than the others. I asked my aunts why they sounded so eloquent. They said, 'We never did baby talk with our children. We don't do "boo-boo" and "coo-coo." That stuck with me. So even though I'm as much of a sucker for chubby cheeks as the next person, when I had my own children, I was conscious of speaking in full sentences and real words, not fake baby words and not speaking to them like they didn't understand. My oldest son, in particular, was rather precocious in his speaking."

Even if your baby doesn't babble back to you, follow Dr. Poussaint's advice and talk to him anyhow. When he was a toddler, our younger son, Miles, might as well have been mute. When Idris was a baby, he chattered all the time. But about all we could get out of Miles were some grunts. He knew how to communicate nonverbally to get what he wanted, but he wasn't using words. Even though we knew a good bit about child development, we have to admit that we were a little worried. Many of our friends' children had been talking by the time they were two. At three, when Miles finally started talking, he developed verbally and intellectually at an astounding rate. The fact that we had kept talking to and interacting with him all along finally started to show. But had we waited to talk to him until he talked to us, he would have been far behind.

The implications of how much we talk to our babies and toddlers turn out to be tremendous.

Now-famous research performed by child development experts Betty Hart and Todd Risley found that tremendous differences exist in the number of words that are spoken in different households and, consequently, in the number of words that children use. These differences broke down along socioeconomic class, even in households that are stable.[26] They discovered that on average, professional parents had a 2,176-word vocabulary, working-class parents used 1,498 words, and parents on welfare used 974 words. Consistent with this, children of professional parents had a 1,116-word vocabulary, working-class children used 749 words, and low-income children used 525 words. (The rate at which children learned new words also varied by socioeconomic status.) Kids in professional families also heard more words spoken in their home—an average of 2,153 words per hour—than children in working-class families (1,251) and low-income children (616). So in four years, the average professional child heard roughly *nineteen million more words* than a working-class child and *thirty-two million more* than a child whose parents received welfare. As a result, they had a larger vocabulary.

"Even when they were little babies, I used to talk to my sons like they could really understand and answer me," says Todd, who describes himself as a "talker." "I would tell them about how much I was grinding to provide them with a good life, I'd give them the play-by-play when the game was on—it didn't matter. People thought I was crazy, but I didn't care. Now I've got two black boys who are extremely articulate and not intimidated about talking to adults—about anything."

And not only do more affluent children hear a greater number of words, they hear more words that uplift them. By the age of four, the average child in a professional home had received over six times more encouragement than discouragement, and the average working-class kid had received two times as much encouragement as discouragement. However, the average low-income child had received only one encouraging word for every five discouraging ones.

"Nothing I do is ever good enough," says Tariq, 11, who attends a highly ranked suburban school. "My mom expects me to do my homework while she's criticizing me. How can I focus when she's so negative?"

When researchers revisited the families when the children were nine and ten, they discovered that the children with the largest vocabularies when they were three had the best vocabulary and language test scores when they were older as well. Of course, by the time that they're ten, children of professional parents benefit in countless additional ways that working-class and low-income parents cannot afford, even if they'd like to.

Fortunately, anyone can build their vocabulary relatively easily—and quite inexpensively. We can learn new words by reading the newspaper, buying vocabulary books, downloading spelling apps, playing spelling bee games, upgrading the degree of difficulty of the books and publications we read, and using the dictionary to look up and practice words we're unfamiliar with. This can even be done as a fun activity that involves older siblings, extended family, friends, church family, and social groups. Also, listen to—and ask your loved ones to tell you—how often you encourage your son.

"The bible tells us that 'life and death are in the power of the tongue' [Proverbs 18:21]," says one pastor who is the father of a twenty-five-year-old son. "Whatever you speak to your son, that's who he's going to become."

NUMBER WORDS COUNT

Dr. Grissmer's study found that how well a toddler understands numbers when he enters kindergarten predicts how well he will do in math—as well as, surprisingly, reading—when he's in fifth grade and perhaps even longer.

But if you look at a group of four-year-olds, their early math abilities will fall all over the map.[27]

"By the time kids are four years old, some are at the same level as some two-year-olds, but there are two-and-a-half-year-olds who test at the same level as four-year-olds," says developmental psychologist Elizabeth Gunderson, assistant professor of psychology at Temple University.

This is another potential gap that we can head off at home. How much young children know about numbers depends on the types of number-related interactions they have with adults. Most toddlers learn how to count to ten, of course, but it turns out that that is the easy part.

"When kids first learn to count, they learn it as a routine like they learn the alphabet and eeny, meeny, miny, mo," says Dr. Gunderson. "Many kids who can count to ten don't necessarily know what it means yet."

Learning what numbers symbolize in the physical world is by far the harder task. So even though we adults know that the number two correlates with a set of two things, young children have a hard time grasping that connection. No wonder when you ask a young toddler who can count to ten to bring you four apples, he may bring you two, or seven.

So what develops a child's level of *numeracy*, or number-related skills?

One important factor is how often adults use numbers in their conversations with him.

Drs. Gunderson and Susan Levine, co-director of the Center for Early Childhood Research and chair of the psychology department at the University of Chicago, conducted research that found tremendous variation in how often parents talk about numbers at home. Some of the parents in their study used as many as eighteen hundred number words in a week, whereas others used as few as twenty-eight.

Including numbers in our conversations improves our children's numeracy; however, relating numbers to real-world objects helps even more.

"Talking about things kids could see in the world and connecting those to words—like, 'Let's count your blocks'—predicted their knowledge later on," Dr. Gunderson says.

It's also important to talk to our sons about big numbers as well as small.

Adults rarely use numbers greater than four with young children. Yet speaking with them about the numbers 4 through 10 led to even greater mathematical success than the number of number words parents used.

"You want to go just beyond where the child is comfortable and challenge them," Dr. Gunderson says. "People tend to underestimate what little kids and preschoolers are capable of. Children soak up language like a sponge."

We can start by adding numbers to our normal, everyday conversations. It's also important to count real objects and label them.

For example, ask, "How many red books do you have? Let's count them. One, two, three, four, five." Or, instead of asking, "Will you bring me your shoes?" you can ask, "Will you bring me your two brown shoes?" And rather than asking him to pass the french fries, ask him to give you seven of them.

Another important math-related ability is the development of *visual spatial skills*.

"The ability to visualize—really, to imagine—is highly important in math and science, even at young ages," says Dr. Levine, who relates the development of these skills to the ability to do science, technology, engineering, and math (STEM) disciplines later. She says that children of any age can develop visual spatial skills with a variety of toys and activities, including blocks, drawing, all sorts of puzzles, mazes, and even Tetris. Children who start playing with puzzles when they are very young have better spatial skills when they reach kindergarten. They also understand the number line better when they learn negative numbers in fourth or fifth grade and have an easier time doing pre-algebra problems during middle school.

NAVIGATING THE DAYCARE CRISIS

Infants and toddlers need adults to encourage them to wonder about their world, ask questions about it, explore, interact with others, and engage in activities to kick-start their brains. But it's hard to find time to engage in these types of activities when you are working full-time, as most black parents are, and may even be juggling two jobs. (We're not going to wade into the Mommy Wars. Few black women can afford to stay home for long. That is what it is, so let's move on.)

It's particularly important that the people who care for our children engage in these types of brain-building activities. Research shows that children who participate in high-quality childcare and educational programs benefit cognitively and in their language and social development. Sometimes the benefits diminish during their early school years, but in other cases experts can still measure the effect well into their later school years and even into adulthood. When we use the term *quality,* we mean that the program does not just meet a child's basic needs, it also offers meaningful learning opportunities, helps them develop their language and literacy skills, and fosters the types of close and caring relationships that we described earlier in the chapter.[28]

Attending a low-quality nursery school is very detrimental to a developing brain. Yet America is experiencing a daycare crisis—and it crosses socioeconomic groups. Highly educated moms (71 percent) are far more likely to place their three- to six-year-old children in a daycare center than are moms who were high school graduates (29 percent)—the greatest gap along educational lines that has ever existed in the United States. Thirty-one percent of black children attend a daycare center, as compared to 26 percent of Asian children, 26 percent of white children, and 14 percent of Hispanic children, so our children are poised to get the cognitive stimulation they need—but only if they can get the quality of care they deserve.[29] The plight particularly impacts low-income children, who are more likely to attend a substandard preschool—followed by a substandard kindergarten, followed by a substandard elementary school, followed by a substandard secondary school—than other children are. Whereas middle-class children may end up with a bad teacher or two, they are far less likely to experience a succession of poor teachers and low-quality educational experiences, which means that one "bad apple" is less detrimental to their long-term success.

In fact, the experts tell us that in some childcare centers, the leaders and the teachers sit down and do almost nothing all day.

"In these types of programs, the adults aren't deliberately trying to hurt children, but they're not doing enough to stimulate brain development that supports executive functioning and the social-emotional skills young black children need to succeed in life and in school," says developmental psychologist Aisha Ray of Chicago's Erikson Institute.

A lack of stimulation has tremendously life-altering consequences, particularly for a developing brain.

How can we find the best daycare provider for our sons?

For those who can afford it, look for a center where the director has child development experience, the teachers have bachelor or master's degrees in early childhood education and are certified by the state, and the teachers earn as much as public school teachers.

The experts tell us that the large daycare chains often have highly qualified staffs—although with price tags to match. More commonly, preschool teachers have two or three credits, or six to twelve hours, of childhood development training and education. Less educated preschool teachers are not necessarily bad for our children, but it is very important that we investigate both the center and the teacher to ensure that our sons will be stimulated.

Before placing your son in a daycare program, observe the classroom he will be placed in—ideally for an entire day. If the center won't let you in or tells you that you can only come at naptime, make a note of it.

"You can observe the place where they're going to wash your car," says Dr. Ray. "But if you can't see the program you are entrusting with the care of your child, you should decide whether that's the best program for you and your child."

The classroom should contain lots of books and evidence that children read and are being read to. Look for signs of alphabet books, counting books, picture books, and chapter books; nursery rhymes and storytelling; activities that involve sequencing things; positive conversations; games with numbers, letters, and sounds; interactive reading; and some of the toys we've described above.

Ask if the teacher uses a daily plan and see whether the curriculum looks enriching.

During the day, your son's teacher should be walking around and be engaging the children. The teacher should also behave affectionately toward the children—and please be sure that the same warmth and gentleness is extended toward the black boys as is expressed toward the other students. The teacher should not be using a lot of commands, fussing at children, or consistently telling them no.

Also, check out the activities. Does the teacher engage the children's hands along with their imaginations? Are they manipulating objects, playing with toys, connecting pop beads, stringing objects together, and engaging in other behaviors to improve their fine motor skills?

Inquire about how the teacher and center handle children who are upset. What will they do if your toddler wants to go home? Can they calm and reassure him that you will be coming back? Will they be sensitive to your son's worries and fears?

"If they say, well, little boys just need to be tough and get over it, that's part of what you need to know as a black parent," says Dr. Ray. "I want my son to realize it's okay to be worried about mom, but it's also okay to be reassured that I'm coming back. I want a program that helps my son learn how to manage his feelings and emotions and to get along well with others. High quality early childhood programs help children learn these important skills along with cognitive learning."

Place your son in a center with as many of these features as you can afford.

"You really have to go visit," says Dr. Ray. "There are childcare programs that don't have highly qualified teachers, but they're lovely programs, and children are learning in them."

Go Natural!

Embrace your role as teacher. Whether you are a parent, grandparent, uncle or auntie, or other member of a child's extended family, each and every interaction with the child will present opportunities where you can teach him. But remember, teaching doesn't necessarily involve worksheets and flash cards—use the sun, moon, and stars; pets; the grass and the trees; and other aspects of his natural environment. And don't forget to keep it light. Old-school toys like Legos, Tinker Toys, and puzzles of any kind—as well as rough-and-tumble play—help construct the parts of his brain that will help him behave and excel academically when he's older.

It's essential that he's literate. Read to him, read to him, read to him—did we say read to him? Also help him to establish reading rituals of his own. Parents who read to their child when he's in preschool help set the stage for him to read well during elementary school.

Use numbers in your daily life. Help him associate the word with the same quantity of physical objects, and don't forget to use the numbers 4 through 10.

Help him become smarter by association. Help him to think critically beginning at an early age and to see the relationships between different areas of and objects in his life.

Accentuate the positive. Speak life into your child by focusing on what he does do and not on what he doesn't do. Use words and phrases that build him up, not ones that break him down.

Finally, we note that less than one-fifth of black children are cared for by their parents during work or school hours between birth and age four—the lowest percentage of any race. However, more than one-third are cared for by relatives. It is important that our grandparents, aunties, cousins, and other caregivers interact with our children, cognitively stimulate them, educate them, and connect with them emotionally. Problems can occur at home that are similar to those that come up in a childcare program. If our caregiver is watching her "stories" rather than caring for our child, we lose much of the benefit that the family ties could potentially offer. We might be better off putting our sons in a daycare center where they receive the stimulation they deserve.

Keeping the Promise

1. **Don't wait for school.** The building blocks of education happen at home, in the earliest interactions between you and your child.

2. **Use words and numbers at home—and turn off the television.** You can cultivate literacy and numeracy just by talking to your child—and you can also cultivate bad habits, like overconsumption of media.

3. **Play, move, meditate.** Early skill development can be fun and relaxing for you and your child and bring you closer together while preparing him for the challenges of school and life.

4

PUT HIS ARMOR ON

How to Talk to Our Sons About Race

One day a friend and I were given permission to leave school because we were sick. My friend had left his keys at home, and his parents weren't there, so he was going to come to my house. We were a block from my house, literally just walking, when two cops pulled up on the side of the street, got out, and asked us what we were doing out of school. We kind of panicked. We had never dealt with the cops like that. So we sort of lied and said that we had a half day. They asked us for information about our school and grilled us about having a half day. Then we kind of told them that we were both sick. It kind of looked suspect, but we were just scared.

The cops looked through the open pocket in the back of

my bag. They were looking for drugs, but we didn't have any. They saw my pills for school and asked what they were; I told them. They were just digging. It was scary.

Then they told us to get in the police van and they were going to take us to the precinct. We swore we were sick and that they could call our school. We had been let out by the nurse—the nurse had signed the sheet—and had permission from our teachers and parents to go home. I told them to call my dad and mom. They did. My parents got mad at them, said that we weren't doing anything, and my dad told them, "Get my son out of the car now."

The cops said they needed a parental signature to sign us off. But my dad was at work, and my mom was visiting with editors to talk about writing this book. In any case, I was in Brooklyn, but they were both in Manhattan and couldn't come back. The cops said they needed an adult at first. I suggested that the editors who were at my house working on our film, *American Promise,* could sign for us. They didn't let that happen. They said they needed a parental signature. But they ended up letting the editors sign for us.

—*Idris Brewster, 18, of an incident when he was a high school senior*

Studies show that black children in general and black boys in particular experience more negative treatment from their teachers—as well as from their peers—than children of other races do.[1] Situations like the one Idris experienced happen to black boys every day of the week, particularly in New York and other cities where stop-and-frisk policies and other methods of intimidation-by-cop prevail.

Among the most important services that black parents can provide is buffering our sons from the onslaught of hostility they will receive from the world and helping them develop a skill set to protect themselves from overreactive teachers, principals, and police officers as well as from other black people, including other black boys, who have internalized the same racially biased ideas. Not only do their personal experiences with racial discrimination undermine black children's initially positive attitudes toward their schoolwork and their academic achievement—especially for black boys—but they can also make our sons feel angry and depressed.

We have the power to educate them in ways that not only counteract these messages but also empower them with a skill set they won't learn at school: how to identify, analyze, and counter racially biased messages, including the ones that they're bound to encounter in their educational environments. But many black parents tell us that they feel tongue-tied when it comes to talking race with their sons. They want to prepare them for the real world, but not depress, anger, or burden their boys with their own baggage.

"My son has friends of different races; I didn't have that," says Flora. "I wish I did and I don't want to layer racial issues on top of that."

Compounding matters, many black children have imbibed the postracial Kool-Aid so often presented in their schools with the best of intentions, as well as their social circles, and are leading the chorus to "Kumbaya." Sadly, the ill will facing black males is so great that most will already be catching hell by the time they reach adolescence. It's up to their parents and their larger Village to prepare, protect, nurture, and console them.

In this chapter we'll examine a variety of ways to talk to your son about race with a level of nuance that reflects both the promise of President Barack Obama and the tragedy of Trayvon Martin:

- We'll explore ways to socialize him about racial issues so that he develops strong self-esteem, a healthy identity, a sense that he can accomplish anything, and the knowledge that stereotypes don't apply to him.
- We'll provide some guidance about conversations that may help him at different ages.

- We'll share some self-defense strategies that extend beyond talks about police stops, hoodies, and sagging pants so that he has a skill set to rely on when the racial mess hits the fan—whether a classmate calls him the n-word, a teacher overdisciplines him, a security guard wrongly assumes that he's stealing, or he experiences a stop-and-frisk or "beef" on the street.

> Promise your son that you will help inoculate him against the stereotypes he will face about who he is and what he is capable of by crafting a narrative about who he is and who you want him to become that includes your spiritual beliefs, your family history, black history, culture, and your expectations of who you want him to become.

REALLY POSTRACIAL?

When Barack Obama became the first black president of the United States, people began to call this a postracial era. But a 2012 Associated Press poll of racial attitudes found that more whites—both Democrats and Republicans—harbor a greater number of overt and covert antiblack attitudes (51 percent and 56 percent, respectively) than they did in 2008 (48 percent and 49 percent), when President Obama was elected. Anti-Hispanic attitudes have gone up as well—from 52 percent to 57 percent.[2]

"The mantra is that we live in a colorblind society, which obviously we don't," says Diane Hughes, a professor of applied psychology at New York University.

But for the most part, black children won't face the racism of their grandparents' generation. The overwhelming majority of Americans condemn and would refuse to be associated with overtly racist behavior, and some of our neighbors are quite thoughtful about issues pertaining to race.

"I realize that being white is a privilege that I've inherited and a privilege I'll pass on to my children, whether I intend to or not," says Mary Ann, the mother of a son and a daughter. "I know that like my immigrant grandparents—who worked hard for what they achieved—it will be easier for my children to find a job, a house, or a cab because of their skin color than it will be for a black mother's child. Of course I want my children to be able to find a job or a house. I want their way to be smooth, just not at anyone else's expense."

Amen.

Many of the black parents we encounter want to believe that their son lives in a dramatically different world from the one that they currently experience.

"I would like to think that the world my sons live in is much better than the one I grew up in," says Joe, the married father of three, including two sons. "I know what I see happening in the world, but I don't want to burden them with my experiences with white people. I want them to be able to have their own experiences."

The experts tell us that this is largely wishful thinking.

From the murder and mayhem that dominate the nightly news to oversexed music videos that air constantly, the media portrays highly negative, stereotypical, and very outrageous images of black males without a counternarrative of positive contributions or even of normal life. A 2011 Heinz Endowment report on media's coverage of black males in Pittsburgh found that even though less than 6 percent of Pittsburgh residents are black males, more than 85 percent of TV news stories and more than 35 percent of print stories were not just about black males but about black males committing crimes. Less than 14 percent of stories showed black males involved in the arts, business, the economy, diversity, community/leadership, education, publishing, or the environment.[3] Experts tell us that this study is typical of what happens nationwide. Negative images have saturated American culture so thoroughly that merely showing many people a photograph of a black male generates fear in the same primal level of the brain that spiders or snakes do.[4]

From health care to the criminal justice system, this fear and contempt that the media stokes pervades America's institutions, including our schools.

"Your child really isn't living in a different world if we examine data on exclusion from the classroom—the way teachers respond to black youth, particularly black male youth, from pre-K through college," says clinical psychologist Howard Stevenson, an associate professor at the University of Pennsylvania's Graduate School of Education. "Those ways of dealing with black boys haven't really changed over the last fifty years."

PREVENTING STICKY STEREOTYPES

No matter how many times you hear someone say, "I don't see race," that's impossible; research suggests that every human being does—and instantaneously.

"There is a ton of evidence showing how we notice race, gender, skin color very quickly, very automatically—and it's not a choice to notice or not," says Nilanjana Dasgupta, a professor of psychology at the University of Massachusetts at Amherst and an expert in implicit bias and intergroup relations.

Unlike in the past, when racial animosity was expressed openly, today black people bear the brunt of *implicit bias,* or thoughts, stereotypes, and attitudes that people of all races often don't realize they carry. (Explicit bias occurs as a result of conscious thought, such as concluding that black people, for example, are genetically inferior, even after considering the evidence to the contrary.)

> **Implicit bias** refers to thoughts, stereotypes, and attitudes about race that people often don't realize they carry, but that are manifested through their actions. Implicit bias has become the primary means through which racial prejudice and animosity are expressed.

"We often use information about people unconsciously, automatically, in making split-second judgments about who this person is—whether they're smart or not, whether they're good or bad, whether they're likely to be a student or an athlete," says Dr. Dasgupta. "We make those assumptions in ways that we are not even fully consciously aware of, so that we don't even know it."

The human brain's inclination to categorize people helps us process tremendous volumes of information efficiently. But there are two sides to this coin. On the one hand, this ability allows us to make split-second decisions when we need to, without first processing every bit of information. On the downside, we may automatically and inaccurately apply what we've learned about one person to members of the whole group.

"Many times this allows us to make quick, fairly accurate judgments, but other times it can be incredibly wrong when we make a judgment or assumption that is patently false about the person," Dr. Dasgupta says.

Black boys walk into a headwind of an unconscionable number of negative assumptions and stereotypes—that they are dumb, threatening, lazy, criminal, animalistic, and overtly sexual, for example, but also that they are good at football and basketball, dance well, can rap, have sexual prowess, and so on. Experts we've interviewed have told us over and over that negative beliefs about black males pervade American society so deeply that many adults have an impaired ability to even see black boys as children.

Both individually and as a society, Americans *project* a tremendous amount of negative attributes onto black males. *Projection* involves seeing in others a characteristic that you possess but deny, don't want to admit, or are unable to see. It is one of about twenty-five psychological defense, or coping, mechanisms that human beings use to deal with stress or adversity. When it comes to black boys, many negative attributes that America projects are actually characteristics of all Americans and American society itself that mainstream America doesn't want to own up to. From the death penalty to school shootings to invading foreign countries, American culture is very violent. But to hear some people tell it, violence is synonymous with black males, not American culture. White landowners often called black people lazy during slavery. But who was lazy—the people who sat on the Big House porch or the enslaved Africans forced to work for them from "can't see in the morning to can't see at night"? And almost every American immigrant group was at some point pegged as unintelligent. Unfortunately, when they were accepted into the mainstream, many then pinned that label on black folks.

But while we can't control what stereotypes society throws at our sons, we do have some say in the degree to which our boys believe them—whether the stereotypes or negative beliefs "stick" to their minds and spirits, that is. *Projective identification* is a term we use to describe the dance that occurs between the person, institution (such as schools or the media), or even society throwing the stereotype around and the person they try to stick the stereotype on—in this case, your son. One of the most important things that a black boy's parents and Village can do is arm him with a deflector shield against narrow, limiting, and stereotypical beliefs so that no matter what people say about him, he doesn't identify with them.

"Everyone thinks I play basketball because I'm tall," says Christian. "Actually, I'm probably the only black kid who don't care about basketball. I play the trumpet, sax, and keyboard. My uncles are always trying to get me to hang out and watch the game. But watching basketball games is boring. I'd rather write music."

No black parent can control whether a person sees their son as, say, unintelligent, but they do have something to say about whether he sees himself that way. As long as he doesn't identify himself as unintelligent—that is to say, as long as he doesn't identify with the projection and the labels don't "stick" to him—he stands a much greater chance of discovering who he is and fulfilling his potential.

"The mother of one of my son's white classmates called me the other day and said, 'My son told me what happened to Charlie and I'm feeling bad so I'm calling you,'" says Carla. "Since Charlie hadn't said anything to me, I asked her what she was talking about. The woman said, 'Apparently one of the other kids told Charlie his music was ghetto, then made a racial joke about niggers.' I thanked her and later asked my son why he hadn't told me. He said, 'Well, the kid is a jerk. He could call me pink for all I care. I'm not pink and I'm not ghetto.'"

Charlie is unfazed because he doesn't buy into his classmate's projections.

A MONSTER IN TRAINING?

But putting a protective coating on a black boy isn't easy.

"We have an enormous amount of socialization in media, in the way systems operate, in surveillance, in the way that news is positioned—every social system we have tends to identify black males as a problem in some way, even by their absence," says Dr. Stevenson.

Our sons encounter this assumption in society at every turn. For example, we can't tell you how often we hear stories about black boys being deemed the culprit for scuffles they didn't start.

"My son was part of some kind of incident on the playground. A black teacher saw the whole thing, then watched a white teacher come over and make my son the perpetrator," says Lori. "The black teacher said, 'That's not what happened; I saw what happened.' Then she told my son 'You've gotta be careful because things are going to happen to you that aren't your fault.'"

"Aden rifled an eraser at me, and the teacher told him to stop it," says Mikel, 12. "But when I threw the eraser back, I got sent to the principal's office—and I didn't even throw it that hard."

On more than one occasion, Idris was blamed for normal "boys will be boys" behavior at Dalton—once, we believe, because the other kids' parents were big donors to the school; we weren't.

But some of these negative expectations come from black people as well. For example, it's not uncommon to hear some black adults make a so-called joke about a toddler boy being "bad."

The negative socialization is so pervasive that grown-ups of all races lose their ability to interpret black boys' behavior through the lens of normal child development. So a three-year-old's tantrum is no longer a mere tantrum; it's an indication that he has some behavior maladjustment or that he's going to be violent one day. An adolescent's developmentally appropriate sensitivity can be interpreted as "emotional instability," a sign of an unstable home life, or a risk factor that he's likely to drop out of school.

"The baggage that so many of us carry—black, white, and everyone—is that the child I have in front of me is an early representation of a monster that is ultimately going to jail," says developmental psychologist Robert Jagers, associate professor and chair of the Combined Program in Education and Psychology at the University of Michigan School of Education. "Because in popular culture—and consequently in the minds of all of us who are exposed to that—black boys are inherently prone towards underachievement, towards being thugs and criminals, and we treat them accordingly. We need to get down to the business of socializing black boys like you would any other young person who is full of potential and promise."

Dr. Hughes, along with student Jessica Harding and her colleague Niobe Way, studied how much *overt* (think name-calling, harassment, insults) and *implicit* (think people fearing them, assuming they're not smart, and thinking they're violent) discrimination middle-schoolers of various racial and ethnic backgrounds experienced in New York City—in school, outside of school, and from their peers of different races from sixth through eleventh grades. Black children in general, and black boys in particular, reported especially high levels of discrimination from adults outside of school. "Way more frequently than they're reporting it from adults in school," says Dr. Hughes.

"Me and my friends, when we get out of school, sometimes we go across the street to the phone store to get more minutes," says Elliott, 16. "They only let a couple of kids in at a time, so the rest of us stand outside and wait. The cops, they know we're just waiting to get minutes, but they fuck with us anyway and try to give us tickets for loitering—that's $150. All we're doing is waiting for our friends. Our teachers see it; it even makes them mad."

Black children in general, and black boys in particular, also report higher levels of stereotyping—such as feeling nervous or afraid around them—from peers, Dr. Hughes adds.

"Don't find yourself in a room with fried chicken, grape soda, or watermelon, and a bunch of white people— someone is going to make a joke," says Eric, 17. "I don't want to say that I've come to expect it, but I'm very prepared for the racist, or inappropriate, or slightly offensive remark."

LET'S TALK ABOUT RACE

Black children—and particularly boys—fare much better academically, socially, and emotionally when their parents proactively talk to them about their race and gender rather than avoiding the subject in order to protect them from hurt or waiting to talk to their son until (the parents learn that) something has happened to him.

"The idea that 'I went through stuff but I don't want to lay that on my kids,' to me, is part of an incomplete conversation that we all have in our society about race," says Dr. Stevenson. "We're more prepared skillfully and emotionally and cognitively to *not* talk about race. And I think that's not simply an issue of fear, it's also an issue of *practicing* how not to talk about race. Talking about race takes a skill set. And sometimes parents' reticence to talk to kids about race is not really about race, it's about racial conflict."

Almost all parents of color as well as immigrants socialize their children with certain racial or ethnic beliefs. African American parents typically engage in one or more of roughly five racial socialization practices.

Preparation for bias. Between two-thirds and 90 percent of black parents prepare their children for discrimination and try to arm them with strategies to handle it. Telling our sons to be on time, to avoid wearing sagging pants or hoodies, and to work extra hard all fall into this category. "It's kind of like, 'This is how the world is; it's not fair, but this is how you cope with it to succeed,'" says Dr. Hughes.

Egalitarian/colorblind. More than two-thirds of black parents tell their children that everyone is equal and that color doesn't matter. "We all bleed the same, we all die the same—those are some examples of those messages," Dr. Hughes says. We hear these kinds of messages a lot when we talk to black parents, particularly those who are middle-class and affluent.

Cultural socialization. An African-centered worldview teaches that self-knowledge is the basis for all knowledge. About one-third of black parents teach their children their heritage, cultural values, traditions, and ethnic pride. Going to see Alvin Ailey when the world-famous dance troupe comes to town, visiting the African American history museum, and having black art and artifacts in your home fall into this category.

We grounded our children both in African American and Haitian culture—Michèle is from Haiti. For example, Miles's name is actually Miles Toussaint—for the last enslaved man in the Brewster clan and the Haitian revolutionary François-Dominique Toussaint Louverture. Depending on our needs, we spin three or four different narratives to our son about who he is and what he is capable of. Michèle would take Idris home to Haiti, we made him learn French, and many summers his Haitian cousins would come to visit the boys here. Seun's parents Tony and Stacey displayed their connection to black culture differently.

"I always wanted my children to have locs," Stacey says. "We were very much into black culture and standing up for African Americans, Caribbean Americans, and other black people. Locs were a way of identifying that my children were a part of that movement."

Promoting mistrust. Only about 3 percent of black parents regularly tell their children that you can't trust white people.

Silence about race. Some parents just don't bring up race at all. Studies do not indicate how many black parents follow this strategy; in our experience, not many.

NAME AND DESTINY

Many black parents pass along their cultural pride and superintend a direction for their son by giving him a name that's significant culturally or religiously.

"Your name is part of your identity and should have meaning," says Nia, who with her husband chose culturally identifiable names for her sons: Kwame and Mandela. Other black parents avoid giving their sons identifiably ethnic names for fear that their sons will be discriminated against.

"They're not discriminating against the name; the name is acting as a proxy," or stand-in, for race, says Nia, whose own name means "purpose." "So when you come to the interview, they're still going to find out that you're black. There's research that looks at twins, and the one with the 'blacker' name did better academically."

A SPACE TO DO REALLY WELL

Which approaches are most effective in raising academically engaged and emotionally balanced black boys?

"Parents who talk to their kids about the existence of discrimination in combination with messages about racial pride and individual self-worth are the kids who do the best, both academically and psychologically," says Robert Sellers, chair of the psychology department at the University of Michigan. "On the one hand, it may make them more vigilant. On the other hand, when they inevitably experience these racial slights, they have tools to understand why this is happening that distance it from themselves."

Psychologist Claude Steele, the dean of the School of Education at Stanford University, says, "Explain the world as carefully and accurately as you can. Be frank, saying, for example, 'Some people may not invite you to their parties, and social segregation is going to happen when you get into junior high school, and they're not gonna cover black people very well when it comes to slavery or many other aspects of American history, and you're going to have to work very, very hard to learn your group's history and your own history, and so on and so forth. But while all that's true, there's nonetheless a space for you to do really well.' That's the goal that I think black parents have to achieve."

The research shows that giving our children the impression that they will receive equal treatment can discount their real-world experiences and leave them vulnerable to discrimination when it occurs.

"The truth of being a black parent is to not encourage a false consciousness—'Oh, there is no prejudice out there'—because that will be dashed very quickly," says Dr. Steele. "Then you'll have no credibility. But we also have to help them have positive, hopeful worldviews."

"Unfortunately, I think many middle-class black parents have bought into the meritocracy notion that if we just try hard enough, go to the right schools, and do the right thing, racism will disappear because enough black people will have risen and white people will embrace us and it will all be cool," says Aisha Ray of the Erikson Institute. "Reality is a hell of a lot more complex than that."

Promoting mistrust is ineffective as well.

"Don't magnify issues into a worldview that will defeat you," says Dr. Steele. "Be accurate and honest about the world, but we have to find a space to live in."

But not talking about race is a mistake for parents of all races and ethnicities.

"Regardless of whether the children are of color, they are learning about race regardless of whether their parents talk about it," says Dr. Hughes.

The experts say that white parents should proactively talk to their children about race as well.

In Dr. Hughes and her colleagues' most recent study, which surveyed parents and their children multiple times beginning in the sixth grade, they learned that parents sometimes underestimate what children know and experience with regard to race. While many black parents intentionally talked race with their children before sixth grade, some didn't want to broach the topic until their child was older. But when Dr. Hughes interviewed the children of these parents, "almost all of them were very, very aware of racial stereotypes and had already encountered them—as sixth-graders," she says.

Ironically, black parents' attempts to shield their children by not talking to them left their kids to their own childlike devices to interpret stereotypes and negative treatment, unopposed by messages reflecting their parents' perspectives and values.

"Sometimes I get called a nigger at school by the white kids. It makes me feel kind of bad," says Timothy, 11. "But I don't really do anything because they don't really mean anything bad by it. Why do you think they do that?"

WHAT TO TELL HIM AND WHEN

It's never too early to start the conversation about race. But it's best to share messages that relate to where your children are developmentally. One way to do this is by taking advantage of *teachable moments,* instances when racial issues naturally arise. It doesn't matter where it comes from, it can come from the news, a TV show, or a movie, because of something someone said to them, or even as you are working out a racial problem for yourself—one that you face at work, for instance. We strongly suggest that you not hold off until you discover that he has had a personal experience of being stereotyped (or worse). By the time you find that out, many incidents may already have happened and he may already be getting depressed or angry or disengaging academically as a result.

"My son came home from school and stayed to himself and seemed mad for a couple of days," says Tanisha. "Come to find out, they had taught slavery in school. He asked me what was wrong with black people that made white people make them into slaves. What in the hell is the school teaching him?!"

"I was subbing as a teacher's assistant to several special needs students in a class where the teacher was teaching about slavery," says Anita. "The teacher says some slave owners treated slaves very well and gave them proper food, shelter, and some money. What?! I was appalled and dismayed. The white kids were even asking, 'How can you get money if you're a slave?' The fourth-grader I was working with and I were both shaking our heads. The teacher saw me and asked me to share my viewpoint. I had to give a history lesson, which he allowed me to do, although he'd whitewash and sanitize it and say, 'We can debate that.'"

Some implicit bias will come from black people who have internalized negative or limiting beliefs about themselves. When Idris was about nine years old, his black basketball teammates, many of whom came from low-income families, started accusing him of "talking white."

But Idris is not the only black boy who has experienced this problem.

"Some of the kids at school tell me I talk white because I speak properly, and I'm gay because I don't sag my pants, I don't wear basketball sneakers, I like skinny jeans, and I like wearing colors. Get over it," says Brandon, 13.

But no matter how well you racially socialize a black boy, some limiting beliefs will likely take root in his psyche. At the tender age of three or four years old, our son Idris rolled down the car window and yelled, "Hey bitch, what's up?" to a black woman crossing the street while Michèle was stopped at a light. Needless to say, Michèle was just mortified, and we can't begin to imagine how traumatized the poor woman was! Miles had never heard that type of language in our home, and we hardly even watched TV. To this day we don't know where it came from. Needless to say, we took steps to eliminate that behavior fast!

Implicit bias affects black children beginning when they're very young, but it's very hard to talk to a young child about people's unconscious motivations. It's your job to protect him from it until he reaches middle school and his brain can begin to process abstract ideas. One way to protect him is to root out your own implicit bias. Also consider communicating these ideas during the following time frames.

Elementary school. During early childhood, be sure to ground him in messages about family, culture, community, spirituality, and group pride and continue instilling those messages throughout his life. To counteract the negative messages he'll receive throughout his lifetime, start crafting a narrative in which you tell him about who he is and why he's important, and tell him your goals and dreams for his life.

"Every two years at our family reunion, we tell the story of our family history," says Gwen. "Every year we learn more and add it on. It's important for our children to understand what came before them and what it means to be a Freeman."

Research shows that the behavior of black children who have a strong appreciation of their cultural heritage is less likely to be interpreted by their teachers as misbehavior or otherwise a problem. This may be because understanding their cultural legacy helps them refrain from demonstrating defiance or hostility.[5]

By the middle years of elementary school, start to counteract messages that black boys aren't as smart.

"That idea is lingering in the air—not just in school, it's in the society—for anyone, including him, to pick up," says Dr. Stevenson. "It's not just the school or the teacher or the predominately white setting. That's not the issue; it's larger than that."

Some schools begin academic tracking—where schools separate students by academic ability—during this age range.

"They start pulling out kids for enrichment activities for higher-level math, higher-level reading. It's very clear to the kids who's getting pulled out and who's not," says Rodney, the father of two sons and a daughter.

And since this is the age range when teaching styles change from learning to read to reading to learn, children with weaker reading skills and literacy begin to fall behind in school, and the other kids

can see it. For example, the 2011 Nation's Report Card for reading achievement shows that among fourth-graders—the time frame when this shift occurs—2 percent of black students tested as "advanced," 17 percent tested as "at or above proficient," 29 percent as "at or above basic," and 51 percent as "below basic," as opposed to Asian students, for whom 17 percent were "advanced," 50 percent were "at or above proficient," 81 percent were "at or above basic" and 19 percent were "below basic." Hispanic students' scores mirrored black students'; white kids scores were closer to those of Asian children. In Chapter 9 we'll tell you about *stereotype threat,* a test-taking anxiety that causes many black children—particularly black boys—to test below their ability level; however, some certainly lag in their reading skills.

In order to protect their self-esteem, some boys may begin to distance themselves from their desire to achieve academically by disengaging or acting out, which we'll explore in depth in Chapter 9.

Also, pay attention to teasing and physical and emotional bullying, the risks of which are at their peak between ages six and nine. Physical bullying drops off rapidly, but teasing and emotional bullying increase at similar rates between ages ten and thirteen. About 30 percent of black students report being bullied during their school careers, similar to rates reported by white (30 percent) and Hispanic (27 percent) students but much higher than Asian students (18 percent).[6]

> **Middle school.** It's extremely important to talk to your children about race during the tween and teen years. It's during this time frame that kids begin to get bored and disengage from school.

Children in demographically mixed or predominately white settings may experience race-related changes in their friendships, and children in both integrated and segregated settings may experience racial hostility in public life away from school, particularly in retail settings.

"There will be more visible markers of race, and developing ado-

lescents will begin to think more about race," says Tabbye Chavous, a professor of education and psychology at the University of Michigan. "Racial divisions and friendship groups start to happen even more explicitly in adolescence, especially during transitions to middle and high school."

But teaching your son that discrimination exists and that his friends may harbor stereotypes can be a difficult message to convey.

"It's hard to grasp the fact that you need to be careful because institutional and individual discrimination exist, but your good friend Brad, who is white, is cool, and you don't have to hate all white people," says Dr. Jagers. "This is a very deep cognitive and emotional thing to learn, and it's not always fully developed at adolescence. And it can put you in a somewhat anxious and not very pleasant state where you're constantly aware of and vigilant about discrimination."

If your son's school system hasn't already started academic tracking, it definitely will during middle school.

And whether your child lives in an integrated or segregated environment, the world's perception of him will likely shift—perhaps dramatically—and gendered racial stereotyping of and racial hostility toward him will likely begin or escalate.

"Being an early-maturing dark-brown boy can feel like the kiss of death in terms of the many nonverbal messages about their humanity. Too frequently, boys are confronted with stereotypic and untoward messages 24/7, without the benefit of reframing by caring adults," says expert Margaret Beale Spencer, a professor of human development and urban education at the University of Chicago. "The biology of the maturation process—a boy's height, weight, and the level of melanin in his skin—can play havoc with his daily experiences before he can even articulate the characteristics that make him special. He knows something is going on, its character too frequently makes him feel uncomfortable. Not surprisingly, he responds to this sense of discomfort by coping in ways that may be misinterpreted or viewed as threatening."

The mother of an eleven-year-old son observed: "My son went from being a cute little boy to a dangerous young man—and it happened almost overnight."

Teachers and others who don't understand the swagger, slang, style, or macho movements that he may express during this time may submit to implicit bias and increasingly interpret his behavior as aggressive, disrespectful, dysfunctional, or even violent. This can turn into a tragic but reciprocal dance, where our sons' emotional responses to rejection, unfairness, and hostility can fuel more misunderstanding, unfair treatment, and bias.[7]

"Kids are very sensitive to teacher expectations and the achievements they've made. Even in first grade they're detectives about 'who's the smart kid, who's the dumb kid,'" says Anne Gregory, an assistant professor at Rutgers University's Graduate School of Applied and Professional Psychology. "Over time kids can internalize 'I'm not good at this stuff,' and it can affect their grades later."

"Somehow my son thought that he wasn't as smart as the white kids. He used to tell us that he was the only one who didn't get what was happening in class," says Yolanda, the mother of a fourteen-year-old son. "Then one day the teacher handed him the wrong kid's test. I think she did it on purpose so he'd know that the rich white kid failed. When she switched the papers, my son had gotten a B. That changed everything about how he felt about himself."

Teacher expectations can even create a self-fulfilling prophecy in a black male's behavior. Dr. Gregory describes an interaction with one young man.

"He just point-blank said to me, 'Well, if they want me to act a fool, I'll act a fool,' which was his way of summarizing that 'because you expect me to have this identity, I can fulfill this identity for you and do even better than you think,'" she says. "If kids don't have places to exert power and a sense of who they are in the school setting except by being a 'bad-ass,' then how are they going to exhibit power? If schools don't have multiple different domains of honoring kids' power—ways of expecting it—then one is going to be in the behavioral domain and acting out and showing that I don't care about the rules. I think kids can take on those identities—of, say, the class clown."

We have heard several stories about how playdates with white children can slow to a crawl or even stop, particularly if his friend is a girl or a boy who happens to have a sister.

"My older son is significantly lighter-skinned than my younger son. Parents are much more comfortable with him, so they invite him over for playdates more," says a mother of two tweens who were born a year apart. "It's heartbreaking, but it shows you how people process race. They can't see that my brown-skinned son is sweet, affectionate, and helpful. My lighter son is more aggressive and pushy."

High School. As your young man gains greater autonomy, he will move in and out of different settings whose history may run deeper than he knows or realizes.

"While it may feel like black love in his immediate environment," says Dr. Jagers, "there could also be black people in his environment who aren't that way and white people he interacts with who have negative perceptions of him," including at school.

If he has friendships or romantic relationships with white girls, they may have an underlying tension.

"I talk to my sons about their interactions with white girls and what that might mean," said one father. "It may be all good among you and your friends; however, if you're in somebody's basement and her father isn't happy to see you or you overhear that something's a problem, let me know so I can handle that as an adult. We don't want that to happen, but you need to know that that's a possibility, and we need to be prepared to deal with it if it happens."

Extend your conversations with him beyond issues of personal bias and prejudice. Be sure to talk to him about *institutional racism,* the policies, practices, and procedures that institutions engage in that disproportionately oppress black people, and *systemic racism,* the value system that underlies both personal and institutional discrimination. Dr. Chavous's research shows that black girls tend to think more critically about institutional racism than black boys do. One way to discuss these nuances is by hipping him to the problematic aspects of mass incarceration. Michelle Alexander's book *The New Jim Crow: Mass Incarceration in the Age of Colorblindness* lays the issues out brilliantly.

"Kids are trying to understand the experiences they're having related to race," says Dr. Chavous. "If they have no framework for interpreting negative experiences such as discrimination, they're more likely to internalize them and develop identities where they're not connected to their group membership and have negative perceptions about being black. Parents' efforts to help their children understand their racial identities and the nature of racism provide them with a framework for making sense of such experiences so that they don't internalize them."

"People tend to talk to boys about what to do in dangerous scenarios because we're more fearful that boys are at risk," says Dr. Stevenson.

But our sons internalize messages about racial pride just like girls do. And black boys whose caregivers impart both cultural pride and cautionary messages do better than boys who receive only reactive and negative messages.

So remember to balance the "watch out" messages with cultural outings and conversations about family, community, and cultural pride.

DUMB, COOL, ATHLETIC, POPULAR

It's also important to engage him in conversations and activities that help him figure out who he is as a person beyond his race. This will also help him build an identity that can withstand stereotypes and prejudices and projections onto him.

"There is a lot of pressure on black boys, especially, to live up to the images that are held on black males in society—to be dumb, to be cool, to be athletic but not smart, to be popular with girls," says Dr. Noguera. "Those images all tend to work against an academic orientation. They also limit the kind of interests and activities boys will get involved in, if that's what they see themselves trying to achieve."

Such images are very pervasive throughout the media and American society, and no institution except the black church consistently puts forth a countermessage. And it's not just white people who harbor these ideas. We need to help him build an identity strong enough to defend him against Uncle Bubba, our son's classmates, others who have internalized limiting beliefs, and the messages in the music and on BET.

For example, who doesn't have family members who want to come to his big game, for example, but have never asked about his grades?

"The messages that black boys are supposed to be violent, tough, dangerous, and threatening—those messages not only are messages that whites have, but if unchecked, black boys begin to think, well, that's what we're supposed to be. That's how everybody is treating us, that's the expectation for us, and therefore that's how we're going to act," says Dr. Jagers. "In many cases you're also protecting them from other kids whose parents haven't protected them."

And let's not forget the ubiquitous messages he gets about our good friend "bud." Marijuana is prevalent among teens across all races.

"Weed is incredibly hard to fight against because it's celebrated so much in the culture that they're immersed in," says Walter, the father of an eighteen-year-old. "All rappers rap about weed and big-booty girls. My son plays football, so he's got the big-booty girls covered; now let's move on to weed."

"Whether you're white, black, Latino, or something else, in L.A. the definition of what it means to be a male can be boiled down to just a couple of things," says one father. "If you're black it means you play basketball, listen to hip-hop, and smoke weed."

The stereotypes set forth for black males are so narrow, so distorted, and so dominant that they can come to define what black manhood looks like if a boy's Village doesn't offset them. A black boy whose identity gets tangled up in narrow and stereotypical definitions of what it means to be a black male—the stereotype of black male as a baller, for instance—may not be that good a ball player at all. But he can never recover the hours and hours he spends learning to dunk. He invests them in developing a skill that probably won't take him very far, and he does it during a developmental phase when many young people he is competing against are learning who they are and what they feel passionate about by being exposed to a much wider range of options. While he's spending time trying to get above the rim, he may be missing out on the chance to discover his true calling, which probably falls outside of the boundaries of a racial stereotype: an astronomer, a marine biologist, or a veterinarian, for instance.

"I like the fact that my son doesn't play football or basketball," says Toni. "I played basketball, and I would be fine if he played it. But I'm glad that he naturally gravitated to other sports."

"I want to be a sound engineer when I grow up," says Zion, 11. "I want to do that or parkour." (Google it; we had to.)

One of our most memorable moments as parents was at a school conference when one of Idris's teachers mentioned the possibility of his becoming a physicist. Idris was surprised to hear that. The fact was, despite our role-modeling and best efforts, our son was more capable of seeing himself as a rapper than a physicist, even though his path was more likely to lead to physicist than professional rapper.

In fact, fitting the profile of a stereotype can have a very attractive upside. Football and basketball players, for example, get attention, popularity points, adulation, girls, corners cut for them—the whole nine yards. And being stereotypically black in some predominately white environments can win a kid cool points. This can make a parent's job of convincing their son to buy in to academics more difficult. Schoolwork requires a kid to delay gratification, whereas sports is rewarding right now.

"It's very seductive to gravitate toward those images," Dr. Noguera says. "But what he's not realizing is that by not investing in his education, he's limiting his options later on."

"If your definition of being a good athlete means that you're not particularly intellectual, that you're not particularly academically oriented, that academics is something that you do in order to be eligible to play sports, then that athletic identity becomes very problematic," says Dr. Sellers. "Too often the message is, 'If you get decent grades, we'll let you play; if you don't, you can't play.' So school becomes work and athletics becomes the reward. It's important that he see both as being important."

Dr. Sellers encourages parents to relate sports to their son's intellectual development by helping him understand how different plays relate to, say, geometry or geospace.

At the college level, he teaches athletes that their education is their payment for playing sports. "Universities, in many cases, make millions of dollars off of them. If your education is your payment for playing sports, then the goal isn't just to go to class so you're not in trouble, it's to go to class to get your payment for the work you do in sports," he says. "If you don't get an education, then you're someone who worked without being paid. Which basically makes you a slave. I'm pretty sure there were slaves who loved gardening, but they were slaves nevertheless."

Another category of societal messages that ensnares far too many black boys involves the socialization that being authentically black means being a gangsta, roughneck, or thug. Atlanta-based sociologist Adria Welcher told us about black children in an affluent neighborhood who were breaking into homes.

"We know that you're from an affluent family; we know that your parents are educated; they have good jobs; you drive a nice car," says Dr. Welcher. "Why do you want to be a thug? Where is that desire coming from? What makes it appealing? Don't you like your comfortable lifestyle; don't you like living in a big home?"

But these boys aren't the only ones whose identity seems to have been ensnared by a stereotype. Even though they are very successful and may, in fact, have found their true callings, we note that Sean Combs (Puff Daddy/P. Diddy), Russell Simmons, Biggie Smalls, and Kanye West are all sons of educators. In fact, Kanye's mom was a college professor. In a different world, perhaps they would have become educators themselves or focused on something more than creating a persona based on stereotypes of hustlers, thugs, and ballers. Tragically, Biggie lived out that mythology, and that choice eventually led to his murder.

KEEPIN' IT REAL?

But in a society in which the definition of black manhood is so limited, a black boy not involved in sports or other stereotypically black activities can have a tough row to hoe. Idris often gets preyed upon by black males from other neighborhoods who see his glasses, skinny jeans, and other apparel as symbols of a type of black manhood they feel is a threat. Even adults need to make sure that they're not unintentionally enforcing narrow norms about what it means to be a black male.

"You have to somehow find an identity space that's valued," says Dr. Jagers. "That becomes particularly problematic because the stereotype for what a black male is supposed to do is so strong. And when you're talking about a black male who doesn't play sports, you have issues of gender conformity and racial conformity."

When it comes to a space to excel academically, many black boys struggle.

"There isn't a clear path for a high-achieving black male," says Mark Joseph, a parent activist and an associate professor and director of the National Initiative on Mixed-Income Communities at Case Western Reserve University. "It isn't like, 'Oh, I can see these kids.' There's not a space they can gravitate to. There's a huge gravity in our culture that says that school's not that cool; it's all about being in the moment and doing things now. This affects boys in general—then you add the layers of race, class, and culture, and you have all these things pulling at them, and there isn't an opposing force."

As Idris experienced when he was told he "talked white," many children are pressured by other black children to conform to racially prescribed ways of behaving. One particular aspect of this dynamic has received a lot of attention. Since the mid-1980s people have studied the notion of "acting white," a phrase people use very loosely to describe a wide range of intra-group peer pressure that can exist among black children. According to research conducted by Ronald Ferguson, when you ask black high school students to explain what the phrase "acting white" refers to when used to describe other black kids, they describe kids who listen to rock music (50 percent), trust their peers even if they're strangers (23 percent), chat on the computer (10 percent), speak standard English outside of school (6 percent), do leisure reading (5 percent), have friends of other races (4 percent), and have a high GPA (2 percent). Interestingly, to hear the media tell it, "acting white" has to do with having a high GPA, the very thing that black kids seldom mention.[8] In another study students listed behaviors that included enrolling in honors and advanced placement (AP) classes, wearing shorts in the winter, and shopping at Abercrombie & Fitch (as opposed to Tommy Hilfiger or the then-existent FUBU), a debate exists about whether "acting white" stigmatizes getting good grades. Some experts claim that the proscription against "acting white" includes pressure to dumb down their grades, while others find no evidence of that claim.[9]

The research clearly shows that black children become increasingly popular among their black peers until their GPA reaches 3.5 (3.25 for boys). Beyond that point their popularity declines—more precipitously for boys than girls. For example, a black student with a 4.0 is as popular as a black student who has a 2.5 GPA, whereas white kids become more popular as their grades rise. (Hispanic kids experience a precipitous drop-off in popularity once their GPA reaches roughly 2.5.) The black students' drop in popularity isn't offset by increases in friends of other ethnic groups. In fact, black and Hispanic students with higher grades actually have *fewer* friends across race than kids with lower grades.[10]

We believe that our sons can benefit from a tremendous amount of social support in their academic environment.

"Part of the achievement gap, I think, comes from social needs that must be fed. In many cases kids will abandon their need to achieve to satisfy their need to belong—I was like that," says Dr. Aronson. "Smart educators marry people's need to belong with their need to achieve. One of the things that we see among Asian students, especially in college, is that they study in groups and turn it into a social affair. But black students in college, by and large they study alone. That means they're not satisfying social needs every time they study. If you can marry these goals, you can often see dramatic gains in achievement."

Interestingly, research by Harvard economist Roland Fryer has found that this phenomenon of black students with higher grades having fewer friends exists only in schools that are 80 percent white or higher. He can find no evidence of it in predominately black settings.[11] Most black children attend predominately black schools, so the notion that academic achievement alienates black kids is, for the most part, not true. And Fryer further notes that social groups seek to preserve their identity and that this activity increases when threats to group cohesion increase. This kind of tension between members of marginalized groups occurs as some members seek to integrate themselves into the larger society and others remain loyal to the group—so this behavior isn't specific to African Americans. In fact, any time you see a movie like *Good Will Hunting,* where someone leaves their blue-collar roots and one of their working-class friends or family members accuses them of thinking they're better than everyone else, you're seeing a similar dynamic in action. People get badgered for being different.

So the research is complicated, but it will always make sense to arm our children with a broad sense of their identity to help them withstand the pressure. It also helps to surround them with peers who excel academically.

"You have to be very conscious of who their friends are," says Dr. Noguera. "When your children are small, you have a lot more influence over who their friends will be. You get to create the playdates and decide who comes over to your house and which birthday parties they go to. Those choices are really important because if you can surround your kids with other kids who have a positive orientation and sense of self, it will be more likely to influence them."

"You need to know your children's friends, listen to their music, watch what they watch on television, and play their video games," says educational consultant Jawanza Kunjufu, author of numerous books, including *Understanding Black Male Learning Styles.*

Even though Dalton is a predominately white school, Idris found a support system among a network comprised of students of color who attend private schools.

And we are inspired by a group of black parents in the Virginia suburbs of Washington, D.C., who created a support group for every black male in the sixth grade—there were fifteen of them—in order to push their sons to excel academically and graduate high school on time. Called Club 2012, the group met monthly at members' homes and held homework sessions, father/son rap sessions, and social and community service activities, according to a story that ran in *The Washington Post*. We believe that this could be a powerful model that black parents should be able to replicate in communities around the nation.

What other methods can black parents, Village members, and educators use to counter societal pressures to conform to a narrow stereotype? By introducing black boys to as many activities as possible and encouraging them to explore them. Take them places and engage in activities with them that society, the media, and perhaps even other black people don't associate with black males. Black people live everywhere and do everything. They need to know this.

"I invite as many speakers as I can into my classroom that show black men doing all sorts of things many of my students have never seen black men doing before," says one teacher. "I love watching their faces and seeing their minds open up."

When Joe was in college, he traveled to South America, and it was one of the most important experiences he ever had. But if he had listened to some of his black friends, who told him "only white folks do that shit," he would have missed out on a liberating experience.

FOREWARNED AND FOREARMED

One reason that black parents struggle to teach their children about race and the world around them is because of their own unresolved trauma about racial issues.

"One of the nuns accused me of stealing a pencil that I never stole—in front of the entire class. She humiliated me," says Brenda, 48, the mother of a seventeen-year-old son. "Another time, the nuns watched these white kids circle me on their bikes and spit on me, but they never intervened."

Dr. Stevenson recommends that parents start by sharing their own racial experiences with each other or with a therapist.

"Storytelling allows people to unearth trauma that they've been practicing burying for years," says Dr. Stevenson. "We're still fearful to talk about race, then we wonder why kids don't fully get our messages."

Only after adults come to terms with their own racial struggles can they begin to teach their sons *racial literacy*, which includes the ability to dissect racially biased images and ideas, debate racial stereotypes, manage stress, and speak up when others perceive racial differences as negative.

"Our sons don't want to upset their friends, yet the consequences of swallowing your voice to hide differences, keep relationships, and avoid being stereotyped are enormous, even in kindergarten and lower school," Dr. Stevenson says. "Over time you forget how to use your voice in other areas."

Racial literacy also includes having self-defense strategies that allow our sons to maintain their dignity in the face of racial insults.

"Being forewarned is forearmed," says developmental psychologist Robert Jagers, associate professor and chair of the Combined Program in Education and Psychology at the University of Michigan School of Education.

"This white kid in eighth grade walked down the hall and called me a nigger, and I didn't even know him," says Alan, a sixth-grader. "I didn't really say anything because I was shocked."

"You don't want your children to be vulnerable the first time they're called a nigger. You don't want that to be a surprise," says Dr. Jagers, an expert in social and emotional learning. "You want them to understand that there is a history, and there could be people in their environment who could have negative perceptions of them.

"Related to this it's important to teach black children *critical-mindedness,* or *critical consciousness,*" the awareness of how their social world works and how they fit in it, says Dr. Jagers. "Because if you don't stand for and aspire to something, you'll go for anything. We have to teach our children what they stand for. You want to put issues in front of them that require them to take and defend a position. That will impact how they think about themselves and behave in different settings."

Talk to them about issues like why so few positive images of black males exist in the media, why police stop and frisk black and brown youth but not others, why black males are disproportionately incarcerated, and so on.

And once again, we encounter the importance of mastering code-switching. "Each environment has different norms and rules," Dr. Jagers says. "The wise person tries to learn what those rules are and adjust accordingly. He says, 'I'm not in control here, so I need to figure out how to achieve my goals. My goal in school is to get as educated as possible. Wherever I am, I need to get the core insights and skills so I can take care of myself and the people I care about.'"

Some people will push back and see this as being a sellout. But there's a difference between abandoning your core and controlling how you're perceived.

"No, always maintain a sense of who you are when you move in and out of these environments—that's your core," says Dr. Jagers. "But figuring out what time it is and what place I'm in is part of becoming a young man."

The American Psychological Association has identified what it calls critical-mindedness and code-switching as being among the skill sets black children need to demonstrate resilience.[12]

PUT YOUR OWN MASK ON FIRST

We participate in fire drills and natural-disaster drills, and we listen to airline instructions about what to do if the airplane's cabin loses pressure. Preparing for emergencies is part of the American experience—but not when it comes to race.

"If an airplane crashes, your chances of survival are nil, but they don't stop giving us the message about what to do," Dr. Stevenson says. "Yet we are afraid to talk to our kids about race—even though we know that the encounters that black youth have with the police or people who see them as dangerous occur frequently."

Encourage your son to share about the race-related experiences he's already had in his life, even subtle ones. Then explore his response to the situation. For instance, let's take this example, an actual story from one of Idris's classmates.

"I was going to tennis practice wearing my tennis shoes, shorts, my shirt that says Dalton and carrying my tennis racquet. You have to walk through this very nice apartment building to get to the tennis bubble. I checked in with the doorman, as I always do; he knew I was there for practice. But when I walked down the hallway to get to the bubble, an older white woman visibly went pale at the sight of me. I went on to tennis practice. Then we got a call. She had complained to the doorman that I wasn't supposed to be there—like I'm a security threat when I'm obviously going to tennis practice. Nothing came of the situation because the doorman knew that I was supposed to be there. But the fact that people think like that is scary to me."

How would you respond if your son told you a story like that? Here are some ideas. "We need to ask: How do you feel about it, how do you journal about it, what do you want to say when this happens that keeps you from getting expelled or in trouble but that doesn't make you feel like you're walking away like a punk—like you're weak—which is a big gender issue for boys?" Dr. Stevenson suggests.

Another response is to practice role-playing negative incidents to work out the best responses to difficult situations. We can do this even before those situations occur, so that when a teacher demeans him, a classmate insults him, or a security guard stops him in a store, for example, he can draw from a tool kit of skills that not only reflects your values and beliefs but also minimizes the chances that he'll stress out, freak out, or knock someone out.

"They need a comeback line that's stylistic, uniquely theirs, informative, but doesn't get them in trouble," says Dr. Stevenson. "He used his voice, he didn't back down, but he didn't kick anybody's ass."

And this kind of preparation should extend to how we train our sons to deal with authority figures. Through community basketball and martial arts workshops, Dr. Stevenson teaches black teens how to stay cool and calm during racial and gender controversy, whether it's beef on the street or being stopped by the cops. We know that young black men often find themselves confronted by law enforcement through no fault of their own. They need to know how to handle themselves. For instance, take this situation experienced by Demetrius, a fifteen-year-old student in New York.

"I was reading my Kindle on the train coming from school, when these two Hispanic guys started fighting down at the other end. The cops came, and next thing, I'm in trouble and get taken off the train. Why? Because I'm black. There was a white kid sitting next to me. He didn't get questioned or taken off the train. I was very upset about that."

How would you want your son to respond at a moment like this, when he's feeling upset and picked on by a police officer? Again, role-playing can help prepare him. Dr. Stevenson encourages parents to play out different situations with their sons by asking hypothetical questions.

"A cop stops you, and you haven't done anything: What are you feeling? What's going on in your mind? What do you want to say?" Dr. Stevenson suggests asking. "Great, you want to cuss them the fuck out, but we both know why you can't do that. What do you say instead that keeps you from getting in trouble but leaves your self-esteem intact?"

This can be particularly important for young men who don't have a lot of men in their lives.

"Many young men who are raised in a feminine context never experience the sound of a male voice in an authoritative way—until it's too late," says Rev. Dr. Alyn E. Waller, senior pastor at Enon Tabernacle Baptist Church in Philadelphia. "So what happens a lot of times is the first time they hear a police officer say in a gruff voice, 'License and registration, please'—and he's supposed to say it like that—the average black male hears that as a threat."

Similar to Dr. Stevenson, Rev. Dr. Waller teaches martial arts and wrestling to black males to teach them how to deescalate conflict, whether with a police officer or when they have a run-in at school or in their community. When asked about the value that being a black belt imparts, Rev. Dr. Waller says, "I have the ability to walk away or use other tools to deescalate, because everything I could gain out of beating you is already flowing within me—I have that confidence. There will be no new news in my kingdom if I beat you, so I don't need to hit you. People fight because they're angry. Anger is a secondary emotion fueled by fear. If you can kill the fear, you can kill the anger, which means that you can respond instead of react. If you can do that, then you don't have to fight. We can teach that in wrestling and martial arts."

In addition to considering martial arts training, talk to your son about how he feels when he's threatened and then help him shape productive responses that will help keep him safe. Dr. Stevenson suggests practicing phrases like "I'm not here to bother anybody," "I was just standing here; I guess I was in the wrong spot," and "My bad"—statements that give nervous cops and edgy knuckleheads room to breathe.

He also teaches young people stress management strategies, such as meditation and deep breathing, which can help them relax when their racial or gender identities come under attack.

"If you're breathing, your peripheral vision and peripheral hearing are more available. So you can actually see fear in other people," Dr. Stevenson says. "You notice when someone is twitching and nervous. Then if you want to, you can say something to make them feel less scared. But if you're hyped, or overwhelmed, you can't do that."

Rev. Dr. Waller teaches young men about fighting within the context of Christianity.

"Jesus had three responses to violence: one time he ran away, one time he stood and fought, and one time he let the other side win," Rev. Dr. Waller says. "The real test of manhood is, are you man enough to run when you ought to run or deescalate; fight for something, even if you're outnumbered; and lose, even if losing in this moment is for the greater good. That's the real teaching of Jesus around fighting."

He verbally plays situations out with young men, asking questions like, "Let's suppose you win; let's suppose you lose. What do you gain? What does it mean to have character? How do you want to be perceived? Where do you get your sense of manhood? And as a practical matter, what do you want after this? Do you want to have to look over your shoulder?"

CHANGE THE MIRROR

Dr. Dasgupta says that no matter what our race is or how biased we already are, we can work to overcome our prejudices by making the decision to change.

The first step involves acknowledging that all human beings pre-judge others, so the fact that you do it as well doesn't make you a bad person.

It's also important to understand that, whether it's Fox News or *America's Most Wanted* or *Cops*, the level of negative messaging about black males is so high that all of us are biased.

Taking the Test

We all have attitudes we're unaware of but that cause us to judge others unfairly nevertheless. The first step toward reducing them is measuring just how biased we actually are. To learn how unintentionally biased you are toward a wide variety of different groups, including black people, try taking an implicit bias test at https://implicit.harvard.edu.

"Our brains are like mirrors that reflect the environment," says Dr. Dasgupta. "If that's what we see, those negative associations get reflected in the mirror that is our mind. But you shouldn't become paralyzed by that."

We all can change, but we must choose to do so.

"If our brains are the mirror, if we then walk over to a different environment, our brains start registering different things," she says. "This is where choice comes in. To some extent we choose those environments."

She suggests that we examine our social networks, the media we watch, the environments we frequent.

"I found in my research that people who have more friends who are multiracial tend to show less implicit bias," she says.

Keeping the Promise

1. **Prevent sticky stereotypes.** No matter what society says about our son, if we teach him a different story about himself, the stereotypes are less likely to stick or modify his behavior.

2. **Understanding the monster in their minds.** Implicit bias can lead to our sons being treated as something different than what they really are—more menacing and less intellectually capable. The only way to combat this insidious bias is to be aware of it.

3. **Don't run from race.** The most successful black boys are the ones whose parents talk to them about race with care and openness, and at the level appropriate to their age.

4. **Teach them racial literacy.** We have to prepare our sons to deal with a wide range of race-based reactions to them, by their peers and by authority figures, through role-playing and other means so that when situations develop, they can remain calm, in control, and safe.

5

HUG HIM AND TELL HIM YOU LOVE HIM

How to Use Parenting Styles that Work

We sat bug-eyed and slack-jawed in front of the computer watching a potential nightmare for Idris unfold—one that he had filmed on his own Flip camera but wasn't even aware was happening. He had recorded himself and some of his white schoolmates in one of the world's most famous retail locations: the FAO Schwarz store on Fifth Avenue. The boys were giggling, playing catch with teddy bears, running up and down the stairs, and being a little rowdy—typical boys being twelve-year-old boys. But we were shocked and had mixed emotions as we watched. On the one hand, we were amazed that our oldest son felt so comfortable in that environment. When we were his age, there's no way that either one of us would have ventured into—much less felt so at home in—such a high-end store. Yet we were also afraid for our son's well-being. We worried that the store manager or a store guard would see him as not entitled to be there, a thief, or even a security threat.

Although Idris was not a teenager yet, the world had already begun perceiving him through the lens of racial stereotypes: threatening, angry, not good in math. We worried that the childish playfulness that he was exhibiting on camera could cause him to be reprimanded, accused of stealing, or even worse. This realization made us feel very sad. We had been raising our son to be open-minded, not to feel constricted by boundaries, and to achieve his full human potential. But we now were confronted with the black parent's dilemma: Should we allow our son to be himself or take this opportunity to prepare him to live in the real world he would encounter as he began to look less like a boy and more like a man—the world that will treat him differently, negatively, look at him as "other"? The time had come for us to begin the years-long process of having The Talk about being black and male in a world that will see him—consciously or not—through the lens of unfavorable stereotypes.

We knew that we needed to think about what to say and how to say it. Handled insensitively, The Talk could scare and confuse our son and hurt him deeply; he could deny what we were saying and identify with his many teachers and peers telling him that racially everything was equal; it could make him feel inferior to or perhaps resentful of his

white classmates and cause him to retreat from them; or, worst case, it could cause a self-fulfilling prophecy in which he might become angry, lash out, and embody the very negative stereotypes we feared. Our parenting approach would make all of the difference.

As we always do when we approach big topics, we considered all of our options. We could have a knee-jerk reaction and lay down the law: "You are not allowed to go to FAO Schwarz. Period. End of story." (Not that we would be able to enforce it.) But while that approach would prevent problems there, it wouldn't help Idris navigate the landmines that exist in other stores, the minefields that cause black parents to tell their sons always to keep their hands visible, to never put them in their pockets when they're in stores. Or we could play Pollyanna and overlook what we'd seen, permitting him to continue to enjoy the naivety of his youth—until someone ended his innocence for him. Because let's face it: The world has changed immeasurably since we were his age. In fact, to hear Fox News tell it, everything is equal. But while we don't want to saddle him with the burdens of our generation, we don't want to leave him in harm's way either. How long would it be before the reality that the media often refuses to acknowledge and his teachers can't see (because they aren't aware that a parallel reality exists that they don't inhabit) came down on him— and how harshly would it fall?

We decided that the best answer for our son could be found in the middle ground. We needed to initiate a

dialogue that we would continue to have for years. He would have this conversation with others as well: his (predominately) white classmates and teachers, his friends, his social network of black, Latino, and Asian kids, the young people on his various basketball teams, his girlfriends, and eventually in college and at work. But we wanted to lay the groundwork for those conversations. Our handling of this difficult teaching moment could shape both his behavior and his willingness to continue the dialogue.

We kept the conversation simple and age-appropriate. If we intended to have it over a lifetime, we didn't need to tell him everything all at once. And nothing bad had happened to him, at least this time. We also knew that Joe's role-modeling would provide a powerful example for how a black male must carry himself. The conversation went something like this.

"Idris, we saw the video from FAO Schwarz," Michèle opened. "It looked like you guys were having a lot of fun."

"Yeah, we were just hanging out," he said.

"You and your friends were just having fun, but you're starting to grow up now and you're getting a little too old to act rowdy in public," she continued.

"We were just playing," he answered.

"We know, but you are black and they are not," Joe said. "People look at you more closely and hold you to a higher standard in terms of their expectations for your behavior."

"I was just acting like my friends were," he told us. It was

clear that as he played Idris had been oblivious. "That's not fair," he continued. "I didn't do anything."

"We know," Joe agreed. "But black boys get more closely scrutinized by security guards and store managers than white boys do. We don't ever want you to find yourself in a situation where you're accused of something that you didn't do."

His eyes widened. He had just remembered something.

"A security guard followed me into the bathroom," he confessed.

"What?!" we gasped.

"He asked me if I had anything in my pocket," he told us. "I thought he was going to arrest me. I was really scared."

"Did he follow any of your white friends?"

"No, just me."

"He racially profiled you," Michèle told him.

"But he was black," Idris argued.

"That doesn't make a difference," we responded, knowing that the security guard had internalized the same messages and may have felt that he needed to hassle black children to succeed at his job. "He probably doesn't even know that he's doing it."

"He said he'd be keeping his eye on me."

Even though our son lives in an era in which the ability to send information all over the globe literally is at his fingertips, he must contend with the same stereotypes that have existed in the country for literally hundreds of years. So much for progress. . . .

THE POWER OF POSITIVE PARENTING

For decades parenting experts looked at the process of raising American children as a "one size fits all" proposition: If advice works for white kids, it should work for everyone else. And some aspects of parenting are universal. But parents of color must raise their children in race- or ethnicity-specific ways for their children to fulfill their potential.[1]

In this chapter we'll examine the latest research about what parenting approaches work best (and worst) for black boys and why:

- We'll hip you to changes that you can make to help the black male that you are helping raise or educate do better in all aspects of his life.
- We'll show you how to shift your own approach to one that will help him get the best results. Since he's worked with most of the other experts in this field, we'll rely heavily on the research of Dr. Mandara and his co-authors.
- We'll also share Joe's insights as a clinical psychiatrist who has worked with countless black boys in community health centers, hospitals, schools, universities, and even the Brooklyn House of Detention.

> **Promise your son that you will hug him and tell him that you love him, set high standards for him, shelter him from the excessively punitive treatment of the world, and be open to making adjustments to your parenting style.**

THE BURDENS OF BLACK BOYS

While the parents of black and white boys have many experiences in common—protecting their emotional well-being, channeling their rambunctiousness, dealing with schools that have been structured for the learning styles of girls, protecting them from bullying, and so on—white parents don't have to prepare their boys to deal with a society that stereotypes and views them as dangerous, as black parents do. They don't have to safeguard their sons from media outlets that broadcast violent and self-destructive images of them. They don't have to protect them from others' harmful projections. (We are constantly telling Idris that he must strive against the negative stereotypes. What an unfair challenge to have to present to your kid!) They don't have to shield them from teachers whose low expectations can undermine their ability to learn.[2] "Boys will be boys" behavior doesn't get white boys kicked out of the classroom or expelled from school (or even locked up) at the same rate that it does black boys.[3] And white parents don't have to fear for their sons' physical safety in the same way that black parents do. Will he get jumped? Will the police stop and frisk him? Will he get shot? They typically don't lie awake worrying about these issues. Black parents do.

"At Dalton, my son had an issue with a bully and finally hit the kid with his book bag," says Lamar. "It was just a 'boys will be boys' thing, but they didn't have any tolerance for it. Meanwhile, the white kids could say whatever verbally abusive, hurtful, derogatory, and demeaning thing they wanted."

But from his parents to his educators to the members of his Village, the adults in a black boy's life can help shield him and improve his academic performance by implementing the parenting styles that work best for black boys. In fact, the latest research shows that child-rearing techniques have a greater impact on his odds of success than even his school or his parents' income, educational level, or marital status do.

This news may seem surprising, especially to black parents, since so many of us have drunk the Kool-Aid that makes us believe that hip-hop videos, underperforming schools, Pookie on the corner, and other nuisances outside of our homes have more influence over our sons than we do. And while these factors do impact them, a growing body of research shows that these outside factors don't "have it like that" over us.

"Parenting style matters over and above the other resources that families have," says family and developmental psychologist Jelani Mandara, a professor at Northwestern University and a leading researcher on how African American families are structured and function. Indeed, studies show that certain parenting approaches can help our sons better withstand racism, underfunded schools, and other systemic and structural forces. Unbelievably, the way we parent our sons can even trump poverty.

"A lot of poor parents do a really great job," Dr. Mandara says. "We have just as many examples of wealthier kids who are disasters."

But the same research that shows that a boy's parents, educators, and Village are more powerful than they may think also shows that the grown-ups who love, raise, and educate them may need a parenting skills makeover. Indeed, the child-rearing techniques that black parents have passed down through generations—the same ones that protected our sons during the Jim Crow era—are not only proving ineffective during this Digital Age, they may actually be contributing to our sons' struggles. Making matters worse, these approaches are employed by many schools, social service organizations, and others, raising the possibility that some well-meaning approaches may actually be doing more harm than good and undermining black boys' success.[4]

CREATING GOOD VIBES

Some aspects of parenting are very universal. For instance, no matter their race, ethnicity, or socioeconomic background, parents of children who achieve the greatest success demonstrate two traits that contribute to their offspring's well-being: they both *respond* to their children and *demand* a lot of them.

Responsive parents demonstrate plenty of love, warmth, nurturing, concern, and emotional support toward their kids. No matter how busy they are, they carve out some one-on-one time to listen to their son's needs and let him know that he's important.

Demanding caregivers push their boy to work hard, hold him accountable for his grades, and require him to behave responsibly. They also create a structured and organized home environment, set rules and enforce them consistently, teach their son how to behave, monitor his conduct, and discipline him when he needs it.

With black boys, two specific parenting behaviors disproportionately affect their success: how warmly adults treat them (a responsive trait) and how effectively they control their behavior (a dimension of demandingness). Sincerely praising their accomplishments and positively reinforcing good conduct can have a particularly positive impact on African American boys. When adults demonstrate these behaviors, they not only help to build self-esteem and understanding of what adults expect, as occurs with other boys, they also gird African American boys to endure the gauntlet of negativity that society dishes out to them.[5]

"Black boys obviously hear praise when it comes to athletics, but that's really the only arena where they hear good things about themselves and feel pretty confident," Dr. Mandara says.

In fact, a growing body of evidence suggests that far too few adults—whether parents, educators, coaches, youth leaders, or other members of their Village—achieve an appropriate balance with black boys. Most unwittingly go light on responsiveness and are heavy-handed with demandingness, and the demanding behaviors they demonstrate emphasize discipline and punishment rather than high expectations, encouragement for hard work, and accountability.

Research from 1997 (the only year for which the data are available) found that 93 percent of white moms, 81 percent of Hispanic moms, and 75 percent of black moms—and 76 percent of white dads, 73 percent of Hispanic dads, and 56 percent of black dads—hugged their child every day. Only 43 percent of black dads regularly tell their child he loves them. Across all races, the parents became less affectionate as their kids grew older.

And some family studies suggest that black parents are less affectionate toward their children than white parents are toward white children. The research is controversial: Most of the interviewers were white, and even if the observations are accurate, there are more ways to show love than through physical affection or saying "I love you."

(Think cooking his favorite foods, wearing last year's coat so he can get this month's sneakers, or overcoming hell and high water to get to his basketball game.) However, this same fieldwork shows that European American parents generally give their children more freedom to make decisions than black parents do, something that many family experts who are black agree is the case.

"One of the hallmarks of a black parenting style is the 'do it because I said do it' approach and the absence of a responsive conversation" between parent and child, says Ronald Ferguson.

And particularly when it comes to discipline, "African American kids—and this includes girls—are punished and disciplined harshly at higher rates than any other kids: at home, in school, and in other environments," Dr. Mandara says. "The group that gets the most negativity from adults is African American boys."

Indeed, often out of fear for their children's safety, many black parents drastically restrict their sons' explorations, even as toddlers, and allow little freedom for their sons to think for themselves, particularly as teens. This domineering approach to raising black boys dates to parents' attempts during slavery and segregation to protect their sons from white authority figures.

Robert, 57, the father of a twenty-five-year-old son, recalls in the late 1960s when the Birmingham police beat one of his best friends to within an inch of his life because the teen's curiosity had gotten the best of him and he had wandered into a white neighborhood. The young man had been at the top of his class and was heading to college. After the beatdown, "he never was 'right' again," Robert recalls. His friend developed mental health problems, underachieved, struggled in life, and died young.

"Any time you have a social structure in which people can dominate others and be mean and unresponsive with no consequence to themselves—and being that way helps them maintain their social position and control others, and there are no norms to stop them from operating this way," you will find a rigid approach to parenting similar to the style that many African American parents employ, says Dr. Ferguson.

Moreover, some parents engage in additional behaviors that are inappropriately demanding such as excessive correcting and faultfinding. When Dr. Mandara takes his sons fishing, "I listen to the parents, particularly in a poor area of Chicago, and the way in which they talk to their children in general," he says. "Everything is so negative: 'Don't do that!' 'What are you doing?' 'Just hold it like this!' Never any kind of praise or anything nice; it's all critical and negative. And it's even worse for the boys." He notes that hypercritical behavior extends into middle-class black families as well.

Many educators also overly censor black boys. "I sit in the back of classrooms sometimes, and even there black boys never hear good stuff: 'Jamal, that's a great idea; you're so smart,'" Dr. Mandara says. "They never hear anything like that—I mean never! They hear: 'What are you doing?' 'Don't do this.' 'Be quiet.'"

Indeed, as award-winning writer Jonathan Kozol observes in *The Shame of the Nation: The Restoration of Apartheid Schooling in America,* many schools for inner-city black and Hispanic children take a militaristic approach of "direct command and absolute control"—one that he's never seen used in predominately white schools but that is "commonly employed in penal institutions and drug-rehabilitation programs."[6]

"Why do we assume that black males need less freedom and more control? Why don't we assume that they need more freedom and less control? I think it comes out of a racist image of them that they're out of control," says Joshua Aronson, an associate professor of applied psychology at New York University's Steinhardt School of Culture, Education, and Human Development. "We insist that our upper-class white kids get lots of project-based learning and freedom to express themselves. I've never been to a school where they say that black kids need more freedom."

Proof positive of this demandingness gone wild can be found in the excessive punishing of black boys in our nation's schools, which we'll lay out in detail in Chapter 6.

Since so many grown-ups demonstrate out-of-balance demandingness with black boys, we may not realize the implications of our own approaches toward our sons—much less the snowballing effect that exists because black boys are overdisciplined throughout society.

But there's good news, and that's what this chapter's about. "When you know better, you do better," as Maya Angelou says.

Almost everyone can make an adjustment—we certainly did. Most of us will find it easy to smile more, hand out more hugs, engage in praise, and offer positive acknowledgments, and some will find it easy to start saying "I love you" on a regular basis. We can also begin to practice more balanced demands. We can develop and communicate our high expectations of black boys, encourage them to work hard, hold them accountable for their grades, and be consistent in our application of rules. And take it from us: Even though the process sometimes feels a little uncomfortable at first, practicing these behaviors on the front side is a lot more enjoyable than control and discipline once the horse has gotten out of the barn.

We can also begin to create environments in our homes, schools, churches, and youth organizations that allow them to practice critical-thinking skills—spaces in which they can be open-minded, ask questions, learn new information, explore fresh perspectives, draw their own conclusions, and communicate their own thoughts and ideas—rather than just parrot ours.

As we make these shifts, we will start to see signs of the results we all desire: higher grades, better behavior, emotional maturity, and more fully developed human beings. And imagine the upside potential if we all make the shift!

WHAT'S YOUR PARENTING "PERSONALITY TYPE"?

We update our hairstyle, refresh our wardrobe, trade in our clunker, and give our living rooms a makeover. So why doesn't it cross our mind to blow the dust off of our child-rearing style? In fact, many of us raise our children with parenting practices that are as old as our grandfather's deuce and a quarter—that's a Buick Electra 225, in case you don't know. They may have worked back in the day, but where else do we rely so carefully on information that is ten, twenty, or even fifty years old? We wouldn't use a relaxer with lye, spin a record album on our iPod, try to ball in some Chuck Taylors, or expect the diaper man to haul off our Pampers. Yet many of us cling to our parents' child-raising techniques.

So perhaps it shouldn't surprise us that few participants in Dr. Mandara's parenting workshops connect their son's behavior problems with how they raise him.

"They think it's just 'this crazy boy and I just want to understand him,'" he says of many parents when they first arrive. During the workshop "they realize 'Maybe he's like that because I didn't do all the things that I could have done.'"

A person's tendency to, say, be affectionate as opposed to distant, or very strict as opposed to laid-back crystallizes into a parenting personality type or style.[7] The mainstream literature often describes four parenting styles: *neglectful,* which some experts term uninvolved or disengaged; *permissive,* also labeled indulgent or spoiling; *authoritative,* sometimes called egalitarian; and *authoritarian,* or autocratic. (Some sources include a fifth style, a hybrid called *strict authoritative* that falls between the authoritative and authoritarian parenting styles.) These approaches differ in responsiveness and demandingness, as the Parenting Styles chart depicts (see page 136).

Neglectful (Uninvolved or Disengaged) Parenting

Parents who employ a *neglectful* parenting style do not demand much of their children or respond particularly well to their needs. Their family's home life tends to be unstructured, and the parents don't provide much emotional support to their children, or monitor them or engage in many family activities. It's important to note, however, that they don't necessarily intend to shirk their responsibilities to their kids—physically, mentally, emotionally, or spiritually.

"There are a lot of mental health problems in this group—a lot of depression and anxiety," Dr. Mandara says. "These parents tend by far to be the poorest, are more likely to be single moms, lower educated, and have more kids than the other groups."[8]

So while we may not approve of the parenting style, a call to child protective services isn't necessarily in order. Some uninvolved parents feed, clothe, and house their kids but struggle in other areas. They may fall at, say, coordinates -2 and -2 on our Parenting Styles chart. Others neglect their child-rearing responsibilities altogether; they may fall at -4 and -4. The children of disengaged parents tend to be very passive, emotionally distant, and socially irresponsible, and they face grave risks.

"They are expected to do poorly on almost everything we have ever measured," Dr. Mandara says. They are more likely to develop mental health problems, perform poorly in school, drop out, struggle to find a job, develop a substance abuse problem, and engage in risky behavior.

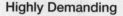

PARENTING STYLES

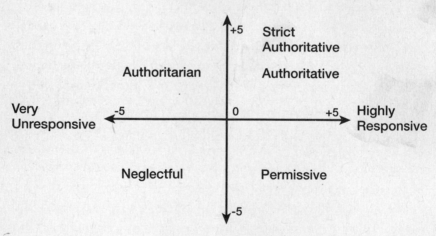

Permissive (Indulgent) Parenting

Permissive parents do not demand much from their children, and while the earliest parenting literature described them as very attentive, some more recent studies show that while they respond to their children's needs, they are not particularly engaged in their children's lives.[9]

The adults who use this style tend to demonstrate warmth and affection, respond to their children's needs, build their self-esteem, and allow them to make many of their own decisions. But they are slower to establish rules, enforce standards of behavior, monitor their kids' whereabouts, or discipline them. In fact, when the offspring of permissive parents misbehave, the parents may avoid correcting or punishing them.

"Permissive parents want their children to like them; authoritative parents want their children to respect them," says educational consultant Jawanza Kunjufu, author of *Countering the Conspiracy to Destroy Black Boys* and other classics on black boys and education.

But while it may appear to outsiders that the children are spoiled or disrespectful or are running all over their parents, many people adopt a permissive parenting style intentionally. In some circles, the style—which tends to be practiced among middle-class parents—is in vogue. The upside of permissive parenting is that the children learn to think for themselves. They become very internally motivated and develop a strong sense of agency. The downside is that they have less self-control and lower self-esteem and tend to lack toughness and resilience; when their teacher marks up their paper or they have to ride the pine, they have a harder time handling it than other kids. Research also shows that coddled kids are more likely to become verbal bullies, and they frequently become confrontational in relationships and aggressive with their parents.[10]

Authoritarian Parenting

Authoritarian parents are on the opposite side of the chart from permissive parents. These moms and dads demand a lot from their children; however, they don't jump through hoops to respond to their needs.

The personalities of authoritarian parents vary widely: some are stoic, some militaristic, and others almost dictatorial (as Michèle's father was). No matter, all tend to be strict and rule-oriented, value structure, expect their children to show self-control, and enforce strong punishments for misbehavior, temper tantrums, and disappointing grades. Cleanliness and order tend to prevail in authoritarian homes, and the children tend to have a lot of chores. But while the kids have a lot of responsibility at home, when they are teens they are not allowed to make their own personal decisions as often as other teenagers are. Somewhat surprisingly, they watch the most TV.

Because they tend to be tough, maintain their distance, and refrain from showing affection, authoritarian parents may appear to be less emotionally connected to their children than parents who demonstrate other styles; however, they may just have a different way of showing that they care.

"Traditional authoritarian parents want their kids to be physically, mentally, and emotionally tough and resilient," says Dr. Mandara. These characteristics were particularly important during the agricultural and industrial eras, when most parents raised children authoritarian-style. Today, authoritarian parenting occurs most often in working-class and poor families.[11]

But while authoritarian parenting creates kids who can tough out difficult circumstances—many coaches rely on the same techniques—it tends to cause three problems.

First, it teaches children to adopt a *subordinate* learning style that leaves them less prepared for the increasingly complex and interconnected world that they live in. Subordinate learners do a great job of seeing the two extremes—the black and the white—of an issue. But they flounder when navigating the middle ground; they are used to their parents thinking for them and punishing them for challenging authority. Consequently their critical-thinking skills tend to remain underdeveloped—a dangerous attribute in a labor market in which "brains are more important than brawn," Dr. Mandara says. "You can make a lot more money with your brain."

Second, authoritarian parenting increases the odds that a child will develop emotional or behavioral problems. We're talking depression, acting out, bullying, and fighting. And during adolescence it also sparks the most arguments about rules. Boys raised in authoritarian homes tend to become hostile; girls tend to become dependent on others and submissive to them.

Finally, the authoritarian approach limits a child's ability to develop emotionally. Children's emotional growth occurs as their intellect develops. Having greater emotional depth, in turn, helps them think deeper and more complex thoughts.

Authoritative (Egalitarian) Parenting

It's easy to confuse *authoritative* parenting with *authoritarian* parenting because the words are so similar, but the two couldn't be more different. In fact, many experts view *authoritative* parenting as the ideal parenting style.

Authoritative parents demand a lot from their kids and are very in tune to their needs. They behave warmly toward their children, listen to their thoughts and ideas, and attempt to address their concerns. When their children become teens, the parents monitor them closely, but they also allow them to make personal choices. In authoritative homes, there are regular family outings, the households are cognitively stimulating, TV-watching is limited, the children don't have to do an inordinate amount of chores, and they aren't forced to attend religious services very often.

Authoritative parents have certain rules that they will not argue about, but they allow their kids to challenge and debate them. And they do not necessarily punish their children when they get a poor grade or have an emotional outburst. The parents view this type of give-and-take as essential to children's development.

"Part of authoritative parenting is being responsive, which means actually talking to your kids and discussing things with them," says Dr. Ferguson. "You want them to know they've been understood, as opposed to believing that it's going to be 'your way or the highway' just because you're the adult and they're the kid."

One of the primary benefits of an authoritative approach is that it enhances kids' critical-thinking skills. As they converse and engage in some back-and-forth, authoritative parents learn what's going on with their kids and try to impart their values, beliefs, and thought processes. The give-and-take gives young people a safe space to question, test, and double-check their ideas—a process that is particularly important during adolescence. When their children make strong points, authoritative parents respond by shifting their own perspectives and even changing their minds, which helps to build their child's confidence and self-esteem. Teens view their parents' willingness to engage them in conversation and debate as respect, which may explain why parents who use this style don't experience a lot of knockdown, drag-out battles.

"People who use an authoritative style are preparing their children to self-advocate, feel entitled and respected, and be heard out," observes Dr. Ferguson.[12] The parents who raise them tend to be economically stable and successful.

But don't necessarily expect your son to go along with your interpretation of what's happening in the world around him.

Between the ages of roughly ten and twenty-four, his adolescent brain will compel your son to push back. So engage and help him develop critical-thinking skills by asking questions like, "Why do you think that's happening?" "What do you think that means?" and "Why do you think that?"

Debate ideas with him to help him see the world critically, develop cultural competence, and learn the values and beliefs that you hold dear.

"Kids debating during adolescence means 'I'm choosing,' or 'I want to choose,'" says Dr. Stevenson. "'The more you tell me what to do, the more I'll resist that. For developmental reasons it's in my nature.' So the best way to deal with that is to fight them and let them win. Sometimes. 'If it's a debate then we're engaged together, so don't pull out the parent card all the time.'"

He'll understand it better by and by.

But while authoritative parents allow dissent, remain open-minded, and are willing to change, these adults always have the last word.

"Authoritative parents allow kids to give their opinions and give them room to debate without knocking them out," Dr. Mandara says. "They are not 'namby-pamby'; they discipline as well. But they rarely have to, because their kids are much better behaved, so the punishments don't have to be as extreme."

In the risk-factor category, the kids of authoritative parents perform well across the board, no matter how much (or little) money their parents make.

"They do better on pretty much everything that we can measure: mental health, drug use, high-risk sex activity, delinquency—starting from an early age on up and even in college," Dr. Mandara adds.

The downside of authoritative parenting is that these "back-and-forth" conversations take time.

"What bothers me about authoritative child-rearing is that it doesn't talk about the drawbacks," says Annette Lareau, Ph.D., author of *Unequal Childhoods: Class, Race, and Family Life*. "It is exhausting to talk to these kids; there is quite a bit of whining and demanding that these middle-class kids do."

You can burn a lot of daylight debating your kids on ideas that you know are ridiculous.

"In our house there's always a negotiation going on," says Michèle, who tries to be strict-authoritative (see below) but whose inclination is to be more permissive. Sometimes she finds the process to be exhausting. But it's worth it.

Strict-Authoritative Parenting

Strict-authoritative parents demand more than their authoritative counterparts but are more responsive than authoritarian parents.

They support their children emotionally, dole out hugs and affection, go on family outings, have close relationships with their teenagers, allow them to make their own personal decisions, and are the most religious families of all. They also keep a very close eye on their teens, give them a lot of chores, restrict TV-watching the most, and punish their children when they get lower-than-expected grades. And while strict-authoritative parents do let their children debate them, they draw the line sooner than authoritative parents do.

The children of strict-authoritative parents tend to do well in every aspect of life. The parents who raise them tend to be economically stable and successful.

KISS "MY WAY OR THE HIGHWAY" GOODBYE

While research shows that these parenting styles exist across all racial groups, for decades people assumed that they yielded the same outcomes for children of different backgrounds. But this assumption had not yet been proven, and Dr. Mandara wanted to know if it was true. So he asked the question: If differences in parenting style do exist across races, could some of the academic underachievement of African American males be attributed to these differences?

To uncover the answer to this question, he and his team of researchers examined data on more 4,750 African American, Hispanic, and European American adolescents as well as on more than 2,600 of their parents. Thirty percent of the study participants were African American, 20 percent were Hispanic, and 50 percent were of European descent. One-half of the adolescents were boys, most about eighteen years old. In addition, the team interviewed more than 5,000 African American and Hispanic youth aged 10/11 and 13/14. They examined the interview participants' responses to a very long list of questions, such as the family's annual income (about half made more than $48,000 and half made less), the value of their home, educational level (they had one year of college on average), the number of chores the children had, how warm the mothers were, how clean and how intellectually stimulating their home was, the ways in which children were punished, how the kids performed academically, whether they acted out, and more.

The results showed that black and Hispanic parents are far more likely to use the authoritarian approach and are less than half as likely to use either the authoritative or strict-authoritative parenting style than are white parents. About one-third of black and Hispanic adults raise their children using one of the two authoritative styles, whereas almost three-quarters of white parents do. Almost equal proportions of black and Hispanic parents were raising their children using the neglectful (uninvolved) or permissive parenting styles.[13] (We would love to know what the statistics are for Asian parents, but they weren't a part of the study.)

These significant differences in child-rearing approaches may contribute to black boys' worse academic performance compared to their white peers of their same socioeconomic group.

PARENTING STYLES BY RACE AND ETHNICITY[14]					
	Neglectful	Permissive	Authoritarian	Authoritative	Strict Authoritative	Total Authoritative
Black	21	19	30	6	24	30
Hispanic	20	20	25	10	24	34
White	7	14	9	37	34	71

Black Parents and Neglect

Dr. Mandara learned that one in five black and Hispanic parents employs a neglectful approach to parenting. This disproportionately high number probably reflects the excessive level of poverty that families of color experience. However, he observes that when black boys enter their teens, some single mothers unintentionally become insufficiently involved because they don't respond to or demand enough of their sons. Most of these moms mistakenly believe that their son needs a lot more room to grow up than he really does. They inadvertently give him too much space, not realizing that he probably needs more structure, rules, closeness, and affection than he would ever admit. Another subset of single mom argues frequently with her son in an attempt to control him, unwittingly pushing him out of the home. Both scenarios can cause the young man to become estranged from his family. Lost, these teens tend to seek each other's companionship and unknowingly reinforce the other's loneliness and alienation.

This risk is, of course, greatest when the boy's father is not actively involved in his life. "It's bad enough when you don't have a relationship with your dad," says Dr. Mandara, "but when you have a negative one with your mother, that's really emotionally distressing. It puts them in a bad place psychologically."

Black boys raised by disengaged parents become cynical, rude, uncooperative, and emotionally unstable. The lack of adult support leaves them defenseless against the systemic and structural forces that confront them: racism, poverty, community violence, underfunded schools, inexperienced teachers, and more. And unless someone steps in, they will experience catastrophic consequences. Later in the chapter we will suggest some ways that the adults in the boys' Village can support these young men.

Black Parents and Permissiveness

Although black folks often shake our heads when we see spoiled white children running over their parents—or at least that's how it looks to our eyes—we are more likely to raise our children permissively. Almost 15 percent of white parents and about 20 percent of black and Latino adults rear their children using an indulgent approach. This method appears to be very common among black middle-class parents.

"Even though we try not to admit it, we've bought into a very European system. I find a level of permissive parenting that goes on in black middle-class experiences where some of us are not doing much parenting at all," says Rev. Dr. Alyn E. Waller, senior pastor of Enon Tabernacle Baptist Church, a Philadelphia megachurch. "Spare the discipline, spoil the development."

"In my research in black two-parent and single-parent homes, parents are on the grind," Atlanta-based Adria Welcher observes of her research on black middle-class parents. "I don't know if the parents are working so much that they just want the children to be entertained, or they're too busy because they have so much to take care of, but the sort of standards that my parents held me to and that my parents themselves were held to are a rarity. Active parenting isn't happening much. The parents work to maintain the bills for the house. The kids have to get in where they fit in."

Black boys with permissive parents tend to do better in school than the sons of both neglectful and authoritarian parents, but they do worse than the sons of authoritative and strict-authoritative homes. Even when they come from stable, two-parent households, they tend to perform poorly in math.[15] (Black girls with permissive parents do better than average academically but are more likely to misbehave than black girls whose parents use other styles.) The black sons of permissive parents exhibit similar behavioral and emotional characteristics as children of other races parented permissively do. And while they're not more likely than average to become depressed, they're far more likely to experience the blues than black children raised by authoritative or strict-authoritative parents. The likelihood that they will act out is also much higher than for the black sons of authoritative and strict-authoritative parents as well as for the white sons of permissive parents. That's a disaster waiting to happen.

"A lot of parents are very indulgent of their boys, especially. They're not giving them any sense of discipline or responsibility. The boys don't know how to negotiate the world, because nothing has been expected of them," says urban sociologist Pedro Noguera, a professor of education at New York University.

> "Kids don't want you to know all the stuff they know. One thing kids hate is adults trying to be cool," says Dave Hardy, president and CEO of Boys' Latin High School, a predominately black single-sex school in Philadelphia. "They want to know that you care; they want to know that you have some knowledge that's going to move them forward. They don't need you to be their friend. They have friends at school; they have friends in the neighborhood. They need guidance."

Although many black single mothers do not start out by parenting their son permissively, as he enters adolescence and she becomes fearful, she may overcompensate by spoiling him.[16]

"In some ways it becomes really bad for her son," Dr. Mandara says. "These boys are not raised to be tough, and it shows when they grow up. They don't know how to deal with pressure. If they lose their job they freak out. They have a very good relationship with their mom but they're as weak as water."

(We do not view this scenario as an indictment of single moms, but we offer the insight to mothers doing their best with too few resources.)

We have experienced our own struggles with what happens when permissive parenting meets a black boy. When Idris was in elementary school, Michèle's mother, who parents permissively, would come stay with us for months at a time. We would tell Idris that he couldn't have something—a toy, candy, whatever—but then find its wrapper under his bed. This happened repeatedly. Michèle's mom would deny knowing anything about it, but she clearly had a hard time telling Idris no. He had her wrapped around his pinkie.

Our approach to parenting is the strict-authoritative style—we try to be firm, provide a lot of structure, and have clear rules and consequences for breaking them. But whether she knew it or not, by spoiling Idris, Michèle's mother was undermining our authority. We reached a point where Idris was not only lying at home to get what he wanted and to evade our rules, he started lying outside of our home; Michèle's mother was rewarding him for being dishonest.

The words *spoiled* and *black boy* don't work well in the same sentence, and *black boy* and *liar* or *black boy* and *thief*—which we worried would come next—are a recipe for disaster. We didn't want his behavior to spiral out of control or for our greatest fear to happen: that Idris would shoplift and end up in jail. Michèle tried to set some limits with her mom, but eventually we had to put our foot down: We banned Michèle's mother from our house, except for two weeks each year. We know this may seem harsh, and as you might imagine, Michèle's mother was upset, but our terms weren't negotiable. She is an adult, and Idris is not. We had to sacrifice her so that we could help him to unlearn his bad habits. Otherwise, we risked a situation that Idris might not be able to recover from. (We should point out that some experts believe that black boys may act out at school when they are raised strictly at home but encounter permissive teachers in class.)

During his thirty-year career as a clinical psychiatrist, Joe has found that about 90 percent of the young people he's seen were raised by negligent or permissive parents.

"Their home environment falls overwhelmingly below the line on the Parenting Styles chart," he says. "The parents are not warm but are often critical and demeaning, and they aren't demanding of themselves or others." Among people who develop drug dependencies and the homeless, he observes, these parenting approaches were the norm.

Black Parents and the Authoritarian Style

Black and Hispanic parents are much more likely to use an authoritarian approach to child-rearing than whites. Thirty percent of black parents, 25 percent of Hispanics, but only 9 percent of white parents are authoritarian. In fact, more black parents use this approach than any other parenting method.

But black boys reared by parents who rely on this rigid style have lower test scores than black boys raised by any parents except neglectful ones.[17] They have about a 30 percent greater risk of becoming depressed, are more than 50 percent more likely to act out, and they withdraw and become distrustful of others far more often than black boys raised by authoritative or strict-authoritative parents. And they are far more likely to misbehave.[18]

"I know I get autocratic, especially when I'm really stressed out," says Savannah, an accounting manager. "I don't mean to be, but it's almost like those reactions become a reflex or a habit. I try to get my friends to help me stop, but they're not there most of the time. Sometimes I know I'm too hard on him."

So then why do so many black parents raise their boy-children this way? As recently as a generation ago, authoritarian parenting yielded the most successful African American males.[19] For hundreds of years, "tough love" parenting protected their sons—and it still does. Once Michèle and Idris went to the pharmacy together. Idris strayed into another aisle. A security guard followed him and then asked if he had anything in his pocket. He didn't. Michèle's knee-jerk and authoritarian response was to tell Idris to stay with her and not wander off. She knew Idris had been profiled and wanted to protect him. (After they left the store, she realized that she should have challenged the guard.)

When setting limits and instituting and enforcing rules with your son, emphasize what to do rather than focusing exclusively on what not to do. He will respond better, and you will get more successful results.

Authoritarian parenting also helped to prepare black males for a lifetime of manual labor—of following rules and doing what they were told. Follower personality types excelled, and independent thinkers and resisters failed.

"Immediately obeying authority figures is a survival skill or survival disposition for black Americans, especially during a certain historical period in the South," says Dr. Ferguson. "It's also a way even today to be successful in menial blue-collar employment, where you can be replaced immediately if your supervisor doesn't like the way you look at him."

But although Jim Crow is over, manufacturing has moved overseas, and what blue-collar jobs remain require critical-thinking skills, many black boys' parents, educators, coaches, and youth leaders still haven't updated their parenting style.

Most grown-ups interact with black boys using an approach from a bygone era that is now ineffective at best and can produce unwanted results.

Far too many people still teach black boys to "follow the rules, listen, and do as they're told," says Dr. Mandara. This undermines their intellectual development and agency, making it "very difficult for them to think for themselves."

Complicating matters, many fathers of all backgrounds intentionally "tough love" their sons to teach them to deal with life's pressures—at least from time to time.

"Certain things that I do with Seun, I do as a man, and sometimes there needs to be a harsh reality," says Tony Summers, who intentionally shifts from strict-authoritative to authoritarian parenting when teaching certain notions of manliness. "Sometimes it can't have any nurturing overtones with it," he adds. "It just has to be harsh, maybe make no sense, or seem crazy."

We have experimented with authoritarian parenting as well. When Idris was about eleven, we signed him up to play basketball for an authoritarian coach who ran one of the best youth teams in New York City. We did it because while both of us can be strict, Joe is not authoritarian and Michèle leans toward being permissive. Joe thought it was important to expose Idris to a disciplinarian so that he would know how to handle stress and to resist and stand up for himself when pushed. And let's face it: From teachers to police officers, the world deals with black males in an authoritarian way. Idris has to learn how to deal with it.

Michèle wanted Idris to learn the same skills. Having experienced an authoritarian father, however, she didn't feel that this approach would help. But since she'll never know what it's like to be a black male and since Joe thinks she nurtures Idris and Miles too much, she consented to the experiment.

Typical Statements Made by Authoritarian Parents

- Do it because I'm the parent and you're not.
- Don't ask questions; just do it.
- Do it because I said so.
- It's my way or the highway.
- As long as I pay the bills, I make the rules.
- Do you pay any of the bills around here?

Now, there's no doubt that the coach intended to do well. He certainly said prayers before practice, showed up week after week, and put a lot of time and energy into the boys. But he yelled at the kids constantly, offered little positive reinforcement, and dished out a lot of negativity. "I'ma whup your ass!" "Get your ass on the bench!" "Sit the fuck down!" "You will never win nothing big." These are the kinds of things he said to motivate eleven-year-olds.

Not surprisingly, Idris struggled with the coach and his team-mates, who bullied him. (You will recall that boys who experience authoritarian treatment act out, bully, and fight.) We spent lots of time talking him through how to handle the pressure, and he did as well as he could. The experience took a toll, though, and after the season we had to rebuild his confidence.

We agreed to disagree about whether the experience had been helpful. Joe thinks that it taught Idris some important life lessons, taught him how to deal with certain kinds of adversity. Michèle thinks that there are better ways to teach toughness, self-sufficiency, and independence and that he is still rebuilding his self-confidence after all the negative treatment he endured during that time. And while we do not believe that authoritarian parenting is synonymous with abuse of any type—physical, verbal, emotional, or sexual—an authoritarian style gone awry can severely damage a child. When Joe treated young black men at the Brooklyn city jail, about nine out of ten of his patients had been abused by an adult—a rate several times higher than in the general population. He saw almost no children who were raised authoritatively.

Black Parents and the Authoritative Style

Only 6 percent of black parents and 10 percent of Hispanic parents practice *authoritative* child-rearing, but 37 percent of white parents do.

Experts view the authoritative approach, including strict-authoritative, as the most effective overall child-rearing style for children of all races and ethnic groups, including black boys. Black boys (and girls) raised by authoritative parents score better on tests than the children of any other parenting style and are less likely to get depressed. The boys have high self-esteem, exhibit self-control, feel powerful, are secure in their racial identity, and are emotionally very well adjusted. They do misbehave a little bit more than the sons of strict-authoritative parents, although significantly less than those of parents who use the neglectful, permissive, or authoritarian style.

"Black boys who receive this kind of parenting do really

outstanding—even poor inner-city boys. They do well academically (in fact, they can even be nerdy); they do really well mentally; they don't smoke much marijuana; in my research they report very low levels of sexual activity; they don't engage in risky behaviors; and they don't engage in delinquency often," says Dr. Mandara. "The effects of authoritative parenting are really profound, but black boys are by far the group least likely to receive it at home and especially at school."

"A lot of educators try to convince me that it's the number of parents in the home or the income of the home or the educational background of the mother," says Dr. Kunjufu. "We have found research that low-income parents without a college degree that are African American have produced thousands of children well above the national average. But these parents listen to their children, give them high expectations, monitor homework, they're involved with the teacher. What parents have to do is simply make their children their number-one priority."

"Kids benefit from structure, kids benefit from very clear guidance and a very clear sense of ethics," says Dr. Noguera.

The authoritative parenting style rubs some black parents the wrong way because it violates certain cultural values about how children should show respect to adults.

"Black people haven't quite made that adjustment," Dr. Mandara observes.

In meetings we've had with black and brown parents from around the country, we've received consistent feedback that authoritative parenting just isn't an African American (or Latino) way to raise a child. Many parents of color have told us that they don't like it when their children come home questioning and challenging, as they're taught to do at school. At home even parents who are successful professionally and know how to deal with white folks effectively may interpret such behavior as disrespect.

Trust us: We get it. When Idris began questioning our authority, there were a couple of times when we wanted to throttle him. But we realized that he was just trying to practice with us the same type of critical thinking that we were encouraging him to engage in at school and that this was a good thing even though it made us extremely uncomfortable.

Joe's psychiatry experience helped him to know that we could not encourage Idris to think critically at school but then punish him at home for the same behavior without creating a conflict within his psyche that he wasn't ready to handle. We didn't want to shut down his intellectual or emotional growth or cause him to act out; we didn't want to be hypocrites; and even though his push-backs made us uncomfortable and sometimes mad, we really didn't want to ask our son to leave his brain at the door.

So we shifted from authoritarian to strict-authoritative parenting to give Idris room to think critically—even if he's thinking critically about us.

Dr. Mandara notes that white parents have about a two-generation head start in transitioning out of the authoritarian child-rearing so common during the agricultural and industrial ages and into the authoritative approach more common among middle-class families.

"Whites were in the same situation not long ago, but blacks are brand-new to the middle class. We're still going through the transition," he says. But black people have to change—and change quickly—if we are to keep our children from being left out in this high-tech, globally interconnected world.

"I'm definitely starting to see changes, but we are not moving as quickly as we need to be," Dr. Mandara says. "Given the situation that black people are in, and particularly males, we don't have a whole lot of time to be wasting. It's imperative that we speed up."

And other adults who participate in black boys' lives will experience better results if they begin to shift.

"You want to strike a balance between support and press," Dr. Ferguson suggests.

"Provide a lot more positive comments, a lot more praise, and a lot more physical affection," Dr. Mandara says. "Say things like, 'You are such a special boy!' or 'I love you so much!' Authoritarian parents may think these things, but they don't say them as often, and that has consequences."

And while we may be inclined to protect or control black boys by keeping them close or otherwise restricting their movement, it's important to let them explore and let teens make some of their own decisions so that they develop a sense of mastery over the parts of their environment that they can control.

Black Parents and the Strict-Authoritative Style

Almost 35 percent of white parents and 25 percent of black and Hispanic parents practice strict-authoritative parenting, the second most common style among black parents.

Black males whose parents use a strict-authoritative technique achieve better results academically than any other parents except authoritative parents. And strict-authoritative parenting offers our sons firmness without the *authoritarian* upbringing's downsides: less-than-optimal critical-thinking skills, a level of emotional development that keeps them from reaching their potential, and the risk of developing behavioral problems, such as fighting, bullying, and being abusive.

As often as possible, we practice strict-authoritative parenting. For us, this means setting very high expectations for Idris, nurturing and supporting him, responding to his thoughts and feelings, engaging in a lot of dialogue, and often playing "devil's advocate" with him as he talks out his ideas.

The other reason we've chosen strict-authoritative parenting instead of simple authoritative parenting is that we find this spin on authoritative parenting best supports our efforts to engage in The Talk. Not only does it allow us to engage in dialogue, it also helps us to draw lines that protect him. And it supports our highly demanding messages to him that he has to perform and behave better than his white peers to protect himself not just from how he may be judged on the street but also from unconscious stereotypes he encounters at school.

Sometimes Idris wants to engage us in a little tug-of-war. For example, he may push back on our conversations about being a black male because he receives the message from his teachers, the media, and society that we live in a postracial era.

Whatever he pushes back about, we'll indulge for a moment.

However, after we've listened to his thoughts, explored his emotions, explained our positions and considered his, we make a thoughtful decision and are done with it.

It also helps us deal with more mundane issues. But it's not always a straightforward success—there's a certain amount of trial, error, and adaptation that has to happen. One year Idris stopped holding up his end of the bargain with the handful of chores that we've given him. He's supposed to walk the dog before and after school and take out the garbage on trash day, but he would "forget." And at one point he really started "smelling himself"—thinking he was grown—and stopped getting up on time for school!

We started out by talking to him about the role he plays in our home and how important his contribution is to keeping our household running smoothly. He kept promising that he would do better but didn't, and each excuse became weaker than the one we had heard the day before. We continued to press him to do his chores—but then decided it was time for some consequences.

First, Michèle took his cell phone away. Idris did walk the dog once or twice after that, but he'd find another way to shirk his responsibility: a basketball tournament or a school trip or something. And depriving him of his cell phone left us without a way to communicate with him, so it not only didn't have the desired effect, we actually needed to give it back to him. So Idris "won" Round One.

One reason he wasn't doing his morning chores was because he was hitting the snooze button too much. The stork delivers some parents highly motivated kids, but if ours could sleep all day, he would; we understand that. So Joe made Idris's life less comfortable by taking his mattress away. Well, having to sleep on his box springs shocked him for a moment, so he walked the dog for about a week—just long enough to get his mattress back. But before long he had returned to breaking his promise or just flat-out lying by saying that he'd do his chores but then slipping out the door. So Joe took the mattress out again—this time for weeks on end. But wouldn't you know it? Our son actually got comfortable sleeping on his box springs or on the floor! Round Two: Idris.

This sent us back to the drawing board. What does a teenager value more than his phone and his sleep, we asked ourselves? Privacy. So Joe took Idris's door off the hinges. Idris fought back by hanging up sheets. We took them away as well. Bingo! Once the semester ended and summer vacation arrived, we could have kept the door down for G.P.—general principles—but we had made our point, and in the summer dog walking is less of an issue, so we let it go. Idris began doing a better job around the house, and Joe gave him his mattress and door back. Outwit. Outlast. Outplay.

But while we joke about there being winners and losers, the goal of authoritative parenting isn't to come out on top; our goal is to develop the type of relationship with our son that will help us to help him develop intellectually, emotionally, and behaviorally. We think it works. Idris went to the junior prom and wanted to stay out overnight. He was going to be at the home of a friend, and he insisted that they weren't really going to "do anything," he was mature enough to handle it, and of course "all of the other parents" were letting their kids sleep over. Whatever. We weren't comfortable with the idea that both boys and girls would be present. Joe immediately said no; his parents certainly would never have allowed it. But as long as the host's parents were present, Michèle wasn't so sure it would be such a bad thing.

In our conversations with Idris and between ourselves—we intentionally had some conversations within Idris's earshot so he could hear us explore the issues—Joe recalled that his parents hadn't always been right. He also remembered doing some pretty mischievous things as a teenager while he was in his own home, climbing out of his back window and into the window of a girl who lived a few doors down, for instance. Joe not only survived, he's done well in his life in spite of many youthful indiscretions. Was Idris really likely to do anything much worse? And if he did, would it be catastrophic? Probably not. So eventually, we decided that he could go to the sleepover as long as we knew the parents and were sure that they'd be home. Idris successfully argued his case and listened to us disagree with each other and talk our concerns through and resolve the situation while respecting everyone's opinions.

But we don't always get it right. And trust us: We've been wrong enough times that we've learned it's okay to change our minds and to admit that he's right. We probably should have handled things differently when it came to Idris's music lessons. The school had told us that Idris had a good ear and had even suggested he concentrate in music. This particularly excited Michèle, whose uncle had played Spanish guitar; she envisioned Idris following in her uncle's footsteps. But when Idris showed an interest in the electric guitar and found songs that he wanted to learn, she insisted that he play acoustic. But Idris's ADD made practicing particularly difficult for him, and we made matters worse by imposing our musical preferences authoritarian-style. Eventually he quit. What did we learn? In retrospect, we should have encouraged our son to learn whatever instrument interested him—a more authoritative approach.

So when our younger son, Miles, expressed his musical interest, we took advantage of the chance at a do-over. Miles was attracted to the piano at a very young age, so we encouraged him, and when his interest shifted to guitar, we allowed it. But instead of pushing him in any particular direction, this time we let our son take the lead. He started out playing rock on the electric guitar, but now plays more blues and moves back and forth between electric and acoustic. In either case we haven't pushed our preferences on him, and he's still very interested.

Only time will tell how we do on the issue of drugs. Marijuana is prevalent among Idris's peer group. We know that he tried it but we decided not to go ballistic, which we did consider even though it would have been an authoritarian reaction. We had a very rational conversation with him instead. To be honest, we think marijuana probably should be legal, but it isn't, so we told him in no uncertain terms that we do not want him getting high—a strict-authoritative approach. We took this position even though Joe smoked weed during his youth and, at one point, cigarettes. (Michèle has never used drugs of any kind.) Joe told Idris that he'd become extremely paranoid on several occasions after smoking marijuana. And although we think the chances are pretty slim, addiction is something more than a theoretical risk since it has happened on both sides of our family.

ut our bigger fear surrounds the potential consequences if Idris
e ever to get caught with pot. "Stop-and-frisk" policing is big in
w York City, and it's overwhelmingly used on black and brown
oung men. More white kids smoke weed, but more kids of color get
stopped. And Idris has already been stopped for "walking while
black." So our insistence that he not get high hinges on the potential
legal consequences. Many parents drug-test their kids, go through
their belongings, or force them to empty their pockets, a route that we
find much too authoritarian. Idris is clear about how we expect him
to behave; we have discussed all of the pros, cons, and potential outcomes. Now we choose to allow him to make his own choices. If
smoking weed does in fact become an issue for him, we're not going
to go authoritarian on him unless he's in danger. But if we feel he's in
danger, all bets are off; we will do whatever we have to do to protect
our son.

KNOWING BETTER, DOING BETTER

So our sons are more likely to succeed if the adults in their lives—their
parents, extended family, teachers, coaches, and youth leaders—shift
from being permissive and authoritarian toward being authoritative
or strict authoritative.

How should we approach this adjustment? It will certainly take
some effort, but it may not be as difficult as we think. The secret to
what changes to make can be found in the Parenting Styles chart (see
page 136). As the diagram depicts, each of the parenting styles borders other styles. For example, the authoritarian quadrant sits adja-
cent to the strict-authoritative and authoritative styles, both of which
yield better results for black boys; the permissive quadrant borders
authoritative as well. Even the neglectful quadrant shares boundaries
with the authoritarian and permissive styles, and at one corner it
touches authoritative as well. So we can change our style by adjusting
how responsive or demanding we behave so that we move toward or
into a quadrant that yields better test scores, behavior, and emotional
development.

Since the well-being of black boys is strongly affected by both the amount of warmth that adults show them and the ability of the adult to strike a balance when they discipline them, we can get great results by adjusting our behavior in those two areas. Recall that warmth is a dimension of responsiveness, which many black parents could stand to display more. Discipline is associated with demandingness, which almost all adults express toward black boys excessively or in an imbalanced fashion that is seldom really about having high expectations for them in a positive sense.

The good news is that nearly every adult is capable of being more or less warm or controlling depending on the circumstances. We know, for example, many parents who raise their children somewhat differently. Who doesn't know a typical "oldest child" or "baby" within the same family? And mothers who "raise their daughter but love their sons" are all over the place. So most people have a part of themselves that can be more or less loving or more or less strict. It's just a matter of tapping into those areas and practicing those behaviors with our sons.

One important key to success is shifting in the direction of a more effective style that aligns with your own natural personality. You don't have to move all the way from permissive to strict-authoritarian, for instance. Let's say that Erica is extremely permissive. She might first practice being a little less permissive—that is, she might practice behaviors that help move her from a -5 to a -2 in demandingness. That adjustment alone will benefit her son. Once those behaviors become more comfortable, she can begin shifting from a -2 toward a +1. At this point she has become authoritarian, a style that helps black boys experience more positive outcomes than when they are parented permissively. That shift alone will dramatically improve the trajectory of Erica's son's life.

We have had a very a positive experience transitioning to strict-authoritative parenting. Idris has clearly become a better critical thinker since we became less authoritarian. He is more emotionally balanced, and even though he acts out from time to time, it's of the "boys will be boys" variety, not delinquency. We do admit, though, that change is a process. We spend a lot more time talking *with* him than *at* him, and that takes up a lot of time. It's been quite a while since we've said, "Do it because I said do it." Instead, we spend a lot more time listening to his opinions and whatever else is on his mind, which helps us understand and appreciate him more—and, we hope, helps him appreciate us. And even when we disagree, we look at it as a teaching moment, an opportunity to engage our son in conversations that will help him become a better thinker, understand our values and beliefs, and become better prepared for life.

Truth be told, in some ways it was easier to tell Idris, "My way or the highway" than to explain ourselves and have a conversation about it. Then again, had we not made the change, we would have spent a lot of time supporting, correcting, and disciplining him while he struggled academically, and the whole process would almost certainly have made him angry and depressed—and that would have required a lot of time and emotional energy too!

Still, we continue to be a work in progress. Some days we do better than others. There are definitely days when we'd want a "do over." If we're tired and overwhelmed, for instance, we may find ourselves being more short-tempered than we'd ideally like to be. On other days we're able to be extremely patient. Nobody's perfect. The goal is for our parenting style to balance out over the long run. It's also important to emphasize the need to be flexible. If one of Idris's teachers had been particularly hard on him, we might choose to be more permissive that day to balance out his overall experience. As long as we parents are in touch with our children's needs, we can demonstrate responsiveness by making adjustments that balance out his overall style.

TEACHERS, COACHES, SCHOOLS, AND ORGANIZATIONS PARENT, TOO

Importantly, caring adults can use the Parenting Styles chart to support boys whose parents are neglectful or otherwise unengaged. If the Village of aunties and uncles, educators, counselors, coaches, mentors, and others becomes more responsive and demanding—effectively shifting their collective parenting of him toward the permissive, authoritarian, or authoritative styles—they will help to improve his academic, emotional, and behavioral outcomes. And when tragedy strikes, as it does all too often in black families, the Village can surround and protect a child.

When Seun was 17, the accidental death of his younger brother, Jabulani, rocked the family. Grief consumed Tony, Stacey, and Seun's grandmother, and the children's needs increased exponentially just as his parents' ability to respond diminished. For a short time there was a gap. Fortunately, the family members really clung to each other, and community members extended many helping hands. In particular, the special education teacher who had been helping Seun manage his dyslexia threw him a lifeline. She talked to him, offered comfort, and told him that the door to her office was open whenever he wanted to come by, even if he only wanted to sleep. Within a few months, his parents had moved through their darkest hours and had become more responsive and demanding again. The community had successfully protected the children, and the teacher had helped keep Seun safe.

But no matter what we do as parents to adjust our approach to raising our sons, for most of the day our boys aren't in our hands; they're in the care of schools, after-school programs, sports leagues, the Boy Scouts, churches, and other entities and organizations. Each of these has an organizational parenting style. Some reflect a specific school of thought; others carry out an organizational mission; still others demonstrate the philosophy of an individual leader, educator, or coach.

While parenting styles vary across institutions and individuals, once black boys walk out the door of their family home, the adults who interact with them—from the bus driver to their coach to their youth leader—almost always use the authoritarian style with them, which arrests their intellectual development and causes misbehavior and depression.

"Oh my God, that explains everything," says Valerie, the vice principal of a middle school in a very prestigious charter school network that is known to be very demanding of the children. "I just had a conversation about this with my staff."

Even before learning this information, Valerie had begun wondering if maybe the school's authoritarian style is counterproductive.

"The teachers are starting to notice boys who act out in school, but when we see them in the community with their mothers, they're very loving and respectful," she says. "I told my staff that maybe we're contributing to the problem—maybe we need to pull back and be more gentle. One of the boys responded immediately: We haven't had a problem [with him] since. So maybe the problem isn't them. Maybe it's *us*!"

Indeed, instead of treating black boys harshly (high demands/low responsiveness), adults should interact with them along *both* dimensions of the parenting chart by being responsive—particularly by treating them warmly—and communicating high expectations of them—a different dimension of demandingness—rather than by over-emphasizing and enforcing rules.

Joe once worked as a consultant to a school district that was integrating a predominately white school with (mostly) high-performing black boys who were the sons of police officers, firefighters, ministers, and other community leaders. At home the boys were probably parented with an authoritarian or strict-authoritative style—they knew how to behave. But soon after they started integrating the new school, they started failing tests, stealing, and misbehaving.

After observing the boys and performing an organizational analysis, Joe realized that the teachers, who were white, expected the boys to fail, so they didn't demand much of them. The boys also experienced constant racial *micro-aggressions*—everyday insults, indignities, and demeaning messages—from both the adults and the other children, which made them angry. Hoping to rectify the situation, the school system hired a black female principal, who inadvertently contributed to the problem. Once she realized what the boys were up against, she felt sorry for them and nurtured them excessively. The low demands of the teachers combined with the high responsiveness of the principal combined to create a permissive environment. Recall that the permissive style tends to create children who are more self-centered, impulsive, disobedient, and rebellious. Among black boys, it also lowers academic achievement.

What was the solution? The answer can be found in the chart. To raise the boys' academic performance and improve their behavior in the short term, the school needed to shift in the direction of an authoritative style. Everyone needed to expect more of the boys and respond appropriately to their needs. Joe coached the teachers to treat the boys as they would their own sons—nurturing, supporting, and treating them kindly while communicating high expectations of them. The principal needed to nurture the boys less and support the high expectations, while clearly communicating and enforcing the rules. Before long the boys began to achieve better results.

Keeping the Promise

1. **Understand your parenting style.** Rather than just assuming that you'll raise your son in the same way you yourself were raised, think carefully about the best parenting style for you and your son.

2. **Avoid overly permissive or authoritarian styles.** Remember that your son needs you to provide guidelines and support—to be his parent, not his best friend or his overseer.

3. **Adjust your parenting style, if necessary.** The good news is that no matter how we ourselves were raised—or what habits we may already have fallen into—there are ways to adjust our parenting style to maximize our sons' potential.

6

YOU BROUGHT HIM INTO THIS WORLD, DON'T LET OTHER FOLKS TAKE HIM OUT

How to Discipline Our Sons for Best Results

I have a lot of victories with boys. The boys in my class excel. They've been empowered by the words I've said to them. But it didn't start out this way. During my second year of teaching, I had a shifting moment. There was a young man I would bump heads with—I mean, every day. Then I met his mother. I saw how they interacted, and I thought to myself in simple terms: I think he has issues with women. Since, in my mind, I reminded him of his mother, I decided to take a different approach. But I had to humble myself to accept and adjust to his reality. And that has been the key to being able to deal with black boys.

I learned that anyone who is bold enough to bump heads with you like that, they have power. So I challenge that power. I give him roles. He becomes an important part of the classroom community. I harness it. I see that in a lot of black boys—that they are actually leaders. But I have to humble myself and be okay with their strength. I don't think a lot of people are. People see it as, he's trying to take over, or he's trying to make me look bad, or he's out of control. In my experience, it's none of that.

You have to be brave; you cannot be scared; you have to defend your ground. Sometimes you have to call a person out—I didn't do anything to you, and you hurt me. But also as a teacher, a grown-up, and a leader, you have to be okay with being vulnerable and apologizing when you hurt a child. I've seen the results of what happens when a black boy feels like nobody gets him, nobody understands him. He's in so much pain. He acts out; he gets in trouble; he fails academically.

Andrea, 38, math teacher

PRISONER OR PROMISING?

He has his father's eyes and your sister's dimples, and his fat cheeks are so cute you could just eat them up, but black children—and boys in particular—encounter a world that doesn't see much beauty in them and treats them very unkindly, even when they're very young.

"Certain times, especially if it's a crowd of us, you can just feel the negative vibes, the bad feelings, the tension from other people," says Carlton, 16.

The tendency of many black parents and Village members to use a more authoritarian and "tough love" approach means that some of our sons don't have a sanctuary to replenish from the opposition that they face when they walk out the door.

"My mother, she yells all the time," says Keenan. "My stomach goes in a knot when I hear her key in the lock."

This tension often exists in their educational environment.

"They treat the kids like prisoners at my son's school," one mother told us. "They are always yelling at them, barking orders, and making them stand in line. I'm quite confident they wouldn't treat white children like that, anywhere, but particularly out here in the suburbs."

"When you look at some of the really successful schools for African Americans, there are a lot of rules and carrots and sticks applied to virtually all behavior," says Joshua Aronson, an associate professor of applied psychology at New York University's Steinhardt School of Culture, Education, and Human Development, referring to schools that wrest high test scores out of kids but at a great emotional cost. "There's little freedom; there's extra school; there's Saturday school. To a human being—an organism that was born to be free and self-determining—this is like putting handcuffs on. And the long-term data suggest that as soon as these kids get into college, many flounder and drop out because they are now faced with freedom for the first time—and aren't prepared for it."

This chapter is about discipline, including the prevailing tendency throughout American society to over-control and over-punish black children, especially boys:

- We introduce this conversation by describing in detail the findings from some groundbreaking studies that lay bare the unconscionable degree to which black boys are punished in educational settings. We provide this backdrop because it's very difficult for a black person to document objectively the existence of bias or racism. This can cause us to wonder if we are imagining things or overreacting—especially in a world quick to accuse us of pulling the "race card" when we attempt to speak to issues involving race. These data provide undeniable proof of the bias our children encounter and beg the question of what we, as parents, the members of their Village, and other adults who care about children, are going to do to fix it. They also counter the stereotype of black boys as "bad" and lay out plainly the role that educators play in making disciplinary choices that deprive our sons of the opportunity to learn and that shove them into what is now known as the classroom-to-prison pipeline.

- We will suggest a definition of the word *discipline* that emphasizes education over punishment.
- We examine just what it means to "spare the rod" as we correct our children.
- Building on our discussion about parenting styles, we will share a repertoire of disciplinary approaches that can help adults balance warmth with high expectations while expressing love and imposing an appropriate amount of control—a goal we think you'll agree is particularly important given the school-discipline data. Approaches to discipline and parenting styles are often related.
- We'll look at the role of spanking and corporal punishment. And we'll share why we believe the time has come for both black parents and the educational community to graduate from physical punishment so that our sons can achieve their full potential.

> **Promise your son that you will challenge excessive punishment in educational and other settings and use a full repertoire of disciplinary approaches to shape his behavior and help him learn self-awareness and responsibility.**

SUFFER THE LITTLE CHILDREN

Black boys are more likely to be suspended or expelled from school than are children of any other race.

"This clear trend has been documented since the '70s, but people are reluctant to talk about it," says Anne Gregory, an associate professor at the Graduate School of Applied and Professional Psychology at Rutgers University and an expert in both racial discipline disparities and techniques to assist teachers and schools educate black boys more successfully. "Black boys have been two to three times overrepresented in discipline of all kinds—suspension, expulsion—for decades now," she adds, also noting the trend of black girls "now getting disciplined at exponentially higher rates of suspension."

> "I get the negative stereotype of oh, he's just the common nigger who hangs out in the street all day; he doesn't have anything to offer to society," says Isaiah, 16. "But if you really knew me you would understand that I'm a really artistic kid. I'm a writer, I'm a singer, I'm a drummer, and somewhat of an actor. I do everything, but people judge books before they get to read the content of the book."

The punitive behavior begins when black children are in preschool, when, we were shocked to learn, they're more likely to get kicked out of school than at any other time, including during their teenage years. Our babies often get expelled for engaging in behavior that's normal for their stage of development. The excessive punishment continues throughout their teens.

The National Prekindergarten Study, a look at 3,898 state-funded, pre-K classrooms nationwide during 2003 and 2004, found that children of all races were three times as likely to be sent packing from preschool than from grades K–12.

Expelling babies! What's up with that?

"No one wants to hear about three- and four-year-olds being expelled from preschool, but it happens rather frequently," said Walter S. Gilliam, director of the Edward Zigler Center in Child Development and Social Policy and an associate professor of child psychiatry and psychology at the Child Study Center at Yale School of Medicine. "Pre-K teachers need access to the support staff they need to help manage classroom behavior problems. Without this support, we are setting up for failure both our children and their teachers."[1]

"Boys in pre-K tend to be more boisterous, rowdy, physical, less verbal, less attentive, more determined in some ways," said Oscar Barbarin, head of the psychology department at Tulane University, at the "A Strong Start" Conference hosted by ETS in 2011.[2] "Girls are more verbal, compliant, and fit into the realm of the classroom better. Even pre-K classes are geared to girls."

Black children were twice as likely as white children—and five times more likely than Asian American students—to get thrown out of preschool. And while boys in general were expelled four and a half times more often than were girls, among black children boys comprised more than 90 percent of the kids who were kicked out.[3]

What gives?

"There's an identification of black boys as black men," says Margaret Beale Spencer, Ph.D., a professor of human development and urban education at the University of Chicago. "Even first and second grade little black boys are getting suspended because teachers—white teachers in particular—are afraid of them. That is, children's behavior is interpreted or perceived by adult teachers through the frightening stereotypes often associated with black men."

Dr. Gregory, who was not involved with the pre-K study but is a former kindergarten teacher, says that earlier in her career when she did mental health work with black boys in schools, she noticed that "in some contexts some of the teachers were really seeing defiance and disruption embodied in them—so we could say the criminalization of black boys and the 'bad seed' theory. And then other teachers were seeing all this potential and engaging them in a very different way."

The results from the pre-K study are consistent with this observation.

"When teachers had access to a behavioral consultant who was able to provide classroom-based strategies for dealing with challenging student behaviors, the likelihood of expulsion was nearly cut in half," Dr. Gilliam said.

A MENACE TO SOCIETY?

The pattern of overdiscipline continues once our kids reach their teens.

A groundbreaking study published in 2011 to improve policymakers' understanding of who gets suspended and expelled took a look at the school records of every student in a Texas public secondary school over a six-year period. Researchers found that nearly 60 percent of all students in the Lone Star State had been suspended or expelled at least once between seventh and twelfth grade. Black students were impacted disproportionately. Indeed, 83 percent of black male students, as compared with 74 percent of Hispanic male students, and 59 percent of white male students, had been removed from the classroom (or school) for at least one *discretionary violation*—a violation of the school's code of conduct but not of the state's rules for mandatory suspension or expulsion. (Seventy percent of black female students had been suspended or expelled for a discretionary reason as well.)[4]

Typical discretionary rules include being tardy, excessive absences, violating the dress code, talking back, using a prohibited electronic device such as a cell phone, or using profanity.

We could spend all day describing the impact that *zero-tolerance policies*—predefined consequences for behavior that must be applied no matter the situation or mitigating circumstances—have had on black children. Even Idris was suspended one time from Dalton's lower school for allegedly hitting another boy—emphasis on "allegedly." Zero-tolerance started off as a get-tough approach for drug enforcement; eventually it was applied to school discipline to address growing fears around school safety. In many jurisdictions it now includes behaviors, such as school dress codes, that have a questionable impact on student safety. Ivory A. Toldson, coauthor with Chance W. Lewis of the Congressional Black Caucus Foundation report *Challenge the Status Quo: Academic Success among School-age African American Males*, notes that the " 'suspend first, ask questions later' attitude" pervades the environment of many schools that educate black boys and includes such threats to student safety as sagging pants. We don't like sagging pants or want our sons to wear them, but are they a menace to the educational process? We doubt it.

"I got a one-day in-school suspension for sagging my pants," says Austin, 14. "Granted, I knew I wasn't supposed to do it, but I'm not the kind of kid you're gonna catch in some skinny jeans. It's a stupid rule; it's just a style."

Perhaps. And if the only tool you have is a hammer, every problem begins to look like a nail.

"I had been sitting at my desk drawing a picture in my notebook when the teacher walked in the room, which was out of control for real, and singled me out for laughing at a joke this kid made," says LeShawn, 16. "Next thing I knew I was in the principal's office and they were calling my mom. It was like, what the hell? Then push comes to shove, and I was getting suspended for two days. Yeah, I laughed—I'll admit it. But if the teacher had seen me two minutes before, she would have seen me with my head down drawing—not tripping, not throwing things, not even clowning around. I wasn't gonna rat out my friends, so I guess I took one for the team."

Despite growing fears, the data indicate that disorder and violence occur in schools today at levels similar to the early 1980s. But studies suggest a connection between the higher rates of suspension and expulsion and lower academic achievement and higher drop-out rates, particularly for black boys.[5]

"They are interrelated processes," says Dr. Gregory, who coauthored a study titled *The Achievement Gap and the Discipline Gap: Two Sides of the Same Coin?* "We know low achievement is associated with more discipline issues, more sanctions. Even if you take into account issues like low achievement and poverty—low-income kids can be exposed to more violence and can have more externalizing behaviors as a result and get into trouble more in school—race is still a big predictor of discipline. Cumulatively, across a lot of studies we've shown that race remains a factor."

By *externalizing behaviors* Dr. Gregory means disruptive, problem, or harmful behaviors that can range from being hyperactive and impulsive to fighting and bullying to engaging in delinquent behaviors such as assault, theft, and vandalism—or, in plain English: acting out.

When Texas researchers honed in on just the ninth grade, they discovered that 75 percent of black males had been disciplined at least once. Of those, more than 25 percent had been given a discretionary out-of-school suspension *the very first time* they violated their school's code of conduct, as opposed to 18 percent of Hispanic males and 10 percent of white males. Black males were 15 percent less likely than white males to be given an in-school suspension for their first discretionary infraction.[6]

The researchers also analyzed eighty-three student attributes—from the number of parents in the home to the socioeconomic status to the quality of the school—so that they could compare the experiences of boys whose backgrounds were virtually identical except for their race. All other factors being equal, the study authors discovered that black males were *31 percent more likely* than white males to be disciplined for discretionary reasons. And despite the negative stereotypes about black males and drugs, weapons and violence, black male students were 23 percent *less* likely than white males to have been disciplined for behaving in a way that violated a state policy requiring that a child be suspended or expelled.[7] Black boys were receiving far more severe penalties for much less severe behavior.

"The Texas study on school discipline came as close as we're going to get to a double-blind experiment in the social sciences," says Dr. Holzman, a consultant at the Schott Foundation for Public Education. "It demonstrated conclusively that out-of-school suspensions and expulsions are simply a factor of racism."

"There's been some research that shows you have two major processes," says Dr. Gregory. "One is differential selection. So you've got white kids and black kids doing the same kind of behavior, but the teacher may hone in on the black kid and say, 'Now you're in trouble.' Then you have differential sanction. The kid gets sent to the assistant principal, who then often issues harsher and longer suspensions— often they have discretion, three to five days—to the African American kid."

"When I was in seventh grade, I got in a fight. Even though the other person was found on top of me, my homeroom teacher said that I was the one who started it," says Carlton, 16. "One of the black teachers pulled me aside and told me, 'As a black kid, you have to refrain from some of the things a white kid can do.' Then he went to the administration and talked to them and, since he witnessed what happened, told them I wasn't the one who started it. He got me out of a lot of trouble. There's a stereotype on me that I'm the one who would start a fight, I'm the criminal, and the white kid would be more calm, the victim. But the teacher cared for me and ended up helping me. That was the first time I realized a teacher cared for me."

Of the students who were suspended or expelled, more than 30 percent repeated their grade at least once, as compared to 5 percent of students who hadn't been kicked out of the classroom.[8] Students who had been suspended or expelled for a discretionary reason were twice as likely to repeat a grade than similar students who hadn't been excluded from the classroom.

Shockingly, nearly three-quarters of special education students of all backgrounds had been expelled at least once, especially those diagnosed as having an "emotional disturbance," "learning disability," or "physical disability."[9] As we will discuss in Chapter 8, black boys are disproportionately likely to get placed in special ed.

"So in addition to the burdens of poverty, poor schooling, and so forth that a hypothetical white kid may also experience, there are race-specific situations, one of which is *push-out*," says Dr. Holzman. "You give a kid two out-of-school suspensions and that pretty much does it" for his educational career.

Educational experts use the term *push-out* to describe policies that kick kids out of schools. Push-out policies increase the risk that a child will flunk, drop out, or get caught up in the juvenile justice system, no matter his race, socioeconomic status, or the type of school he attends.[10]

You can't teach students who aren't in schools. The Schott Foundation's report *The Urgency of Now: The Schott 50 State Report on Public Education and Black Males* identifies that "black and brown students have fewer learning opportunities and more days out of school than any other group," with one of the main contributors being how states and schools approach discipline.[11]

Push-out describes policies that remove kids from schools. These policies often lead to a higher risk of children flunking, dropping out, and, eventually finding themselves caught in the criminal justice system.

"Even if you look at a student and think, well, they're already heading toward dropping out, we know that suspending them actually increases their chances of dropping out," says Dr. Gregory. "Whatever academic trajectory a kid is on, that suspension can actually make it worse."

"I told them, 'You should give yourselves a pat on the back for disqualifying me from my education,'" says Elliott, a sixteen-year-old who does not live in Texas but is bored with school, cuts class frequently, and was suspended for leaving school grounds. "Then I said, 'The meeting's over; I have make-up work to pick up.'"

Not surprisingly, Lone Star State students who were suspended or expelled were significantly more likely to come in contact with the juvenile justice system. The more discretionary disciplinary actions the Texas students experienced, the more likely they were to come in contact with juvenile authorities.

"The most serious rule-breaking happens when kids are not in school," says Dr. Gregory. "The more you start sending them out into the neighborhood, the higher the chances that they're going to be interacting with law enforcement."

When asked what he would do during his suspension, Elliott said, "I'll stay home or hang out with friends. My grades are all in the 80s. It's really stupid the way education works."

One in four black Texas students was disciplined four or more times, and 26 percent of black males were in contact with the juvenile justice system. This compares to 22 percent of Hispanic males and 14 percent of white males. (At 14 percent, black girls were almost twice as likely to have contact with the juvenile justice system as white girls.)[12]

"A snowballing can start to happen when kids are excluded from

school," Dr. Gregory says. "That snowballing, particularly for black males, can culminate in incarceration"—the school-to-prison pipeline.

The Schott Report notes that students who have been suspended three times are more likely to drop out of school by tenth grade than students who have never been suspended. Students who drop out, in turn, have three times the chance of being incarcerated later in life.

While the racial data on punishments meted out in accordance with Texas's zero-tolerance regulations fell in a reasonable range of difference, "The local school discipline rates were extravagantly tilted against black kids—in spite of the prejudice against Hispanic kids in Texas," Dr. Holzman says. "And that's what the national statistics show."

RACIAL PROFILING IN SCHOOL?

Speaking of national statistics, a 2006–2007 study[13] of more than 9,000 middle schools in eighteen of the nation's largest school districts found that 28 percent of black males and 18 percent of black females were suspended at least once, as compared to 10 percent of white males and 4 percent of white females. Eleven districts suspended more than one-third of their black male students, and Palm Beach County (Florida) and Milwaukee really went off the chain, suspending more than half of their black male students.

The study also found rising suspensions of black males between 2002 and 2006, while suspension rates of white and Hispanic male students declined. And while the percentage of white and Hispanic females being suspended barely rose at all—0.4 and 0.3 percent, respectively—suspensions among black females increased by 5.3 percent. Fighting was the most common reason that young people were suspended, followed by abusive language and attendance problems, disobedience, and disrespect.

The racial disparities were egregious enough that the authors wrote, "Regarding the causes for the disproportionately high rates at which students of color are suspended, some argue that minority chil-

dren, particularly male students of color, tend to misbehave more frequently in school than do white children. Research on student behavior, race, and discipline has found no evidence that African-American overrepresentation in school suspension is due to higher rates of misbehavior."[14]

They also wrote, "The profound race- and gender-based disparities . . . raise important questions about both the condition of education in our urban middle schools and the possibility of conscious or unconscious racial and gender biases at the school level."[15]

"The important policy question this raises is whether we as a society are comfortable with putting this many students out of school, especially since we know about the negative effects of being out of school," said study author Russell Skiba, a professor of educational psychology at Indiana University, an expert on equity in school discipline.[16] An earlier study performed by Dr. Skiba and coauthor Daniel J. Losen found that "only 5 percent of all out-of-school suspensions were issued for disciplinary incidents that are typically considered serious or dangerous, such as possession of weapons or guns. The remaining 95 percent of suspensions fell into two categories: disruptive behavior and other."[17]

Not surprisingly, many educators insist that punishing children reduces chaos, improves outcomes at school, and lessens the likelihood of urban violence or another Columbine or Newtown. But most of the infractions that get black children suspended fall in what Dr. Skiba and his coauthor called "mundane and nonviolent misbehavior" that may not even disrupt the educational process, much less place anyone else at risk.[18]

Drs. Toldson and Lewis analyzed data from seven thousand school districts and seventy-two thousand schools nationwide compiled by the U.S. Department of Education's Civil Rights Data Collection. Consistent with Dr. Skiba's findings, they found that no matter their race, children who routinely came to class late, often missed assignments, and admitted that their schoolwork was too difficult were more likely to get suspended than either those who brought drugs, alcohol, or weapons to school or those who admitted to fighting or injuring others. Students being educated in the South were more than twice as likely to be suspended than students in the Northeast, the Midwest, or the West.

The data also showed that the higher the students' grades, the more they perceived teachers as caring for them; they perceived teachers as punishing students with lower grades more often. Black students were more likely to report getting lower grades, being more disengaged from school, and engaging in aggressive behaviors.[19]

Drs. Toldson and Lewis identified that black males can become disengaged from schools for many reasons, ranging from curricula that don't include them, racial biases, poor relationships with teachers, not being socialized to the academic environment, and having attention or learning disabilities that had been misdiagnosed or are misunderstood.

What's more, "there is greater physicality in the lives of black kids," says developmental psychologist Robert Jagers, an associate professor and chair of the Combined Program in Education and Psychology at the University of Michigan School of Education, who was not involved with these studies. "Part of that is the toughness, the physicality, having to deal with adversity—all of that is so much a part of how many of our kids are growing up. But how do you deal with that when you're in a zero-tolerance environment? How does a kid negotiate that? Some of the things you're taught in your neighborhood and in many aspects of broader society about how to deal with conflict simply don't translate in a zero-tolerance environment."

KNOWLEDGE IS POWER

We encourage you to examine these studies with your own eyes, particularly the Congressional Black Caucus study, which includes recommendations for parents, schools, and communities as well as resources such as the telephone numbers for the congressional representatives of the districts serving the largest number of black students, which you can use to voice your displeasure (see endnotes for the sources). Also examine the Schott Foundation report, *The Urgency of*

Now. As you read, recall the research, mentioned in Chapter 4, that NYU's Diane Hughes and her colleagues conducted on the experiences of children of color with school and community bias. The children believed that they were treated better at school than they were out in the world. But look at these data! If they are correct, then the amount of prejudice that children of color must experience outside of school is mind-boggling. It also makes you wonder what their still-developing brains make of all this.

After you read the studies, why not research the disciplinary practices for your son's school and school district? Also visit the Civil Rights Data Collection website, as Drs. Toldson and Lewis did (http:// ocrdata.ed.gov). There you can view data on discipline, bullying and harassment, restraint and seclusion as well as other vital information broken down by race, ethnicity, gender, disability, and other factors. Get the information for your children's school and school district, and come together with other parents, community leaders, and teachers who are "key opinion leaders" to analyze the trends together. Ask school leadership what they plan to do to remedy the disparities that likely exist, and let them know that you intend to hold them accountable.

You can encourage teachers, administrators, and school safety officers to also look at the data proactively and develop solutions together. The authoritative parenting paradigm of high warmth and high demandingness (see Chapter 5) applies in school settings also.

"What you're doing is developing a relationship with these kids," Psychologist Claude Steele, dean of the School of Education at Stanford University, advises teachers. "You might have seen movies and all your life the culture might tell you that you need structure and discipline and all that sort of stuff. But I think a lot of teachers and parents realize that you first have to build trust. Discipline can be a part of that, but they have to understand that you're really in there for their best interest—that you can see who they are and still believe in them, like them, and value them. Teachers who do that will be very successful with those kids, and the teachers who don't, won't be."

Whether at home or in the classroom, encourage your young person to use his math, writing, critical thinking, and leadership skills to, say, analyze the stats for his school, write a report describing the data, and work with other students and teachers to address any changes that need to be made. Students and families can connect with grassroots organizations such as the Youth Justice Coalition (http://youth4justice.org), Dignity in Schools (http://www.dignityinschools.org), and Solutions Not Suspensions (http://stopsuspensions.org), which are working to stop schools from excluding young people from classrooms.

But don't get it twisted: Schools may not welcome inquiries about these topics.

"Schools have a hard time absorbing the information and not deflecting," Dr. Gregory says. "They start getting into the blame game, where they say, 'It's because they're acting out more, or are low achievers.' We really need to get school districts and teachers to self-reflect, because it's not just outside-of-school factors or the achievement gap that is leading to the discipline gap. The issues around race are still there."

And don't necessarily expect that you'll win the victory for your child. State laws and school and school district policies can take years to change, although some states, cities, and school systems are already examining their policies to address race and discipline disparities. Yet the more light we shine on the problem, the more heat school administrators are likely to feel. So don't underestimate the potential of your impact, and be willing to fight for the good of the next generation or somebody else's son.

"We always say, it's not *if,* it's *when;* and, It's not the man, it's the plan," says Asad Shabazz, head of an organization called Young People in Action. "If we understand these things, then we don't let you do this to another person's child—not under my watch. We're going to educate the next person on what to do."

DISCIPLINE FOR SUCCESS

As the school data clearly show, many people who would probably believe that they love our sons mistakenly equate discipline with punishment—at least when it comes to black children.

"The crux of disciplining our children is teaching them how to behave and make good choices in future situations," says Ursula Johnson, a postdoctoral fellow at the University of Texas Health Science Center in Houston. "Because if they don't understand that they can't do certain things and why, other people are going to make choices for them."

But when we talk about discipline, we're not just talking about punishment. We believe that *discipline* describes a lifelong process of educating children and shaping their behavior over the long term. It includes loving them, keeping them out of harm's way, passing along our values, helping them organize themselves, teaching them a healthy sense of right and wrong, developing an internal sense of responsibility in them, and guiding them so that they learn how to "check" their own behavior.

We see punishment as a form of discipline, but one whose use is limited to correcting behavior right now. A wide variety of ways of disciplining a child exist, many of which are far more effective long term. Quite often a person's disciplinary strategies and parenting style are related. We'll explore a number of approaches to discipline; undoubtedly you already use some of them.

SPARE THE ROD, OR NOT?

Whether or not they call themselves Christian or go to church, many black parents follow Proverbs 13:24, which reads, "Those who spare the rod hate their children, but those who love them are diligent to discipline them." People popularly refer to this notion as "spare the rod, spoil the child," although that phrase doesn't actually appear anywhere in the Bible.

But while it informs our approaches to correcting our children, many of us are not clear about what "spare the rod" means.

"In the spare-the-rod-spoil-the-child context, 'rod' means discipline across the board. Rod doesn't mean that you have to hit, but it does include the concept of negative reinforcement," says Rev. Dr. Alyn E. Waller, senior pastor of the Enon Tabernacle Baptist Church in Philadelphia. "So the larger context of 'spoil the child' is, 'Spare the discipline, spoil the development of a human being.' Permissive parenting ultimately will not produce a positive citizen."

This brings us to the subject of spanking. Whether you can get them to admit it or not, almost all American parents use corporal punishment at some point, usually mildly or moderately.[20] Now, when people talk about corporal punishment, they usually mean spanking, beating, whipping, paddling, or going upside a child's head. But just for the sake of a good discussion, let's throw swatting, popping, pinching, and thumping into this conversation, as well.

Almost 95 percent of parents of three- and four-year-olds report that they've spanked their child during the previous year.[21] Studies show that parents of boys, Southerners, the poor, moms with less education, younger moms, evangelical and conservative Protestants, and black people tend to spank more than others.[22]

When Dr. Johnson conducts parenting classes, she finds, "There's a small minority that is extremely opposed to spanking—they wouldn't do it, haven't done it, will not do it. Then you have people who have done it but don't want to do it—they want to learn new approaches. Then you have the hard-liners, who say, 'I believe in it; I'm going to do it; you can't stop me.'"

Some 77 percent of black women and 82 percent of black men, as compared to 67/62 percent of Hispanic women/men and 61/77 percent of white women/men, agree or strongly agree that "a good hard spanking" is sometimes necessary.[23] Many black parents say they spank because their parents spanked them. We can't tell you how many times we've heard a parent say, "If it was good enough for my parents, it's good enough for me" or "I got spanked and I came out okay."

Then again, many black parents spank because they know that their son is walking on a tightrope through the world that requires him to demonstrate tremendous self-control. These parents don't want their son to "become a statistic" and are doing the best they can to prevent their greatest fear from happening. It seems that some black parents don't have a wide repertoire of disciplinary tools and don't want other black parents to look down their nose at them for having an unruly child.

The research about whether spanking helps or hurts black children is mixed. Some studies show that spanking can cause children to become more aggressive, antisocial, and depressed, among other negative outcomes, while others suggest that it may not cause the same psychological harm that it tends to bring about in white children—at least when black parents raise their children using the authoritative or strict-authoritative parenting style.[24]

"If you live in a community where people spank kids, they know it doesn't mean you don't love them; it's no big deal," says Dr. Ferguson. "But in a community where no one spanks their kid, they think, 'My parents don't like me' or that it's perverse."[25]

"In sixth grade I was talking to some white kids about being beaten. They were like, 'Oh, my god!' They had never heard of that," says Davon, who's now sixteen.

Recall that only 30 percent of black parents practice either the authoritative or strict-authoritative style that the spanking research associates with positive outcomes; the other 70 percent use another style. That is to say, spanking does not always yield beneficial results in the long term, even though no one can deny that most children immediately react to getting popped.

It's also hard to know whether people in studies actually tell the truth about the type of corporal punishment they use in the privacy of their homes.[26]

Spiritually, Rev. Dr. Waller believes a difference exists between popping a child out of principle when you're not angry and hitting a child when you're mad at him. "When my mother hit me, she had not left the place of love but could recognize that her son had done something that required an immediate negative reinforcement because she didn't want that behavior to live in me down the line," says Rev. Dr.

Waller. He contrasts it with parents who allow a behavior to continue until they feel mad at, disrespected by, or fed up with their child. "That mother can do the same physical thing that my mother did—pop her son—but she is doing it out of a different relational nexus," he says. "Now, in the spirit realm she is sending something else into her child because she's also hitting with an angry spirit."

Importantly, the American Academy of Pediatrics (AAP) advises against spanking, which may seem to work at first but loses its impact over time. The AAP notes that because most parents don't like to spank, they're likely to be inconsistent with it, which sends their children mixed messages about discipline. Spanking makes a child more aggressive and angry, rather than teaching him responsibility; many parents lose their temper in the process and later regret their behavior; and it can lead to physical struggles and even harm to your child. Compared to people who were not spanked, children who were spanked are more likely to become adults who are depressed, use alcohol, have more anger, hit their children, hit their spouses, and engage in crime and violence. Plus children don't see the difference between their parents hitting them and them hitting their siblings or peers—which is not a good idea for a black boy.[27]

"Parents are modeling how to deal with feelings all the time, and children are watching and learning from their parents," says Kathleen Walls, a former teacher who now teaches emotional literacy to individuals of all ages.

We don't support corporal punishment when it's used on any children—at home or at school. We note that black students are also more likely to receive corporal punishment in school than any other children. In 2006, the year for which the most recent data are available, black children comprised about 17 percent of the student body but about 36 percent of those paddled. Black boys comprised less than 9 percent of the school population but 26 percent of total paddlings.[28] In the thirteen states with the highest rates of paddling—it won't surprise you to know that they are disproportionately, although not exclusively, in the South—black boys were more than twice as likely to be paddled than you would expect, given their proportion of the student population. And although girls are paddled less at school than boys, black girls are more than twice as likely as white girls to be paddled as well.[29]

No, you probably won't wreck your child if you spank him, but you increase the odds against him. He's more likely to drop out, go to jail, and harm others. He's also less likely to become a father himself. Our job as parents is to promote communication and conflict-resolution and critical-thinking skills and to demonstrate them by example.

HOW DOES IT FREE US?

Both of our parents believed in Proverbs 22:6, which reads, "Train up a child in the way he should go and when he gets old he will not depart from it." This advice covers corporal punishment, too.

Joe's father was a minister. He would spank his children briefly with an extension cord. Then one day when Joe was about eleven, his dad said, "I can't do this anymore" and never hit his children again. Michèle's father beat her with a belt. He also made her kneel facing a wall for hours. He had been abused in Haiti back when he was a child, where the use of a whip dated back to slavery, and wayward children were forced to kneel on gravel in front of a wall for hours at a time.

We didn't feel that corporal punishment turned us into better people. We also don't believe that it destroyed us. So while we can't say that corporal punishment is evil, we would like to paraphrase a question that poet Sonia Sanchez often asks: "Yes, but how does that free us?"

We don't think that physical punishment does free us, especially given the history of how physical punishment has been—and continues to be—used on black people. And it's important that we make sure that we don't inflict on our children the abuse that's been inflicted on us. That's why we didn't use it when Idris was a toddler. Yes, it was helpful during an era where parents needed to protect their sons from white supremacy and when a successful black male was a black-and-white thinker working on yesteryear's assembly line.

But that was then, this is now.

Having not used corporal punishment for more than ten years, we strongly believe that if you want to raise a high-performing teacher, a surgeon, engineer, professional, artist, or entrepreneur—in other words—a thinker—physical discipline is not helpful.

When we spank children, we lose the chance to engage their pre-frontal cortex and unintentionally make it harder for them to become sophisticated thinkers.

"We often want to do it the way that my father did it, for example, or his father before him—get the switch," says developmental psychologist Robert Jagers, associate professor and chair of the combined program in education and psychology at the University of Michigan School of Education. "I'm not judging that, but it depends what you're moving toward as to which strategy you want to utilize. If you want to control him and have to check his behavior immediately, then go ahead and beat him. But if you want to raise a thinking, self-sufficient young man who doesn't require a bunch of external rewards and punishments, then you have to find another way."

There's no way to spank or pop or wallop or even pinch hard or often enough to get a child to agree that it's good for him to do his homework, become more engaged in his classes, or get a good education. It won't take long until your son develops defense mechanisms to protect himself from physical punishment. Hitting is also more likely to harden him or to cause him one day to strike out at you and, perhaps later, his lover or his own children or to make a misstep while using violence to coerce a loved one that will land him in prison. Is it worth that risk? We don't think so.

PASSING THE TEST

Even if you do spank your young child, at some point the spanking has to stop. The techniques you use when they're five don't work when they're teens, and you may suddenly find yourself in over your head. Dr. Mandara now laughs as he recalls looking down at his mother trying to spank him—already at age twelve he had outgrown her.

"When I was fourteen, my mother tried to spank me once, and I just started laughing at her," says Johnny, now seventeen. "At first it just made her even madder, but then she realized how ridiculous it was and she just gave up. It was stupid."

Having said this, there's another side to it. As your son grows older, there may be a moment when he challenges you aggressively. You have to be prepared to respond. "There is a period during which boys test their fathers," Dr. Ferguson says. "The father can't lose that test—you have to win that encounter. It usually doesn't take much."

"I'm not a big believer in corporal punishment, but every blue moon you may have to 'wax that ass,'" says Giovanni, the father of four children, including three boys, who range from thirteen to twenty-eight. He recalls an encounter with his then-sixteen-year-old son: "When my oldest kids were teenagers, I'd let them run their mouths a bit and warn them when they were getting close to the line. Usually they'd pull back—you know, that's part of the process. But one time my son tried to 'flex' and jump all big and bad with me, so I had to remind him who was in charge. I punched him in the chest—not hard, but hard enough. I hated to do it—I felt so badly afterward that I couldn't take it; I apologized to him later on. But I did it intentionally. In that moment, he had to know who was boss."

"Oh my god, he fucked me up," laughs Giovanni's son, Michael, now twenty-five. "The punch hurt, okay, but actually it didn't hurt as much as it shocked me. My dad is basically a pretty cool cat. When we would give him too much lip, he would send out this warning shot, like, 'All right now, I brought you into this world and I'll take you out.' But everyone says that; you know they don't mean it. He always talked to us when he was mad or maybe yelled a little. But when he hit me—and in the chest at that—I was like '*Day-um!* My dad is *crazy*! I better pull up.'"

What You Can Do

Parents and the Village

1. Behave warmly and lovingly toward all the children in your life, including our boys and young men.

2. Use a wide range of disciplinary approaches to emphasize education, not punishment, and reduce your reliance on spanking with the goal of eliminating it.

3. Obtain the discipline data for your school and school district and push for policy changes that would require annual reporting of data disaggregated down to the school level.

4. Let officials at your child's school as well as local and state boards of education know that disparities in race, gender, and disability are not acceptable.

5. Support training to help teachers teach diverse learners more effectively.

Educators

1. Use disaggregated discipline data to make reforms that will eliminate racial, gender, and disability disparities.

2. Invest in accurate reporting and use data on discipline in early warning systems.

3. Change school policies and practices leading to high suspension and expulsion rates.

Policymakers

1. Require states and districts to report disaggregated disciplinary data in public, including lost days of instruction.

2. Include suspension rates among the factors schools and districts use to measure performance.

3. Step up federal civil rights enforcement to address discipline disparities—especially in high-suspending districts.

4. Support evidence-based interventions and implement systemic improvements to school discipline.

5. Provide teacher training in classroom management.

6. Include classroom management skills as part of teacher evaluations and make sure that teachers and principals have sufficient training in these areas.

But we challenge the assumption that even moments of confrontation between a parent and a teenager have to become physical. Precisely because the world does behave so harshly and violently toward us, we strongly believe that black parents and children must communicate with each other using nonviolent approaches. This requires learning to listen to each other, developing conflict-resolution skills, and encouraging the use of critical-thinking skills. Of course parents have to model these behaviors, especially as children grow older, when your actions speak louder than words.

A lot of different disciplinary strategies yield better long-term results than corporal punishment does. We hadn't had a lot of exposure to them, so we had to do some research of our own. No matter where you are in this process, you can start by swinging less and talking to him more, and when you talk, challenge him to explore sophisticated ideas. Among them: Why do you think that I am upset with your behavior? Do you understand what I'm concerned about? How do you see the situation differently? What do you think that the punishment should be for your actions, and why?

Talking to Idris and Miles and using time-outs and other ways of correcting them that didn't include corporal punishment—these approaches have helped our sons learn how to think about their actions, understand the consequences of their choices, and regulate their own behavior so we don't have to do it for them. And we feel good that we have been able to correct them when they misbehaved without buying into or piling onto the punitive world they experience outside of our home.

Yes, corporal punishment yields more immediate results. But we can tell you from our own firsthand experience: Talking is cheap, and it pays off over time.

FOURTEEN WAYS TO DISCIPLINE YOUR CHILD

We're the first to admit it: Having been physically disciplined ourselves, we struggled at first to incorporate new ways of correcting our sons into our repertoire of disciplinary measures. When we started using time-outs, we didn't realize that we didn't know how they worked. We didn't yet understand that when Idris was in time-out, we couldn't be in the next room writing a term paper, or the next thing we knew, he would be in the kitchen pouring himself a glass of orange juice or scooping out some ice cream. If we put him in time-out, we would have to sit and have a quiet discussion with him: "This is why you are in time-out; this is how you get out of time-out; this is how you prevent it from happening again." These conversations helped us get him to buy in to behaving better later on.

Below you will find fourteen approaches to guiding and correcting a black boy, ones that allow us to add warmth to our relationship with him, while letting him know that we expect a lot from him.

Some of these approaches also develop his prefrontal cortex, the part of the brain that helps him control himself. Better to teach him to control himself than for the world to control him for him—especially since we know where that can end up. So even if you have the discipline thing down, you might want to consider this list. You may find, as we did, that you and your son can benefit from a larger repertoire of approaches than you currently use, especially since children are wired to challenge their parents as part of their drive to become independent.

1. **Set the example that you want your son to follow.** He can't fly with the eagles unless you show him the route to take. This is the simplest and, in many ways, most important form of discipline. From the earliest ages, our sons model our behavior. Trying to later correct them for doing things that they learned from us just teaches them another bad lesson: how to be a hypocrite.

2. **Demonstrate affection.** Hugging, kissing, and speaking warmly are cornerstones to effective discipline. "Far too many people focus on correction but not affection or protection," says clinical psychologist Howard Stevenson, Ph.D., an associate professor at the University of Pennsylvania's Graduate School of Education and an expert in adolescent psychological adjustment, including anger and aggression prevention. "There's no love in a sense that kids can see and feel. They don't feel that people are watching their back. Even many teachers are just waiting to catch them doing something wrong—and that's the height of their educational inspiration."

3. **Spend time with your child.** Our kids are more likely to listen when they know that we love and respect them and will tend to their needs. And it's important to sow into their spirits daily to let them know that we love and appreciate them, to make them feel safe, and to offset

outside negativity. Try to build in ten to fifteen minutes of one-on-one time with your son each day. Dr. Johnson recommends playing, reading, or, for older children, helping you in the kitchen.

"Parents of black children have to carve out time for their children," says Aisha Ray, Ph.D. "Some parents absolutely insist that they have dinner together two or three times a week as a family—no excuses, no explanations; nothing can interfere with this, this is our time. Mom and dad can't talk about their work. No one can have their cell phone at the table. It's about fellowship, companionship, and making sure that everybody's okay. It need not be dinnertime—that might not be practical for every parent. But the idea is to have regular, predictable, scheduled time together as a family with your children."

"If you're working two jobs, you're working hard, you're a single parent, or whatever, it's hard to spend time with your kid. If you don't and if you don't put him in situations where there's good people giving him advice, he's gonna get advice but it's gonna be from idiots," says Dave Hardy, president and CEO of Boys Latin High School in Philadelphia. "Look at the way drug dealers do it: They get a kid, the kid goes up to the corner, and they start talking to them about sports and sneakers. 'Wouldn't you like the latest sneakers?' They give him money to go buy sneakers. They send him to the store, and give him a few dollars. All of a sudden they have a relationship and then that kid's out on the corner slinging drugs. They have a better relationship with those kids than their parents do. Now it's weird, it's not healthy. But they knew the steps it took to establish a relationship. Why can't adults do that?"

4. **Share control.** Nobody likes being bossed around all the time, and children seek opportunities to express their growing competence and independence. So let your children choose activities and lead some of your time together. "Do you want to wear the red shirt or the blue one?" "Do you want to go to visit your favorite cousins or

the amusement park?" Can't make up his mind? You decide. You can even work with teens to create their own punishments.

5. **Praise them.** Since the world is on the lookout for things our sons do wrong, it's our job to catch them doing things right. "It's important to praise their really good behavior so that they're getting the attention for the good and not for the bad," says Dr. Johnson.

6. **Distract them.** You can easily correct an infant or young child by getting him interested in something more appropriate—say, hit the pot with the wooden spoon, not his sister—and by explaining the reasons why their previous behavior wasn't acceptable. This applies to children of all ages.

7. **Explanations.** Rather than assuming that our sons can read our minds, we can prepare them for different situations by laying out beforehand what's going to happen and how we want them to act. Whether why the sun rises in the east and sets in the west or why your family has the traditions it does, take time to explain life to your son. This is especially important when it comes to activities—say, keeping his room clean or doing his homework—that are not immediately gratifying, but pay off in the long run.

"Parents don't realize just how confusing the world can be for young children," says Dr. Ray. "There's a lot that doesn't make sense; there's a lot that's really scary. Helping our children understand how the world works and their place in it is a critical parenting role. We need to answer their questions, engage them in conversation, and explain things that do not make sense to a three- or five-year-old. When we do this we model ways of understanding and coping that are very important. These are invaluable lessons for our children."

8. **Directions.** Sometimes adults inadvertently give children more tasks than their developing brains can keep up with. Provide young children with two or three directions at a time; when they accomplish those, follow up with more. Older children can handle more instructions, but not as many as an adult brain, so shorten the list a little.

9. **Create transitions.** Young children, in particular, may have a hard time switching between activities. Give them advance notice that the activity is going to change, then continue to remind them every few minutes that the change will be taking place. Imagine how you would feel if you had no way to tell time and were constantly finding yourself jerked away from doing things you enjoyed? We can help smooth those transitions for our sons.

10. **Time-outs or cooling-off periods.** Time-outs aren't just a tool of early childhood; used as cooling-off periods, they can help older children also—but only if you've interacted with him beginning earlier in his life in a way that has built a family culture of respect and discipline. Decide in advance what behaviors warrant a time-out and explain them clearly. Warn him once when he enters the danger zone. If he keeps it up, make him sit in a chair, on the steps, or in another mind-numbing location that doesn't have any distractions (or ways he can hurt himself if he's upset). A bedroom full of toys, his iPod, and a TV won't work. You may need to stand with or perhaps even hold a youngster in place. Time-outs for little children should last one minute for every year of age. With teenagers, call a fifteen- or twenty-minute cooling-off period, then continue your conversation in a more constructive manner.

When we first began using them, Michèle's experience of using time-outs with Idris was that they were ineffective. Joe suggested that she stop what she was doing and supervise them. We were learning that our time-outs were too long. Five or ten minutes is like a lifetime to preschoolers. At first Michèle's response was, "So if he's on punishment, I'm on punishment?!" Well, we discovered, yes and no. Taking time out of our schedules accentuated how important the discipline was to us and emphasized how much we cared for him. It was a win-win. Once we realized that we had to do this, both Idris and, later, Miles responded quickly to this form of correction. At first she would supervise them for two minutes. Over time, we were able to cut our time-outs down to as little as ten seconds and still have the impact we wanted. So although it took us a while to figure out how to use time-outs effectively, in the end they ended up being far less time consuming than we had believed—and a lot better than dealing with the yelling, and stomping, and crying, and door slamming, and re-correcting, and bad vibes that result when physical punishment is involved. We got control and respect without hitting and negativity.

11. **Natural consequences.** As long as it doesn't place your son in danger, consider overriding your instincts to rescue him and letting the situation play out so that your son can learn from it. Sometimes children—and especially teens—learn best when they experience the repercussions straight, no chaser.

12. **Logical punishments.** More often than not you'll have to create the consequences that you want your son to experience. Be clear about what you mean, stay calm and firm, and follow through with the consequences immediately and make them last for a reasonable amount of time.

"White kids have to go to their room. They can't come out for a short period of time," says William, 15. "You can't leave your house for three weeks." Overpunishing sends the wrong message.

13. **Withholding privileges.** Tell your son that if he doesn't behave in a certain way that he'll have to give up

something important to him that is related to his misbehavior.

"There came a point where for my mother to use a belt on me was a joke simply because of my physical prowess. But for my father to deny me the keys to the car was traumatic," Rev. Dr. Waller recalls.

14. **Actively ignore mildly negative behavior.** Focus on and reward him for what he does right not does wrong. Rather than immediately chastising him, simply discuss the bad consequences of mildly negative behaviors with him at another time so he can think about and internalize those lessons on his own.

Helping our sons excel emotionally, academically, and behaviorally in ways that prepare them for the future requires us to employ a wide variety of disciplinary approaches.

"You want to have a lot of tools in your toolkit as a parent," says Ursula Johnson, a doctoral fellow at the Children's Learning Institute at the University of Texas Health Science Center in Houston. "Do you always use a hammer to construct something? No. You use a Phillips head; you use a wrench; you use whatever you need to make the job run more smoothly."

"There is teaching and training; there is positive reinforcement of good behavior, and there is negative reinforcement of bad behavior," says Rev. Dr. Waller, whose training lies in marriage and family counseling. "But it is all done in the context of the spiritual principle of 'speak the truth in love.'"

Keeping the Promise

1. **Understand the issues.** Black boys are subjected to harsher discipline than other children, putting them at greater risk. There are resources to help us understand, and combat, the issue.

2. **Discipline is more than punishment.** In fact, punishment is a very narrow form of discipline. Discipline includes loving them, keeping them out of harm's way, passing along our values, helping them organize themselves, teaching them a healthy sense of right and wrong, developing an internal sense of responsibility in them, and guiding them so that they learn how to "check" their own behavior.

3. **There are many alternatives to corporal punishment.** And these alternatives are better for our children—and better for us—in both the short- and long-term.

7

PROTECT HIM FROM TIME BANDITS

How to Teach Our Sons to Manage Their Time

My son is a jock. He spends a lot of his summer running and working out so he'll be ready for football in August. After he works out, he feels exhausted. I push him to read, and he can be a voracious reader of certain kinds of books. But he spends way too much time playing video games. During the summertime he might use 20 percent of the day to read and the rest of it on video games and playing b-ball in the driveway.

We would fight every day about video games. They are like crack—they consume your child's mind. But if I'm being honest with myself, a video game means that my teenage black boy is in the house in the basement. I can reach out and touch his ashy behind any time I want. That's preferable to him running around with his boys. When he's not in the house, my ass is on edge all the time. We live out in the suburbs, but I'll take the video game over the street in a lot of cases. He probably picked up on that and manipulated it: "If I stick around here, I can do whatever I want? Word!"

A lot of middle-class black boys manipulate the hell out of their situation. They're smart and savvy about their surroundings and people's reactions to them. They know about the dire straits that black boys are in and know they're a rare commodity—it's like brothas who get a good job and are running women. They know people will treat them differently because they're getting better grades and aren't in the criminal justice system, but then they'll use it to get over as often as they can. It creates a culture of laziness. Because even though they don't do as much or try as hard as other kids do to get results, they get results that are almost as good as the white kids or good enough. I see it in my son; I see it in the sons of my friends.

If my son's average is 90 or above, his point of reference isn't to compete against the kids who get over 90, it's the other black boys who aren't doing as well. He thinks he's good, but I'm not impressed. You studied one hour on the night before the test instead of for three nights in advance. You did what you needed to do to get over. But why not match the Asian kid who got a 97? The subtext when he explains it to me is, "Why kill myself, not have a social life, and miss parties and video games, when I can get a 90 and still get into Harvard?" Maybe he could have gotten into Harvard if he had worked harder, but he didn't work hard, and while he's going to a good school, it's not Harvard.

—Jason, 48, the father of a nineteen-year-old son

TIME MANAGEMENT IS THE KEY TO SUCCESS

Succeeding in school requires our sons to manage their time so that they complete their homework and papers, study for quizzes and tests, and do college research and get applications in on time. Success also requires that they resist temptation, whether from their iPod, *Call of Duty: Black Ops, NBA 2K,* or the latest girl "blowing up" his phone.

In this chapter we will introduce you to several studies that examine how our children use their time:

- We will do a deep dive into our kids' consumption of electronic media.
- We'll talk about the importance of teaching our son how to manage his time at school and at home afterwards, so he will not only understand more of what the teacher is trying to teach him, but he can also deepen that learning, practice new skills, and demonstrate the knowledge he's acquiring by completing his homework with a high degree of accuracy.
- To assist you with this, we'll introduce a way of thinking about time that we believe will help set black boys up for success.

> **Promise your son that you will protect his future by limiting the amount of time he spends consuming media and using electronic devices, by setting rules about the types of content he can consume, by creating a college-bound home environment, and by teaching him a mind-set that prioritizes his future success.**

CHASING ASIANS

Contrary to the negative stereotypes about black children not caring about how well they do in school, studies show that black children do, in fact, want a good education. They report that they want to do well in school at least as often as other children do, with some studies reporting that they care somewhat more.[1]

"I know I need to get good grades so I can go to college and get a good job," says Akil, 15. "There's people in my family that went to college before, but none of them ever graduated. I want to be the first."

But competing on equal footing can be difficult when you have to come from behind to catch up.

Research undertaken by Ronald Ferguson, the head of Harvard University's Achievement Gap Initiative, on children in high-achieving suburban schools, indicates that when children's skills are less well developed than their peers, their efforts may yield less payoff. Ferguson finds that despite their desire to achieve, black children in these schools complete less of their homework than their white classmates do, even though they spend about the same amount of time trying. That is to say, black honors and AP students study as much as other honors and AP students, and black students who take the general curriculum study as much as other students taking the general curriculum—but because skills gaps exist, black children have to spend *more* time on their homework just to achieve the same homework-completion rates. Bottom line: catching up requires working harder than the people you're trying to catch.

Students of Asian descent out-hustle children of all other backgrounds, studying for half an hour longer than other students who take the general curriculum and about forty minutes longer than kids in honors and AP classes—every weeknight.

Let's just do some simple math: thirty minutes a day of additional homework times 180 days in the typical school year yields ninety more hours of study time each year. That's the same as if the Asian American students in the study hit the books full-time for two more weeks (assuming an eight-hour school day) than other students did. If you multiply ninety extra hours of study per year by thirteen years of schooling, you discover that the Asian children in the communities Dr. Ferguson examined studied almost thirty weeks more, over their secondary school careers, than children of other backgrounds did. Their willingness to grind harder than everyone else is just one part of the so-called Asian Advantage. If we want our children to have a place at the table in the global economy, it needs to become the new black standard.[2]

But if our children are ever to catch up, we think that black adults will need to reconsider our position on digital devices. As we lay out in painful detail, the extra number of hours per day our children are spending using consumer electronics—often with the content unsupervised—is embarrassing. And we strongly suspect that our kids are paying a price—and that price is academic success. We hope that you will be as mortified by the data as we were and that it shocks you into action to save your son!

BLAME IT ON THE BOOGIE?

A tremendous upside opportunity exists for all parents—but particularly black parents—to help our children perform better academically by being more demanding about how they manage their time.

As a backdrop to this conversation, let's assume that our sons get out of school at 3 p.m. and go to bed at 10 p.m. on weekdays. That means they have seven hours that they spend outside of school each school day—or a total of thirty-five hours a week. Assuming that they're awake from 10 a.m. to 10 p.m. on weekends, or twelve hours a day, they have another twenty-four hours on weekends. That adds up to roughly sixty hours of time each week that's not accounted for by school or sleep. It's not as though they're doing nothing during this time, of course. They spend it commuting to school, doing home-work, completing their chores, participating in sports and other ex-tracurricular activities, working, hanging out with their friends, watching TV, playing video games, and so on. But we can position them to thrive in the global economy by getting them in learning mode for as many of these hours as possible.

Research by Dr. Ferguson as well as a large study of the media consumption habits of millennial children conducted by the Henry J. Kaiser Family Foundation, a nonprofit health organization, suggests that our children need us to be more proactive in helping them invest that precious time in ways that support their academic goals.[3]

Because whether it's television, radio, the Internet, cell phones, video games, or whatever other kind of media, black and Hispanic children spend a breathtaking thirteen hours, on average, using elec-tronics each day—often with more than one device running at the same time. Compare this to a somewhat less outrageous (but still over the top) eight hours and thirty-six minutes for white children (Asians were not included in the Kaiser study). Yes, you read that right: black children are using electronics for four and a half hours a day more than white kids, who are also using them too much.[4] And between 2004 and 2009, the time difference *doubled* from two hours and twelve minutes to four hours and twenty-three minutes more per day. Black boys are the heaviest media consumers.[5] And this media-consumption gap crosses educational levels, socioeconomic status, and two-parent and one-parent homes.[6]

"Black kids spend a lot more time watching television than white kids do," says Dr. Ferguson. "In fact, I would bet a lot of money that they spend more time with electronics more generally."

But as our media consumption has gone up, the amount of time we've spent reading to our children has gone down. Between 2005 and 2007, reading rates dropped in almost all families except white families, where they held steady. The percentage of three- to five-year-old black children whose parents read to them frequently plummeted in just two years, from 50 percent to 35 percent. Although we cannot be certain that using more electronics definitively caused less reading, we don't really have to convene a commission to figure out what's happening, do we? We believe that black children's excessive use of electronic devices is having tragic consequences for their academic competitiveness.[7] In fact, almost half of children who are heavy media consumers report getting more fair or poor grades (Cs or lower) than other children, whereas about 65 percent of moderate and light media users report that they get good grades.[8] And don't forget that the electronics gap is in place by the time our children are pre-kindergartners.

The stories that our TV, movie, music, and video consumption patterns are telling us suggest that we need to lock these gadgets up during the week, if not throw them right out of the window.

Television

Across every socioeconomic group, black children watch the most TV by far, both during the week and on the weekend. In fact, on weekends our kids watch twice as much TV as other children do, with Hispanic kids not far behind.[9] But the fruit doesn't fall far from the tree. Research by Nielsen Media Research shows that across every single age group, black adults watch more TV during every single time slot—daytime, prime time, and late night—than do members of any other group.[10]

In line with this, Dr. Ferguson discovered that in middle-class families, more than 80 percent of black first- through sixth-graders have a TV in their bedroom. Compare this to 70 percent of Hispanic children, 40 percent of white children, and 36 percent of Asians.

"My son's Jewish classmates came over, and guess what they were excited about when they went to his room? They were excited because he had a TV," says Ellen, whose son is twelve.

"We didn't have much when I was growing up, so I want my children to have all the things I wanted," says Kenneth, a lawyer and the father of two sons and a daughter. "We have a flat-screen in every room of the house, and, yes, a game is always on."

"Well-to-do black parents say, 'I didn't have that,' or 'I work hard to give my kid that,'" Dr. Ferguson says. "For not-so-well-to-do parents, it's a rite of passage—everybody else has one. The fear is, if you don't give your kid a TV, they'll think you don't love them. It's not that any one family by itself made the wrong choice to put the TV in the bedroom, it's just that they were all part of a culture where that was the norm," Dr. Ferguson adds. "If you deviate from the norm, then your kid thinks something's wrong."

In Dr. Ferguson's study, 30 percent of black elementary school–aged children reported that they watch TV more than they do anything else, as compared to 14 percent of Hispanic, and 13 percent of Asian and white youngsters.[11]

The Kaiser study found that children with a TV in their bedroom watch more TV than children with no TV in their bedroom; children in homes where the TV is left on all of the time watch more TV than children in homes where it's rarely or never left running; and children in homes that have media rules consume significantly less media than those in homes that have no media rules.

"There's way too much TV," says Dave Hardy, president and CEO of Boys' Latin, a Philadelphia charter high school that serves 450 boys, most of them black. "There's nothing good about TV when kids come home. They should do their homework, read a book, have conversations, and then talk to somebody. They haven't learned how to do that."

"Kids with TVs in bedrooms report being sleepier in school," says Dr. Ferguson, "although it's hard to know the degree to which the TV in the bedroom is just a symptom of other issues."

Black children are also more likely to watch TV during meals, which is worrisome given the important role that family meals can play in helping us check in with our children, learn what's happening in their lives, and help them to process their experiences.

"People are watching TV and eating McDonald's or a pizza and calling that dinner," says Hardy. "That's not dinner. You just ate in the same proximity; you didn't have dinner. Have dinner and a dinner conversation, and your kid will do much better. Because you learn more at the dinner table than you do in the classroom anyway."

"Upper-middle-class people often give their children advantages in schooling. First, the parents read to their kids on a daily basis. They turn off the television. They develop their children's vocabularies. They have face time, for example, during family dinner hours," says Dr. Lareau. "Some parents are also able to telecommute or work part-time. It is a great privilege. But if they have that luxury, then they are able to be home between 3 and 6 in the afternoon. Often, they make up the hours later, but they are available to their children during that critical time period."

Cell Phones

Black children spend more than forty-five minutes talking on a cell phone plus more than two hours texting each day, as compared to twenty-five minutes and one hour and twenty-two minutes for white children and thirty-seven minutes and one hour and forty-two minutes for Hispanic kids. Less than 30 percent of black seventh- to twelfth-graders reported having any rules about the amount of time they could spend talking on the phone, and less than 15 percent reported having rules about the number of texts they could send per day.

Movies

On a typical day, almost 20 percent of black youngsters as opposed to 7 percent of white kids report going to the movies on any given day. The average moviegoer of any background spends more than three hours there.[12]

Music

Black and Hispanic children spend almost two hours and forty-five minutes listening to music each day, compared to one hour and forty-eight minutes for white youth. Since we first set foot in this country, music has sustained and saved African Americans and other people of color on many levels; however, it's important to protect our children from negative content or at least to get them thinking critically about it.

"We have to engage in self-critique," says Margaret Beale Spencer, Ph.D., a professor of human development and urban education at the University of Chicago. "In our communities, unfortunately, we have not universally and successfully resisted the internalization of dehumanizing beliefs about black people."

Our children are also in danger of hearing loss from having their headsets on too long and too loud. If you can hear the music when your son's headsets are on, it is too loud to be safe on his ears.

Video Games

Black (one hour and twenty-five minutes) and Hispanic (one hour and thirty-five minutes) teenagers spend about a half-hour more each day playing video games than white children do.

"I go to bed early, then I wait until my mom goes to bed and get up and play video games 'til four in the morning. I sleep during second period," says Matthew, 16, a C student.

OPPORTUNITY KNOCKS

But even with our children using so many electronic devices, as parents we are significantly less likely than other parents to have rules about time limits on different types of media or about what kind of content they can and cannot consume.

In fact, only 26 percent of black parents have rules limiting the amount of time their children spend watching TV, and only 43 percent have rules about the types of shows that our children can watch. The same pattern—few black households with rules about electronics—holds across other media, including music. This is particularly worrisome given the negative images about black males, in particular, that abound.

"Not only is the planet communicating uncensored values and views to your child, but unavoidably your child is responding to what he's hearing without the benefit of a translator to support both his family and community," says Dr. Margaret Beak Spencer.

When an adult challenged Jackson, 10, about why the bad guys in an online auto-theft app were black and brown and asked if he had ever played a game with a white car thief, he looked puzzled for a few moments before responding, "Get over it. It's realistic; this is how the world is."

Really?

No parent of any race can keep up with every website their child visits or every app he plays (especially on his friends' cell phones), but the lapses in oversight taking place in black homes—the only place where we can ensure that someone will challenge, refute, interpret, and push back on these images—leave our sons' developing minds exposed to negative information about themselves without adequate adult protection. If we don't take this on in our own little dominions, who else will care enough to do it?

"Right now, my son isn't very happy with me," says Susan, the mother of a thirteen-year-old son. "I only allow him to use his iPod Touch for two hours a day on the weekends and occasionally during the week—but only for a few minutes. In the meantime I have to deal with permissive parents who don't monitor their children's texting at all. He's upset because he feels isolated because his friends are all on Instagram, and he can't communicate and make plans with them. Well, I'm figuring out how to deal with this on the fly, but we've already been through this: His grades dropped as soon as he got his iPod. He can be mad at me if he wants. It's my job to protect his future."

Now, we'll be the first to admit it: Both of our sons are fixated on video games, and we're not quite sure what to do about it. We learned from parenting Idris that we could negotiate with him about playing video games to get him to do other things. Now, our younger son Miles wants to play video games, but we want him to study. We've established that Miles is only allowed to watch TV or YouTube or play games on his cell phone beginning on Fridays at 3 p.m. and ending on Sunday at dinnertime. He can't do those things on weekdays—we make few exceptions. On weekends we limit him to eight hours of electronics or barter additional electronics for more reading, writing, and arithmetic time. So far it's working, but we've got our fingers crossed.

The good news is that even though black parents tend to be overworked and, by the time we arrive home, exhausted, now that we understand the magnitude of the problem, we can take advantage of the extraordinary opportunity that exists to shift our children in a more academic direction—for as many as four hours a day, which is a tremendous amount. If we take this issue on individually in our homes, and collectively in our churches, communities, and organizations, the upside could be tremendous.

GETTING IN THE ZONE

Indeed, our children need a tremendous amount of support from both their parents and their community if they stand a snowball's chance in hell of defending their futures against the consumer electronics and entertainment industries, which are hell-bent on tempting them to exchange their potential for the addictive pleasures electronics offer them right now.

In the famous marshmallow study—in which seven- to nine-year-old children were offered a choice between one small reward (typically a marshmallow) to eat right away or two rewards if they could wait until the researcher returned in fifteen minutes—the children who waited eventually scored 250 points higher on the SAT. This is the same behavior we want to encourage in our kids—the ability to delay gratification. We think the work of psychologist Philip Zimbardo, author of *The Time Paradox: The New Psychology of Time That Will Change Your Life,* provides us with a road map we can use to teach our sons about how to manage their time.

Dr. Zimbardo has studied the relationship between people's time perceptions and their success, and he has found that each person's decisions are influenced by their sense of time, whether we're aware of it or not. Because even though when we think of time we often consider it as being objective—that is, there are sixty seconds in a minute, sixty minutes in an hour, and twenty-four hours in a day— our perception of time can speed up or slow down. For example, we've all had situations when we lost track of time while, say, we were driving on a great road on a sunny day, listening to our favorite album—or when a driving vacation dragged on forever when the air conditioner broke and our children were in the backseat bickering.

Dr. Zimbardo's research shows that the tendency to live mentally in the past, present, or future varies from person to person. When it comes to decisions, every person has an unconscious bias toward one metaphorical *time zone:* the past, the present, or the future. *Past-oriented* people tend to reflect on previous experiences, which in turn strongly influence their future choices. *Present-oriented* people tend to think about the immediate circumstances around them. *Future-oriented* people assess the consequences their actions will have moving forward. The children who held out to get the second marshmallow turned out to be future-focused.

Within each time zone, two additional tendencies exist, creating a total of six possible habits. Past-oriented people can be *positive* (focused on the good old days) or *negative* (focused on failures or regrets). Present-oriented people can be *hedonistic* (focused on pleasure, taking risks, and seeking sensations) or *fatalistic* (believing that what happens in life lies beyond their control). Future-oriented people can orient themselves toward *life goals* (meeting deadlines and achieving objectives) or be *transcendental* (strongly influenced by their belief in spiritual life after death).

WHAT'S YOUR TIME ZONE?		
Past	**Present**	**Future**
Positive	Hedonistic	Life Goals
Negative	Fatalistic	Transcendental

These time perspectives are not genetically determined—our culture, social class, nationality, ethnicity, and individuality strongly influence them. Case in point: The American Dream once rewarded a future orientation that corresponded with reaching life goals. Our nation got in trouble when we shifted to conspicuous consumption—think: insider trading, the collapse of Enron, and the financial crisis and real-estate meltdown that have ravaged the global economy.

Or, as one friend recently put it, "When I came to the United States, my dream was to buy a house. Now my son wants to buy a car, and my grandson wants to buy sneakers."

How does this relate to the education of our sons?

One daycare center owner described the issue perfectly: "The low-income parents think about today but not tomorrow. Sometimes they ask, 'Why is he getting homework at this age? I have enough to do at night.' I tell them, 'It's about him not about you.' The educated parents think long-term but not short-term. They drop their kids off and don't give them a hug or forget to tell them they're coming back to pick them up—sometimes you have to be in the moment. Lots of well-to-do parents have a big disconnect and aren't parenting at all. The nanny is raising them, but then the nanny gets fired, gets married, or has her own family. Where does that leave the kid?"

Whatever time zone we gravitate toward becomes a mental habit that we unconsciously overuse and that biases our decision making. Dr. Zimbardo describes growing up in a Bronx ghetto in a Sicilian culture that was overwhelmingly past- and present-oriented and having to work to change his time orientation to one that correlates more with success. He has found that low-income people tend to be both present-oriented and fatalistic and that hedonistic people get the worst grades. The entertainment industry encourages us to be both present-oriented and hedonistic—particularly children, whose immature brains tend to be present/hedonistic naturally.

And Joe observes in his practice that many of his clients with a criminal background have either a present/hedonistic or past/negative perspective. Their conversations often sound like, "This is what happened to me. I got caught. This is what The Man is doing to me." They don't talk about their future very much; partially because their thoughts remain stuck in the past, their lives tend not to get better.

Our children's electronics consumption is conditioning them to be present/hedonistic, which Zimbardo's research shows correlates with low grades. For our sons to excel academically, we have to fight against the hedonistic tendencies that are increasingly a part of American culture and encourage more future-oriented thinking.

Dr. Zimbardo observes that people who feel fearful and threatened become more present-oriented, whether that fear is real or imagined. We believe that this has significant implications. Consider, for example, how fear might undermine the ability of people who live in high-crime neighborhoods to plan for their future—including their children's ability to study for an upcoming test. And with so many middle-class black people worried about racism's impact on us and our children or about our financial stability, we wonder if our fear may bias us toward focusing too much on our present.

Highly successful people shift time zones as they change situations.

The optimal profile for success includes being high in past/positive, moderately high in future orientation, moderate on present/hedonism, and low on past/negative and present/fatalism characteristics. This combination roots a person to his family, his personal identity, and his sense of self in a positive and empowering way; provides him with energy and joy to learn about himself as well as the people, places, and things around him; and provides an excitement about future destinations and challenges.

We think that this profile fits in nicely with some of our racial-socialization objectives: grounding our children in their history and family identities, teaching them to enjoy learning, and encouraging them to focus on their ability to overcome challenges and demonstrate control over their choices.

When Joe talks to his patients about the value of time, he tells them to envision every person they pass with a thought bubble over their head like you see in a comic book. Imagine that each bubble corresponds to their salary: $12,000 or $35,000 or $100,000 or $300,000. The income in their thought bubble almost always corresponds to the amount of time that person has spent investing in their education.

CREATE A COLLEGE-BOUND ENVIRONMENT

By changing the way we organize our homes and family life, we can center our children less around entertainment and more around education.

Start by tracking how much time your son (and your other children) spend using electronics each week. Ask them to help you identify small shifts that you can easily accomplish, focusing on changes that you can make every day—think: turning the television off during dinner, cutting down on the number of electronic devices running at a time, and reading for twenty minutes a day. Then give your family a heads-up about when the shift is going to take place. Explain that the changes will help them do better in school and behave in a way that will up the likelihood that they'll get to go to college. Celebrate everyone's small successes by giving high-fives, creating a rewarding family ritual, or going out for a treat. But most of all, be patient. The tortoise beat the hare, after all.

Moving forward, communicate your priorities and expectations, says Stephen Jones, associate dean of students and strategic planning at Villanova University. "Every week have a discussion about what's happening in their classes and what their teacher's expectations are," he says. Then organize your household around achieving these goals.

Teach them to do their homework as soon as they arrive home from school, while what they've learned is still fresh. Have them work on upcoming projects at least several days in advance. Ask questions like: How can you make sure your work is done on time? What's your plan to make sure that happens? Set rules around telephone, texting, TV, and video games to help them succeed. Email their teachers so that they know that you care and are involved, and go online each week to review their grade report.

He should be using a date planner by the end of elementary school.

"Most students don't have a time management system," says Dr. Jones, who leads weekend and summer programs for black engineering students and teaches time management and study skills.

"They just look at the assignments each day and do what they can."

Have him write his assignments, upcoming projects, and tests in his planner so that he (and you) can see what's coming up.

The Optimal Time Profile

- High past/positive,
- Moderately high future orientation
- Moderate present/hedonism
- Low past/negative
- Low present/fatalism

"A lot of students are disorganized and have papers everywhere—rolled up, balled up, folded in their pockets," says one teacher.

"I got a D in social studies," says Marcus, an eleven-year-old who loves social studies. "I was doing my homework with my mom, but I kept forgetting it in my locker."

Help him create a study schedule, emphasizing that days that appear to be free time may not actually be free. He should be doing homework, reading, developing himself, and studying for tests a week in advance.

Encourage your son to take notes in every class, writing down what the teacher writes on the board as well as any new terms, their definitions, and questions he needs his teacher to clarify. If your son's notes are messy or disorganized, have him rewrite and reorganize them each day when he gets home.

Set aside a quiet place for him to study where he won't be distracted. Depending on your household, there may be too much commotion for him to study at the kitchen table; his bed, on the other hand, may make him fall asleep. If you have room and can afford it, get him a desk. Millennial children can multitask; however, neither TV nor Jay Z should be playing. Have him try jazz, classical sounds, or spa music instead.

Struggling with Homework?

Not smarter than a fifth-grader? Don't sweat it. Many parents struggle to help their children with homework, particularly with math, which is taught differently than it was back in the Stone Age. And parents who attended poorly performing schools may not have learned the subject themselves. Some adults will be able to guide younger kids by asking open-ended questions that lead him to the answer. Questions like: What do you think? What would happen if you did it this way? Is there another way that you could try it? Michèle's mother had only a sixth grade education, but she supported Michèle during elementary school by helping her put her projects together. During junior high school she supported Michèle by sitting with her as she did her assignments. But don't allow your son to fall behind. And older children in particular must learn how to ask for help.

Learning when and how to ask for help is one of life's most important lessons. By high school, teachers in most schools are available after hours to provide additional help. And almost all schools and school districts have peer tutoring and other resources available to students and families. Teach your son that asking for help is a sign of strength, not weakness or failure. (If it takes a few tries, don't worry; it took Idris five years to ask for help.) And make sure you role-model the behavior by asking for assistance when you need it.

"We don't ask parents to support their kids doing their homework because that assumes that the parents know how to do it. There are some that do, but in high school you're supposed to learn how to do your own homework and to go to your teachers when you're having a problem," says Hardy. "We tell parents that if their son comes home complaining about his homework, the first question to ask him is, 'What are you going to do about it?' That question puts it back in the boy's lap. That doesn't mean you can't help, but he has to figure out what steps he's going to take to get help. The parents can't call the school all the time. You have to let him do it."

Before he wraps up, be sure to check his homework. Is it complete? Did he follow directions? Is it accurate? Will his teacher be able to read it or does his handwriting look like chicken scratches?

Help him organize his books and homework in a central location. Then make sure he gets to bed at a decent hour so that he's in shape to learn, to behave as you have trained him to, and to make good decisions the next day—including decisions about how he manages his time.

"A lot of our children are not getting enough sleep. Parents are not being hard-nosed enough to insist that they go to bed, above their kids' objections," says pediatrician Michelle Gourdine, a clinical assistant professor at the University of Maryland School of Medicine. And don't forget the impact that electronics are having on sleep time. "Kids are gonna tell you, 'Oh, I'm fine; I'm good,' but they're not. It's important that they get eight to ten hours of sleep each night so their body can repair itself, rejuvenate, and reset so when they wake up they're at their maximum capacity to learn. When we talk about academic performance, a lot of it has to do with our kids' nutrition and sleeping habits."

"If you really care about your kid's learning, you gotta make sure you care about their sleep," says NYU psychology professor Joshua Aronson. "A lot of the black kids that I observe in school are tired and sleeping in class. Many live in noisy, stressful environments."

"When I come home from school, I go to sleep for a couple of hours," says Darvon, 15. "Then when my mom comes home, I eat dinner, do homework, go to my room and watch TV until she goes to sleep. I text and play video games until like four in the morning. Then I go to sleep." Darvon often misses first period and admits that he falls asleep in class.

Digital Dangers

Black children spend about an hour and twenty-five minutes a day online, doing social networking, watching YouTube videos, playing games, instant messaging, surfing, and otherwise messing around. Only two minutes of that time is spent reading a magazine or newspaper.

Only 35 percent of black parents limit their children's time on computers, 44 percent have restrictions about computer content, and 30 percent have rules regarding their children's social-media profiles.

Source: Henry J. Kaiser Family Foundation, *Generation M2: Media in the Lives of 8- to 18-Year-Olds.*

STOPPING SUMMER SLIDE

Some studies suggest that much of the achievement gap between lower- and higher-income kids can be accounted for by how children spend their time over their breaks, especially over the summer.

When educators administer the same test at the start and at the end of summer vacation, kids score lower in the fall, a phenomenon called *summer learning loss, summer slide, or summer setback*—the loss of knowledge that all children experience when they're not engaged in mind-expanding activities.

One study that tracked more than eight hundred Baltimore students from first grade until age twenty-two found that disadvantaged children (most of the parents with a high school diploma or less) actually progressed at a *slightly faster pace* during the school year than their peers with more advantages (mostly parents with at least some college). But beginning as early as the fall of first grade, they lost ground academically every summer. The researchers discovered that two-thirds of the achievement gap between the less-advantaged and more-advantaged peers that existed at the ninth grade was caused by summer slide during their elementary school years—a time when higher-income families would push their children forward academically by having them read, attend sports camps, go to museums, go to exotic and interesting countries on vacation, and participate in other enriching activities.

In fact, the researchers discovered that the gap that grew over summers during primary school reduced the odds that children would take college-placement classes, increased their risk of dropping out, and lowered their chances of attending college.[13] They also wondered whether high-poverty schools are doing a better job of educating students than people realize—only to lose their edge to summer setback.

Parent groups, the Village, schools, churches, and communities can come together to create summer and break-time enrichment activities—from reading to trips to the zoo to community clean-up and, particularly for older children, local social justice projects. They can also press something researchers questioned: why schools administer placement tests at the start of the fall semester, when all students—and particularly the most vulnerable ones—score lower.

> **Summer slide** refers to the loss of knowledge children experience when they're not engaged in learning activities. But just because our children are not in school—as in the summer—doesn't mean we can't keep them stimulated.

Keeping the Promise

1. **Help our sons manage their media consumption.** Black children consume significantly more electronic media than other children—with detrimental results.

2. **Time management is a vital life skill.** Helping our children learn to manage their time—from getting the right amount of sleep to teaching them to use a day planner—is one of the most important things we can do for them.

3. **Make the breaks count.** Even during the summer, we can help our children make the most of their time.

EDUCATION TO MATCH HIS NEEDS

How to Understand Our Sons' Learning Styles and Special Needs

All through kindergarten and first grade, my son did very well and had no problems at school. But all of a sudden in second grade, the teacher starts telling me he wasn't behaving well and he was having problems in reading and writing. Mind you, he had a very strong teacher—also a white woman—in first grade, and none of these issues existed. But, okay, we met with his second grade teacher.

She said, "Maybe the problem is that he's an only child."

I said, "Well, there's nothing that we can do about that. Do you have any other strategies that you can suggest?"

She says, "Well, maybe if he was around girls more. Does he have any girl cousins? Maybe they can help his writing style."

Is my son at age seven going to sit down with his girl cousins and write a letter? It's just not gonna happen. But I said, "Well, let me see what you're referring to."

So I had him write a letter to a friend. Basically the letter said, "Dear Jimmy, Come to my house. We'll play PlayStation. We'll have pizza. We'll have fun. Bye."

Then I asked the teacher to show me a letter from a girl. It was long and flowery.

I said, "My husband has a master's degree. It takes pulling teeth to get him to write a letter. Maybe it's just a boy/girl thing; they're probably just different."

So I go back to his first grade teacher for help. She tells me, "You gotta get him out of here, because he's cute now, but when he gets older, he's gonna be threatening to them. They're going to be intimidated." So we did.

—Tamika, the thirty-six-year-old mother of a
fourteen-year-old son

In this chapter we examine some of the reasons black boys disproportionately get placed in special education and get passed over for G&T, honors, and advanced placement classes:

- We'll help you understand the importance of learning styles and supportive educational environments.
- We'll give guidance on navigating the special education system.
- We'll help you understand how learning differences and disabilities work.
- We'll talk through the difficulties of G&T programs.

Promise your son that you will help his teacher customize his educational experience to his learning needs, that you will communicate your high expectations both to him and to his teachers, that you will help him understand that he must learn no matter what anyone else thinks of him, and that you will respond quickly to ensure he obtains appropriate help if you, a teacher, or another member of his Village, notice possible symptoms of a learning or developmental difference or disability.

HE DOESN'T FIT THE PROFILE

Many experts we've spoken to believe that schools are better suited for girls than boys, leaving males of all races at a disadvantage from the time they begin school.

"Boys' fine motor skills and executive function develop more slowly than girls' do," says David Grissmer, research professor at the Center for Advanced Study of Teaching and Learning at the University of Virginia. "If you get a boy in kindergarten, he's eight to ten months developmentally behind in two key skills needed to take advantage of kindergarten. He hasn't got the basic comprehension skills, and if he happens to be young in his class, that puts him further behind."

Boys also tend to communicate more directly than girls do and interact through physical activity and movement. They like hands-on activities that rely on large muscle movement rather than their fine motor skills. When boys are young, they tend to have less control over their behavior than girls do. But schools strongly reward children who communicate verbally, sit still, work quietly at a desk on tasks that require fine motor skills, and demonstrate a high degree of self-control—that is to say, girls!

Kids who don't fit this profile are often viewed as poorly adjusted, are often accused of misbehaving, are subjected to punishments, and get assigned to special education more often.

"We've designed a female classroom for large numbers of male students," said educational consultant Jawanza Kunjufu, author of *Countering the Conspiracy to Destroy Black Boys* and other classics on black boys and education in a radio interview.[1] "If you know that boys have a higher energy level, allow more movement. If you know that boys have a shorter attention span, then shorten the lesson plan. If you know that girls mature faster than boys, then there's no need to put boys in remedial reading classes or in special education. Allow for the maturation difference. The research shows that girls mature about three years faster than boys in terms of a K–12 experience."

"You have to allow boys to be able to express themselves so it's not such a pent-up environment that they're unable to be who they are in a constructive manner," says a high school vice principal.

The fact that boys start behind girls in pre-reading skills ups their odds of being miscategorized as learning disabled during their early school years.[2] In 2011, 9 percent of boys as compared to 6 percent of girls ages three to seventeen had been diagnosed as having a learning disability.

"Boys catch up later," says psychiatrist Alvin Poussaint. "But teachers may gravitate toward the girls and see the boys as slow. They may not understand the difference developmentally."

With black boys the differences in race, gender, and often socioeconomic class that exist between them and their teachers complicate these developmental differences. Eighty-three percent of full-time teachers are white, and 84 percent of elementary school teachers are females; only 7 percent are black.[3] In general, boys don't encounter male teachers, much less black male teachers. Importantly, even though they go on to instruct an increasingly diverse population, new teachers receive little to no education that would make them cross-culturally competent.

"Many teachers think that everybody is the same in terms of resource history, the challenges they're confronted with, and what they're trained to do in terms of teaching," says Dr. Spencer. "Serving as a source of support for children's learning is critically important. Traditional teacher training may not include supporting youngsters whose experiences include a lot of challenges linked to race, color, and gender complicated by low socioeconomic status. That's a very,

very complex interaction that's not in the training or the cultural sensitivities of many traditionally trained adults, both black and white. For blacks the tension might be due to social class. For whites dissonance may occur due to unquestioned and unanalyzed stereotypic assumptions about how social class interacts with race and ethnicity. Contemplating these complexities in non-pejorative ways is not part of traditional teacher training programs."

One consequence? Although only 9 percent of the school-age population nationwide consists of black males, 15 percent of black males end up with an individualized education plan (IEP), which contains customized objectives for children with disabilities.[4]

And while giftedness is dispersed equally throughout the population, black boys are disproportionately unlikely to be placed in gifted and talented (G&T) programs or honors or AP courses, even when they qualify.

"Today 9.1 percent of black male high school students are in special education, compared with the national average of 6.5 percent; and 14.5 percent of black males are in honors classes, compared with the national average of 25.6 percent," says Ivory Toldson, author, Howard University counseling psychology professor, and deputy director of the White House Initiative on Historically Black Colleges and Universities. Dr. Toldson adds this important-to-remember detail: "Yes, there are more black males in honors classes than in special education."

BOREDOM AND LEARNING STYLES

Different children, regardless of their race or their gender or age, have different learning styles.

The term *learning styles* describes the way a person naturally or habitually uses their senses to extract and process information in their environment, including at school. For example, *visual* learners prefer seeing pictures, graphs, timelines, films, and demonstrations; *aural* learners prefer hearing, reading aloud, sounds, rhymes, and music; *interactive* learners tend to love group activities and bouncing ideas off of people; and *kinesthetic* learners learn through bodily sensations, hands-on experiences, role-playing, and movement.

"Yet the classroom still tends to be set up to cater to one type of learning style," says pediatrician Michelle Gourdine. "So if you don't fall into that category, then we're sorry; good luck; hope you do well."

> "My son's teachers complain that my son is always looking out the window," says Tahira of her ten-year-old son. "Yet somehow he always gets As and Bs. They claim he's disengaged. No, you are boring. He reads, likes going to museums, and Is very excited about learning at home. Somehow they just can't seem to get that."

A number of factors contribute to this disconnect.

Many times a mismatch exists between the learning style of a student and the teaching style of their instructor.

"When you have what we call a kinesthetic learning style—kids who have to do, who have to be active, who have to have hands-on—most classrooms aren't set up to adapt to that learning style, which is unfortunate," says Dr. Gourdine. Requiring students to work quietly by themselves on a worksheet or read a textbook is not the best way to engage them.

"Last year I led a group of students to Costa Rica," Chris, a charter school teacher recalls. "There were three boys, and two of the three boys were in nonstop motion. One sits because he draws so much, but his papers are full of drawings. The other didn't stop moving for a week. It's so much easier to teach him when we're outside and moving around. He walks in and out of your conversation. He might say, 'I want to learn a language' and then walk away and start interacting with people. Then he'll come back and ask, 'How do you say *pretty* in Spanish?' because he sees an attractive girl. But he was the one who could speak the most Spanish at the end of the trip. And he was the one bouncing around the organic cow farm asking all these questions about cows. He was not a nuisance. But when he's in some people's classroom, he's a nuisance. Even when he's excited about what he's learning, he can't follow the rules. But I'm so over the idea of there being four walls and five rules."

"Teachers may not know if they have an auditory learner versus a kinesthetic learner," says Bryant Marks, director of the Morehouse Male Initiative at Morehouse College in Atlanta. "They need to engage in appropriate strategies to reach all the kids. Am I aware of how to teach the same concept in two or three different ways?"

When a teacher doesn't have this ability, students may become bored and inattentive in class, do poorly on tests, or become discouraged.

"Boys can tend to be more hands-on and physical," says one principal. "But if you're holding fast to how you learn and holding the child accountable because they don't learn like you do, you're doing the child and yourself a disservice. Because the child's going to get frustrated, you're going to get frustrated because they're frustrated and giving you problems, and it's going to spiral downward from there."

But a child who looks bored may also be masking more vulnerable emotions that are important for their teachers to attend to.

"It's not always easy to tell the difference between a bored student and a student who feels rejected and scared," says Joshua Aronson, an associate professor of applied psychology at New York University's Steinhardt School of Culture, Education, and Human Development. "When people are scared of looking foolish, of being rejected, they often look numb or bored. So you look at your students and say, 'You're bored,' or 'You don't care,' when actually a lot are just scared to engage. The stakes in American classrooms can be very high. By attending to children's need to feel comfortable in classrooms, you often get a dramatic improvement in achievement because you often take away that fear. We should also address boredom because there's a lot of boredom in schools."

KEEP IT MOVING

"If two-thirds of children and an even larger percentage of African American males are right-brain learners (visual-pictures, oral/auditory, tactile/kinesthetic), but 90 percent of lessons are oriented toward left-brain learners (visual-print), then Houston, we have a problem," Dr. Kunjufu writes in *Understanding Black Male Learning Styles.*[5]

"I saw one teacher's lesson and asked her why she thought her children don't learn," one principal told us. "She was like, 'They need to pay better attention in terms of how and what I'm teaching. If they don't get it, then it's their fault.' Suffice it to say that I wrote that teacher off. In my opinion it's never the child's fault; it's our responsibility to teach the child, not to teach ourselves."

According to Dr. Kunjufu, a large percentage of African American males are tactile and kinesthetic learners, a learning style that's not embraced in many schools. What's more, kinesthetic learners need forty-five minutes of daily physical education. Sadly, only 4 percent of elementary schools, 8 percent of middle schools, and 3 percent of high schools provide PE or its equivalent every day.[6]

"Testosterone makes you aggressive," Dr. Poussaint says. "It's important for boys to blow off steam and run around the yard. That's why boys gravitate to sports."

"In an all-boys school, you have to have sports or these boys will drive you nuts," says Dave Hardy, president and CEO of Boys' Latin High School in Philadelphia.

We learned very early on that physical activity would need to play an integral role in Idris's life. Even before we received his formal diagnosis of ADHD, it was very clear that physical activity helped our son focus and study. When some boys get into trouble, the first thing their parents do is pull them out of sports. With Idris, we realized that sports wasn't an extra activity, sports needed to be a priority. So we had him engage in some sort of physical activity every day before school, even if it was just going outside and dribbling.

"Exercise is sort of an essential nutrient," said John Ratey, an associate clinical professor of psychiatry at Harvard Medical School and the author of *Spark: The Revolutionary New Science of Exercise and the Brain,* at a 2011 conference hosted by Harvard University's Achievement Gap Initiative. Dr. Ratey explained that when you keep children from playing, they "do less well on their SAT scores, they have a harder time socially, they become bullies or bullied—and we see this with our children today who are sitting and have all the media input in the world but are not interacting."

A DIFFERENT WORLD

Far too few of America's teachers of any race receive any cultural competency training to qualify them to know how to teach black boys, particularly when the boys come from low-income families. Additionally, a study of white teachers' experiences with black students identified that many teachers have a limited amount of personal and professional encounters with people who are racially, ethnically, linguistically, and culturally different from themselves and that student teachers have expressed their dissatisfaction with their training in teaching diverse students.[7]

Adding insult to injury, teachers of black boys tend to have less experience in education than the average teacher. And because many new teachers cycle in and out, they may also be new to the school.

"The younger ones come in and may not stay very long. Before they become master teachers, they're out," says Dr. Marks.

"Many times the teacher really wanted to work in a suburban school district, but she didn't have enough years teaching," Dr. Toldson says.

Some research shows that when low-income and minority students consistently have high-quality teachers, they make significant gains. But other studies show that even experienced teachers can lack confidence in their ability to teach black boys.

For example, a study conducted in Maryland found that even "highly qualified" teachers don't always believe they can teach black students successfully. The fifty teachers, administrators, and counselors whom the researchers interviewed were quick to blame the students and their families for failing to meet academic standards, describing factors like the students' "lack of preparedness," "negative dispositions toward learning," "lack of math, time management, and critical-thinking skills," and "broken families" for the boys' academic results. We know that some of these problems do exist—among all students and, in some cases, disproportionately among black students. Yet "almost none of the teachers who participated in our focus groups said that they themselves were responsible for the limited achievement of African American students in their schools," the study authors wrote. Surprisingly, the students' educators did not identify structural factors, such as the systematic underfunding of public education, as factors that may have impeded students' learning. Many of these teachers were black. The researchers concluded that many of the beliefs that teachers had about black students were consistent with racist ideologies and internalized oppression.[8]

Education requires that a relationship exist between the student and the teacher but, more importantly, that the student trust the teacher. Teachers who are most effective are not only knowledgeable about the subject they teach, they also understand and appreciate the life experience of each student.

"Show some interest in who they are as individuals and who their families are," says psychologist Claude Steele, dean of the School of Education at Stanford University. "Then you can have an impact on their reading skills, their math skills, or whatever."

"The more you know about the student, the better chance you have of educating them and the less likely you are of accepting their failure," says Hardy. "If you wanna know why public school teachers in big cities so readily accept failure from kids, it's because they don't know them. They come in just in time for school, and they leave as soon as the bell's over. If they don't get paid for activities, they don't do them."

This doesn't mean that teachers who aren't black can't do a good job of teaching black children—or that black teachers are necessarily more effective with black children.

"The strongest teachers for raising achievement among white children were black teachers whose daddies were professional," says Ronald Ferguson, of Harvard University's Achievement Gap Initiative. "The strongest teachers with black kids were white teachers whose daddies were professionals and black teachers whose daddies were not."

In fact, research shows that teachers from all walks of life can teach children that they love and care for, and that has certainly been our experience with our sons.

"Teachers of all kinds of backgrounds can care and deliver, but they do need to have a certain empathy and impulse to really connect at the same time they have an impulse to hold kids responsible and accountable," Dr. Ferguson says.

"I don't care what color or what race you are, every human being needs to feel like their presence, their existence, is important, needed, wanted, valued," says one teacher. "You need people to look you in the eye and say 'I love you, you're beautiful, you're appreciated, I affirm you—even when you mess up, even when you're imperfect.'"

"My ninth grade history teacher was this small white woman who changed my work ethic," says Benjamin, 17. "She was a strict disciplinarian, and I found value in that. I had a research paper and I worked with her like 24/7—like meeting with her a lot every week. It wasn't like I was doing bad, but I showed that I really cared and she showed that she really cared, and I ended up doing so much better. Not only because I worked harder, but she was able to see my effort. She ended up writing me a college recommendation."

INTERESTED AS A PERSON

One important aspect of black children's learning is that they tend to be significantly more sensitive to whether their teacher likes and believes in them than white children are.

"Teachers of black children have an incredible amount of power, and often they don't realize how much power they have," says Joshua Aronson, an associate professor of applied psychology at New York University's Steinhardt School of Culture, Education, and Human Development. "They have tremendous responsibility—black children are much more sensitive than white children to what they think their teacher thinks of them."

"I've had an adolescent boy say to me, 'I want to go to college, but Mrs. Jones doesn't like me, so I'm not going to work for her,'" says Tabbye Chavous, professor of the combined program in education and psychology at the University of Michigan. "He wasn't saying, 'I don't care about school,' he was saying, 'I'm resisting this individual teacher who devalues me as a person.'"

Studies show that black children learn best when they believe their teachers are fair and when they like and value them.

"With black boys in particular I think it's a point of fairness. If they see you treating one group this way and another group that way, they're going to flip out; they're going to be defiant; they're going to raise questions of favoritism," says a middle school principal. "Lots of times teachers don't want to come to grips with that. Most adults can figure you out in five minutes—whether they should fight or flee. I think children are much better at knowing if someone's a danger to them—when someone is their companion, their confidante, their friend, and has their best interest at heart."

"My social studies teacher is an asshole," says Mark, 15. "He's always trying to catch the black and Spanish kids not knowing something and embarrass you by calling you to the front of the class or by 'louding' you. He doesn't do that with the white kids. And the fucked-up thing about it is, he's black. Half the time I know the answer, but fuck him; I'm not telling him."

Indeed, when researchers ask high-achieving black students about their teachers, they report that their teachers are interested in them "as a person," treat them fairly, encourage them to get extra help when they need it, and let them know when they do a good job.[9]

GREAT EXPECTATIONS?

Black boys are already heading into a world that doesn't understand them or think that they will amount to much. The kinds of expectations placed on them by their parents and in schools can make a big difference.

"There's probably quite a bit of acceptance of underperformance in schools," says Dr. Ferguson. "We take certain kids and don't push them as hard as we otherwise might. That can be both social class– and race-based."

"Before he even went to kindergarten, our son's pediatrician and preschool teachers were telling us that he was way ahead of other children," says Jocelyn. "When he was in first grade, he was already reading at a third grade level and spelling at a fourth grade level. But somehow now that he's in third grade, his teacher, who is new to the school, put him in second grade reading and second grade spelling. We found out when our son started to tell us that he must be stupid, because his friends are doing harder work and the teacher only gives him easy things. When we asked that he be retested, she resisted. When we went to the principal and insisted, he was moved up two reading levels in two weeks."

"In third grade my son's teacher sent him home with a list of vocabulary words that included words like *box* and *fox*," says Angela. "I called the teacher and was like WTF—last year he was in advanced spelling and had placed out of word study. The teacher said he didn't do well on the part of the DIBELS test that assesses his mastery of complex consonants and abstract vowels. But what does that have to do with *fox* and *box*? Why are you not scaffolding him? Why are you holding him back completely? When I used the term *scaffolding*, she realized I knew what I was talking about. It was a Thursday or Friday; I told her that by Monday he needed to be scaffolded. If he needs to be put in two different groups at the same time, do that. But don't put him back completely. Needless to say, she didn't like me or him after that. He would come home telling me that she would roll her eyes at him and sigh at his answers."

We've heard stories like these a lot. . . .

In education, the term *scaffolding* refers to the temporary and individualized support that a teacher provides a student when he is learning new information to help him reach his educational goals. It can include role-modeling, coaching, providing additional guidance, offering hints, using additional learning tools, and so on. It's a key way that students learn new things without being held back.

But teachers aren't the only ones who think too little of black boys. Too often their parents don't demand enough of them either.

"There is a rumor that in Asian homes, in terms of expectations, anything less than an A, changes will be made—there will be less television or playing outside," says Dr. Kunjufu. "In white homes, anything less than a B, changes will be made. But the rumor is in African American homes, as long as you pass, as long as you get a C, there's no need for changes."

"We have the lowest expectations for these boys. And it's not the white man, it's not the Republicans—it's family, friends, teachers, and neighbors," says Hardy. "The biggest obstacles black boys face are set up by the people who are very close to them. People who know them and say they love them are not doing them any favor by accepting less than the best from them."

"I got As, and two Bs, and a C," said one nine-year-old, whose C was in math, the subject his mother teaches; whose B was in language arts, which his father teaches; and whose other B was in gym, although he plays team sports. When told by a neighbor that his grades weren't good enough and that next time he needed to do better, he finished the neighbor's sentence before she could get it out of her mouth, saying, "I know, I need to get straight As."

Our sons will encounter people who don't vibe with them, understand them, think much of them, and more than a few who won't have their best interests at heart. But we have to tell them that it's not about the teacher; they're in class to learn the subject no matter whether the teacher likes them or not.

"Whenever my boys start complaining about the teacher, I tell them, 'I don't want to hear it. The teacher ain't got nothin' to do with whether you learn,'" says Jason, the father of two boys. "You can't give anyone that kind of power over your life."

"I had this teacher who I saw as my adversary. Every day he called my name—it was like he was picking on me," says Mario. "One night when I was struggling with my homework, I said to myself, 'I am not going to let this man get the best of me.' I started to race home every day just to do his homework. I would take notes and review every word until I could recall them. It got to the point where he wouldn't ask me questions anymore because I always raised my hand. After a while class became more than just facts. I found myself craving knowledge more and more. He sparked a passion for learning within me. I wanted to be successful."

ATTENTION DEFICIT POLICIES?

In addition to having different learning styles and sensitivities than many schools and teachers can easily accommodate, boys of all backgrounds appear to have more learning differences and learning disabilities than girls do.

Boys have higher rates of *attention deficit-hyperactivity disorder* (ADHD, which for our purposes will include ADD, *attention deficit disorder*), which is a learning *difference,* not a learning *disability.* As we experienced with Idris, ADHD can interfere with both a child's ability to learn and their behavior.[10]

"I remember in middle school, I would be doing work with my friends, and when we would start trying to focus, they could just automatically change gears," says Idris. "I would be looking at everything and be distracted by anything and everything you could think of. That's why I was seen as sort of disruptive in school. I wasn't really being disruptive, I just wasn't focused on what they wanted me to be focused on for too long a period of time. I was just so distracted by everything around me."

Just as we did, most of the black folks we talk to believe the urban legend that ADHD is overdiagnosed in black males. They're wrong.

"The chances that an African American individual—child or adult—will have the option of benefiting from treatment are much lower" than they are for white people, says psychiatrist Javier Castellanos, the NYU physician who diagnosed Idris with ADHD. "There is a perception that there's an overidentification of ADHD, but it's been demonstrated over and over again that this perception is inaccurate. I can tell you that people with means and power aren't avoiding the diagnosis or treatments," he adds.

"I know that they like to label black boys especially," says Jenay, the mother of a seventeen-year-old son with ADHD. "But I'll tell you what white folks do: They get the diagnosis and take advantage of every single resource they can possibly find. Black parents, because of the stigma of labeling, do not want their kids to be tested, or they don't want to wrap their head around the fact that their kid has a learning difference. So their kid fails in school or gets labeled as lazy."

"If the parent is African American and particularly if they're interacting with a white institution, there's the initial suspicion that there's nothing wrong with your kid but that they're mistaken or being racially biased," observes Dr. Ferguson, who navigated the same issue with his youngest son. "But don't be too self-assured. Ask questions and collect information to test both your own and their hypotheses. Your hypothesis is, 'This is racism'; theirs is, 'Your kid has a learning disability.'"

"I understand the diagnosis is a double-edged sword," says Jenay. "But it's like someone with diabetes—you're not diabetes, you just happen to have it and adjust accordingly. You take pills or change your diet or implement compensatory strategies. You can get extra time to take the test, a person to help note-take, audio books—stuff like that. But our kids don't get those resources."

"If more of the education and special education experience were a strengths-based model, parents wouldn't be so embarrassed to speak," says Kathryn, the mother of two teens, one of whom has ADHD. "If there were more recognition of what he *can* do rather than just what he *can't* do, IEP meetings would be more meaningful. But even in our own families, we are hesitant to talk about these issues—to say that we don't know what his difference will mean during the course of Thanksgiving dinner. And family members who don't have the problem may not be predisposed to care."

"I would read through the IEP and get upset about he can't do this, he can't do that," says Amanda. "I would get upset and cry about what they would say before I got there. In some ways I wish I had saved my sorrow and anger for the meeting. I never allowed them to know what impact it was having on my son and me for them to lead with his deficits."

While Dr. Ferguson agrees about the value of "asset based" approaches, he cautions us that they can sometimes prevent us from dealing with deficits that we can fix if we face them head-on. That is, *we can't fix what we refuse to talk about.*

But just because ADHD is underdiagnosed by medical doctors, it doesn't mean that a lot of folks who aren't qualified to make a diagnosis don't throw the label around inaccurately and indiscriminately.

"I cannot tell you how many patients have come to see me with their parents saying, 'The teacher wrote me a note that my kid needs to be placed on ADD medication before he can return to my classroom,'" says Dr. Gourdine. "That infuriates me to no end. It is so common—teachers self-diagnosing 'disruptive children' without having some sort of clinical diagnosis. They are not qualified to diagnose, but many just slap another label on the kid and send them to the doctor, expecting the doctor to write the prescription—which I won't, not without proper evaluation. I have also seen among some physicians a willingness to go ahead and prescribe meds to treat ADD for kids who have not been properly evaluated."

"If you're a teacher and you've got to get twenty kids from Point A to Point D because that's what the standards say, you don't have time to engage somebody who's out of bounds," says John H. Jackson, president and CEO of the Schott Foundation for Public Education. "We created attention deficit policies, and based on the policies, we label the students as having attention deficit disorder."

"When I moved to a new city, it was just me and my son. For him, adapting was a culture shock until I got him into what I thought was the right school," says Sara. "Every Friday his fourth grade teacher would send home a disciplinary report that would say that he hadn't been turning in his homework and that she kept having to move him. He kept saying 'I'm not doing anything,' and I wasn't having any problem with him. But I had just moved him across the country; maybe it was too much. So I was disciplining him and holding him accountable at home. He started being depressed and discouraged all weekend. Then I had him start working with a tutor. She wasn't experiencing the problem either. But the teacher wrote my son up so much that the teacher got the school counselor involved. They wanted to tell me that my son had ADHD, was hyperactive, and couldn't focus and complete his assignments. But my son was on the chess team that the same teacher ran and wasn't having any problem concentrating at all. Anyhow, they put him on an individualized education plan (IEP), and we ended up in this assessment that could determine whether he got kicked out and put in an alternative school for troubled kids. Well, that turned out to be the best thing that could have happened. It turns out that my son did not need medication. The teacher had a son on ADHD medication; her husband was also on ADHD medication. They determined it wasn't my son; her classroom was overstimulating and chaotic."

In retrospect we have to take responsibility for some of Idris's academic problems. We were a little embarrassed by his learning difference and rationalized that their observation was yet another example of the system going after black boys—a dynamic they'd given us plenty of reason to worry was in motion. But when black parents do as we did—hold on to the discrimination conclusion like a dog holds on to a bone, while ignoring other options—we are less likely to get our child the assistance that he needs in order to advance.

In our effort to get our son to respond, we were feeling frustrated, yelling and sometimes being more authoritarian with him than we like to admit. Eventually we agreed to his request to get evaluated for ADHD.

"I was kind of intrigued, excited, and nervous at the same time," says Idris. "We had been discussing it for years; I just wanted to have either the validation that I was or wasn't ADHD. I wanted to know if it was true or not, so we could stop staying in ambiguous territory."

While researching this book we learned that ADHD is more common among premature and low–birth-weight babies.[11] Idris wasn't born prematurely. However, we also learned that there can be an association with bipolar disorder.

"The overlap between ADHD and bipolar disorder is very high, and bipolar is a highly heritable disorder," says Charles Nelson III, chair of pediatric developmental medicine research at Boston Children's Hospital and professor of pediatrics and neuroscience at Harvard Medical School. "Perhaps he got some variant of those genes and it presented itself as ADD."

In addition to having more ADD, boys also seem to have more *learning disabilities*, an umbrella term that we use to describe neurological disorders that make it hard to develop certain academic and social skills. About 10 percent of boys aged three to seventeen versus about 6 percent of girls have a learning disability.[12] Dyslexia is perhaps the most well-known learning disability.

Although learning disabilities affect a person's ability to listen, speak, read, write, spell, reason, or do math, the fact that someone has one doesn't mean that the person is unintelligent or that they're lazy. Learning disabilities can be caused by a wide variety of factors—from heredity to problems during pregnancy and birth (low birth weight, prematurity, drug and alcohol use among others) to problems after birth (serious illnesses or injuries, poor nutrition, or exposure to toxins). They become more common as children grow older, with 3 percent of preschoolers, 7 percent of children aged five to eleven, and 11 percent of young people aged twelve to seventeen identified as having one.

Children who have public health insurance are almost twice as likely to be identified as having a learning disability of one type or another as children covered by private insurance. And black children (10 percent) are slightly more likely than white children (9 percent) but significantly more likely than Hispanic (6 percent) and other (5 percent) children.

Finally, many people are quick to see the downside of a learning difference or disability, but few are as easily able to see their upsides. Many people with disabilities and differences go on to excel in life—Magic Johnson, Carl Lewis, and Harry Belafonte (dyslexia), Michael Jordan (ADD), and Tiger Woods and James Earl Jones (stuttering) among them.[13]

> "My son's not going to be able to tell the news in the school newspaper with the written word," says the mother of a teenage son with ADHD. "But if you give him a camera, he sees the world differently. He can contribute as a videographer or photographer."

THE SPECIAL ED TRAP?

From classrooms for girls to active learning styles to learning differences and disabilities to changes in educational standards—a wide

variety of factors form the "perfect storm" that lands a disproportionate percentage of black boys in special education, including many
black boys who do not belong there.

"We all have different attention spans, levels of anxiety, suscepti-
bility to distraction, social acuity, etc., which are controlled by past
and present circumstances as well as our unique chemical makeup,"
write Drs. Toldson and Chance W. Lewis in *Challenge the Status
Quo: Academic Success among School-age African-American Males,*
a report published by the Congressional Black Caucus Foundation.[14]
In fact, many black boys who end up in special education don't have
a disability at all. "Rather, they have circumstances that spur behavior patterns that are not compatible with the school environment,"
Drs. Toldson and Lewis write.

Although it was originally created to provide support and services
to children with disabilities in order to help them learn to their full
potential, special education often has been used to segregate children
of color and children with disabilities from mainstream students. This
often keeps them from receiving the equal education that special education was intended to facilitate.

"Special education is supposed to be an intervention to support a
child in order to get him back on track, not a life sentence. Too many
young men tell me, 'Once you're in special ed, you're always in special ed,'" says Ron Walker, a former principal who is now executive
director of Coalition of Schools Educating Boys of Color.

Indeed, Drs. Toldson and Lewis write, "There is research evidence
that black males are more likely than other races to have false negative and false positive diagnoses, due to culturally biased assessments,
unique styles of expression, and environmental stressors."

"Over the past decade, education has moved to a standards-based
reform agenda. So anything in the process that is not standard—
a student who's not from a standard cultural or socioeconomic
background—their needs are never addressed," Dr. Jackson says.
He notes that on the Nation's Report Card, 36 percent of white
males are not on grade-level proficiency in reading. "So what we
identify as standard—none of the students are meeting that model,"
he adds.

Today black boys are 2.5 times more likely to be classified as mentally retarded than white boys are.

Dr. Gourdine reminds parents to make sure that our sons are in condition to go to school.

"A lot of kids are labeled as being slow when they're not slow at all. Far too many of them don't have proper fuel in their body to do what they would otherwise be able to from a cognitive standpoint," says Dr. Gourdine. "They're not 'dumb'; it may just be that they're not eating right or getting enough sleep. Academic performance has a great deal to do with your nutrition, eating, and sleeping habits."

Which doesn't mean that some boys don't belong in special ed programs. But once there, it's important that we make sure they're getting the resources they need to succeed—many parents have told us about the lack of special education resources within their schools.

"To this day it sticks in my craw: In fourth grade his special education teacher took family leave," recalls one parent. "But instead of replacing her with another special ed teacher, the school sent a lovely woman who was a general education sub for at least a semester. At a very critical time he didn't have a special educator in math or reading. I feel he has a deficit to this day as a result of losing that time."

LOCKED OUT OF OPPORTUNITY

Black boys also find themselves locked out of both gifted and talented programs and advanced placement classes.

Black boys are 2.5 times less likely to be enrolled in gifted and talented programs, even if their prior achievement indicates that they could succeed.[15]

"The disproportionality in gifted and talented programs is quite extraordinary," says educational consultant Michael Holzman, a consultant to the Schott Foundation for Public Education. "There are entire community school districts in New York where none of the kids are tested for gifted and talented programs. So they don't have a chance of accessing those resources."

In New York City, for example, 21 percent of kindergartners are tested for gifted and talented programs. But the chances that your son will get tested depend on the neighborhood you're raising him in. In some areas as many as 70 percent of youngsters are evaluated, while in others, as little as 7 percent are. The difference occurs along socioeconomic lines. This type of educational *redlining,* the "unethical, sometimes illegal practice of limiting residents' access to vital services in certain communities," means that 30 percent of children in some neighborhoods are admitted to G&T programs.[16] In others? As little as 1 percent. We don't have to tell you who doesn't get admitted, do we? The districts with the highest percentages of black males averaged 3 percent eligible admitted out of 17 percent tested.

"This policy reinforces a depiction of black males as being viewed as less gifted. Psychologists tell us that 'giftedness' is, by definition, evenly distributed among children. In New York City, what is not evenly distributed is the opportunity to learn in such enriched environments,'" stated the authors of the Schott Foundation's report *A Rotting Apple: Educational Redlining in New York City.*[17]

Research shows that African American teachers are more likely than white teachers to describe their black students as "intellectually gifted." The trend to lock black boys out holds true in AP placements as well.

Among ninth-graders nationwide, only 15 percent of black boys, but 22 percent of black girls, 27 percent of white boys, 33 percent of white girls, 18 percent of Hispanic boys, and 21 percent of Hispanic girls, took an honors course.[18, 19] Of black males who had the potential to take an AP class, 20 percent took the subject, but 80 percent attended a school not offering the subject or just didn't take it. Among white males, 38 percent of those qualified for AP took it and 61 percent did not.[20]

Many schools serving black and low-income students don't even offer AP classes. Students who want to enroll in them may have to take public transportation across a busy city in the middle of their school day.

"We need to make sure that every high school has a college-bound curriculum. And we need to make sure that every high school has the kinds of courses that are required at a minimum for the most competitive public state university. A lot of public high schools omit important classes like physics, and calculus, even algebra II," says Dr. Toldson.

To find out if your children's school locks them out of opportunity, visit the Civil Rights Data Collection website at http://ocrdata.ed.gov.

"I think push-out and lockout policies are quite vulnerable to pressure," says Dr. Holzman. "Only a fool would defend them."

The bottom line? Each of our sons is different—whether he is in G&T and/or has ADD. In this era increasingly marked by standardization and competition for limited resources, we are going to have to roll up our sleeves and exercise ingenuity—individually and collectively—to support as well as protect them. For the very first time, many of us have access to hard data that can tell us quite what is happening with greater precision, so that we no longer need to rely on either the system's accounts or community hearsay. We also have a wide variety of digital tools—from email, to Facebook pages, to Twitter—that make it easier than ever to connect with and engage our son's teachers, administrators, as well as other parents, and to share information so that our son's needs neither get lost in the shuffle nor brushed under the rug.

Keeping the Promise

1. **Support your son's learning style.** It's critical to understand your son's particular learning style in order to find the best learning environment.

2. **Understand ADHD and other learning differences and disabilities.** The more we know about our son's specific issues around learning, the sooner we can get him the right help and resources.

3. **Advocate for change.** Where schools are failing—whether through underresourcing special education programs or using discriminatory practices to lock our sons out of G&T programs—we should push for change.

9

WORKING HARD WILL MAKE HIM SMARTER

How to Teach Our Sons to Combat Stereotype Threat and Develop Persistence

My son had an incredibly racist first grade teacher—she diminished him and just couldn't interact with him. For example, she said that he couldn't read, but he had been reading since he was three. Yes, he could read; however, the fact that she wouldn't talk to him or call on him in class let him know that she didn't like him. That's when he started to get very anxious when he had to read out loud.

His third grade teacher became concerned that he was having some difficulty, so we had him tested by a psychologist. The psychologist said that he was reading on a seventh grade level silently and his own grade level when he read out loud. This is a kid who reads constantly for pleasure.

When I met with the teacher, I tried to tell her that it was anxiety—that he worried that she was judging him. But even when you try to talk race in a non-accusatory way, teachers struggle with how to process it. I think they are afraid of being accused of racism, even when that's not what you're saying. And if you try to bring up issues about racial dynamics, they think you're saying that they're being mean and unfair. The point is they shut down.

—Holly, 37, the mother of two sons

SIZABLE DIFFERENCES

Black children score an average of about fifteen points lower than white children on IQ tests and about 100 points lower on each section of the SAT test—that is, they're likely to score 100 points lower on critical reading *and* 100 points lower on math *and* 100 points lower on writing.[1]

"Those are sizable differences, enough to affect a person's opportunities when tests are used to base admissions decisions on," says psychologist Claude Steele, dean of the School of Education at Stanford University and one of the foremost researchers on standardized testing.[2]

This performance gap exists across socioeconomic groups. And even though being from a middle- or upper-income socioeconomic group tends to narrow the gap, it doesn't wipe it out completely. Many different theories exist about the origin of this performance difference. Experts point to the role that environmental factors such as socioeconomic differences and lower-quality schooling play in undermining test scores.[3]

But this doesn't explain the lower scores black children achieve, even when they live in integrated environments, attend high-quality schools, and come from families that are middle or upper class.

Some researchers have honed in on a phenomenon called *stereotype threat,* a type of performance anxiety that can affect people from diverse backgrounds in a wide variety of situations. Studies show that stereotype threat has a particularly detrimental effect on black boys when they take tests. That's in part because African American children know, beginning at a young age, that negative stereotypes exist about their intellectual abilities.

"Kids are very aware of the stereotypes of them," says urban sociologist Pedro Noguera, a professor of education at New York University. "Particularly in academic settings like testing situations, kids—especially black kids—become aware that 'people like me don't do well in these situations.' Unless there are ways to counter those stereotypes, it can have an effect that limits the ways kids see themselves and interact with others."

And a body of research, much of which has been led by Dr. Steele, shows that when you place a black child—but particularly a black boy—in a situation where he wants to do well but faces a negative stereotype about himself, the anxiety he develops causes him to underperform and then, ironically, confirm the stereotype.

"As you go up the socioeconomic ladder, and as kids go to school increasingly in integrated situations, the problems are not so much structural, socioeconomic problems and disadvantages—quality of teacher, and quality of schools, and the turnover of teachers—the problems are much more these socio-emotional issues," says Dr. Steele. "Not only is it true in the United States, it's true anywhere you have a stigmatized group."

In this chapter we'll challenge some common but outdated notions of intelligence so that parents and educators can create environments that allow your child's intelligence to shine and help him feel confident when he takes tests and earn scores that reflect his true abilities:

- We'll explain how stereotype threat works and what parents, teachers, and schools can do to reduce the insidious hazards to black boys' academic and socio-emotional well-being that are floating "in the air," as Dr. Steele states.

- We'll also tell you why it's important that we not coddle our son but instead challenge him to reach his full potential, engage in activities that push him beyond his comfort zone, and even stretch himself so far toward the frontier of his abilities that he occasionally falls on his face. Yes, that's right: He should occasionally fail!

Promise your son that you'll teach him that the power to get smarter lies in his own hands. Promise to teach him the importance of dedicating himself to studying hard, of investing time in his academics and in any other activity that inspires him, of embracing challenges at school and in life. Promise to show him that it's good to stretch himself and even, sometimes, to fail.

NATURE OR NURTURE

Until recently in the United States, many people believed that intelligence was a fixed characteristic you were endowed with at birth. If you were lucky enough to be born to the right parents, you had it; if you weren't, too bad, so sad.

This idea was often interpreted in a remarkably literal way. When we met with Joshua Aronson, an associate professor of applied psychology at New York University's Steinhardt School of Culture, Education, and Human Development, he framed it like this: "When I was a kid, we were told that you had a certain number of brain cells and that you shouldn't drink, smoke, or do anything that would kill them."

But researchers have learned that that belief is inaccurate. Today, scientists understand that there are many different types of intelligence—from musical to interpersonal to kinesthetic and beyond. They also know that the brain produces new brain cells and that no one is born with a predetermined amount of intelligence. All of us have the capacity to make ourselves smarter. But while scientists have long understood these ideas, for some reason Americans have been slow to get the memo. People living in most other developed cultures understand that you can increase your intelligence by working your brain, just like you would exercise or lift weights to strengthen your muscles. Children from many Asian cultures understand this, and the willingness of many children of Asian descent to outwork our kids is an important source of the so-called Asian academic advantage.

But while we can increase our intelligence by working our brains harder, intelligence can be very fragile as well.

"We can crush people's intelligence by the conditions that we put them in," Dr. Aronson says. According to Dr. Aronson, many threats to human intelligence are vestiges of the primal threats that humans experienced in the earliest days of our species. For example, the threat of rejection is one of the greatest threats to our intelligence, and he describes it as being "crazy scary" to human beings.

"When we were evolving as a species, getting tossed out of a group meant you were no longer going to be able to share in the group's resources and protections so were going to die," Dr. Aronson says. "As a result we've all evolved very powerful mental systems to detect whether we belong, fit, or are safe in a given situation. If we get signals that say we are not safe or that people don't respect us, like us, or want to be around us, our brain and body re-prioritize where the blood rushes in our brain."

When we fear for our safety—or fear, as Dr. Aronson describes, that we're not wanted—our brain and body redirect our blood to help us protect ourselves. For example, they increase the amount of blood that flows to our arms, legs, and the primitive parts of our brain that are associated with our self-protective, fight-or-flight-or-freeze instinct. And they reduce the amount of blood that flows toward both the higher-functioning parts of the brain—those associated with executive function and cognition, for example—as well as parts of the body that manage less urgent functions, such as our digestion, reproduction, and so on. Once the threat subsides, blood flow resumes to the higher-functioning parts of the brain, and the body carries on with many of its less-essential functions.

Why does this matter?

"When people feel that they don't belong and if they're not socially comfortable, it's exceedingly hard for their brains to learn," Dr. Aronson says. "We don't get good at algebra when we're under the threat of rejection."

"Good teachers often understand that before a child can be engaged at the cognitive level, the child has to have a trust in the situation," says Dr. Steele. "The challenge a teacher has in a diverse environment is to develop the trust of all those students—that she cares about them and realizes that they have real potential. Without that trust students are not likely to engage. If they do, a variety of curricula may work."

It's also hard for students to perform their best on a test if they feel uncomfortable.

"It actually impairs people's intelligence when they are in a situation where they feel they don't fit in," says Dr. Aronson.

THE THREAT IN THE AIR

How does rejection relate to pop quizzes, exams, and SAT tests?

Researchers now know that anything that triggers a person's fear that they don't belong can depress their performance in all types of high-stakes performance situations, including when they take tests. This phenomenon, called *stereotype threat,* is defined as the nervousness and anxiety people feel when they know that a negative stereotype about their group or about themselves exists in a given situation and they fear that they might do something that would confirm the stereotype.

"When we are in a performance situation and want to do well on something that's difficult and we're worried that someone will judge us through the lens of a negative stereotype, our concerns about what others will think make us underperform," says psychologist Nilanjana Dasgupta, an associate professor at the University of Massachusetts.

Though we usually think of threats as being physical, stereotype threat exists "in the air," says Dr. Steele. To understand, just consider how prevalent the following notions are and how often even well-meaning adults make black boys aware of them: Black boys aren't as smart; they aren't doing well in school; they have behavior problems; they're an "endangered species"; they can't afford to become "a statistic"; they're "more likely to go to prison than to college"; and so on.

Stereotype threat is defined as the nervousness and anxiety people feel when they know that a negative stereotype about their group or about themselves exists in a given situation and they fear that they might do something that would confirm the stereotype.

These types of messages can crop up in any area of life and come from anyone, and that's part of what makes them so dangerous.

"So the students, even though they're standing there on the same campus, in the same room, with the same teacher, they're really in very different environments," wrote Dr. Steele. "And that's what's been difficult for we educators to appreciate, the difference in those environments."[4]

We'll give you a less academic example of how stereotype threat plays out—and how anyone can be affected. Researchers at Princeton University discovered that when you tell white students that you're going to measure their "natural athletic ability," they golf a lot worse than when you don't tell them anything. Why? Because they are aware of the stereotype about white folks and sports—that (at least compared to black people) they (supposedly) have less "natural athletic ability." You've heard the stereotype before—in fact, they even made a movie out of it: "White men can't jump!" But tell black students that you're measuring their "natural athletic ability," and it has no effect on their performance. Because the stereotype is that black people are naturally athletic, and we know that. But tell black students something about their golf performance that triggers their fears that a negative stereotype will be applied to them—for example, that their score reflects their "strategic ability," which puts the stereotype about their intelligence into play—and their golf score will suffer. White students given the same message will golf normally. On a course that typically took about twenty-three strokes to complete, researchers found that white students took three more strokes and black students took five extra strokes to complete the course when they thought a negative stereotype about themselves was relevant in that situation.[5]

But golf is just a game. Imagine what happens when your grades or your ability to get into a good college—or to qualify for a certain type of job—are on the line.

It turns out, as well, that researchers can depress the test scores of "very strong white male math students . . . Stanford students whose . . . average self-rate math skills were very strong."

When told that they were taking a test in which Asians do better than whites, these students scored three points lower on an eighteen-point test than white male participants who were not told anything.[6]

"Even white males at the top of the math bell curve can be made to mess up on a math test, simply by telling them that we're going to compare them to Asian students," says Dr. Aronson. "This had a big effect, which, interestingly, is about the size of the full black-white test score gap."

Say what?!

Even when you confront people who some would argue are among the most privileged members of American society—white, male math students at Stanford who haven't had their group's math inferiority "hammered into their heads"—with a negative stereotype about themselves, you can rattle them so much that their test performance plummets by the same amount as a black boy who worries that someone will think he's less intelligent.[7] This is the same test-score gap that some experts attribute to genetic inferiority, poverty, and coming from a family without a lot of education. Imagine how our Stanford math students might perform if they faced this threat all day, every day.

Then again, maybe we don't have to imagine. Maybe we only need to look at the example of former president George W. Bush, a Yale and Harvard graduate from a family with tremendous intergenerational wealth and cultural capital. From addressing foreign leaders in the wrong language to calling them by the wrong titles to using the wrong words, President Bush clearly experienced performance anxiety when he had to speak in public. But even though people joke about him being dumb, Dr. Aronson points out that he got a respectable 1330 out of 1600 on his SATs.

"As he was fond of saying, people 'misunderestimated' him," Dr. Aronson says. "We often 'misunderestimate' our students if they are forced to perform in an environment that is making them nervous about whether they are going to confirm a stereotype. You can see that no explicit bigotry is required. All of us can put ourselves in this kind of situation because we are human beings."

STEREOTYPED AND STIGMATIZED

Minority students are most at risk of stereotype threat.

"It doesn't matter which culture you look at, whichever group is outcast or marginalized—even if they share 100 percent of the genetic makeup of the dominant group—they will always do worse on intelligence tests and always do worse in school," says Dr. Aronson.

"Anywhere in the world when a group is stereotyped and stigmatized, you see the same thing: the underperforming in school, the behavior problems," says Dr. Steele. "This is not just something about African Americans, every similar group in the world has precisely the same kinds of problems. If you look at the Barakumin in Japan, you see the same problems. But when they migrate to the United States and look like any other Japanese, all of these problems go away."

African Americans—especially boys—"feel this threat, this pressure, in any situation in which intellectual abilities are at test or at issue," says Dr. Steele.

"It's psychologically threatening to be told that your group doesn't do well on this measure and, oh by the way, here's this measure," says Dr. Aronson. "Performance pressure, test anxiety—this happens a lot more to black students than white students. I think that black students' test results often cause them to be underestimated. Worrying while you're taking a test is distracting."

Our use of the term *African American,* rather than *black,* in this context is deliberate. Because black boys who are born in America—and particularly those whose parents trace their lineage to slavery—test lower than black immigrants from Africa, the Caribbean, and other parts of the African Diaspora.

"Immigrants come over here, and they haven't been brought up in this stew of racist images, so they haven't internalized them," Dr. Aronson says. "So you can put them in a stereotype threat situation, and it doesn't resonate with them; they don't feel inferior."

But just give American culture time.

One study found that while first-generation West Indian students perform better under stereotype-threat situations, second-generation West Indian students show declines in performance similar to those experienced by African American students.[8] And even though first- and second-generation black and Hispanic immigrants may not identify with broad American racial categories and therefore may be more resistant to stereotype threat than are domestically born African Americans, an achievement gap exists relative to their equally qualified white classmates. Not surprisingly, some second-generation immigrant students begin to experience certain of the academic-performance-depressing elements of stereotype threat that African American students do.

The data is limited but they are beginning to suggest that over time, the children of black immigrants become American—African American.

THE FLIPPED SCRIPT

The flip side of stereotype threat is *stereotype lift,* which occurs when a person performs better than usual because they know a positive stereotype applies to them in that area.

"If you remind a guy that he's a guy before a math test, he does better," says Dr. Aronson. "If you remind a girl she's a girl, then she does worse."

The same holds true in other areas of performance.

"You may be watching them rain threes during practice, but you know you're going to beat them," says one father who coaches his son's basketball team, describing the stereotype lift black children may experience on the basketball court, an area of life where the stereotype works in their favor. Even if a black boy's not the greatest basketball player, "he can endure a lot of frustration without feeling discouraged in the same way because his group is seen—stereotyped—as belonging there," says Dr. Steele.

So if you put a white male in a situation in which he has to recall his race and gender before a test—say, when filling out the demographic information before the SATs—he's going to perform better. But move the demographic information from the front of the SATs to the end, and the advantages that white boys experience tend to disappear. When researchers test this theory, white girls' scores go up in math and black students' scores go up overall.

The impact of stereotype threat is so compelling that stereotype threat researchers have pressured the Educational Testing Service and College Board to remove the request for demographic information, and the companies' own research bears the concern out, Dr. Aronson tells us. Parents, educators, and allies of other races should press for this change so that our young people achieve results that accurately reflect their abilities.

DOUBLING DOWN

We want to add some complexity to the negative stereotype that black children don't care about their academic performance.

"Certainly for middle-class families education is such an essential value in the African American community, and people don't realize that," says Dr. Steele. "People look at you funny when you say that, but it's true. It's always been seen as part of the way up and linked to mobility."

For example, if you ask parents of ninth-graders of all races what level of education they expect their student to attain, black parents

(28 percent) are far more likely than Asian (23 percent), Hispanic (24 percent), or white (16 percent) parents to say that they expect their child to get a J.D., Ph.D., or other high-level professional degree.[9]

In fact, the first response that many black children have when they experience stereotype threat is not to quit but to try extra hard.

"The way it interferes with performance is not by getting people to give up so much as it causes them to try too hard," says Dr. Steele.

Ironically, this increased effort ratchets up their anxiety, causing them to underperform once again relative to their abilities.

At this point they get confused because they have less-than-fully-developed brains, and often they don't have anyone to talk to about the reasons that their results are lower than they expected. Confronted with parents and teachers who also do not understand what is going on and are disappointed and worried that they may be about to "become a statistic," our children double down on their efforts. They often study more and try even harder. But the extra anxiety may undermine their results and, again, their test results won't reflect their efforts.

"Without language it's hard for them to describe this aspect of their experience," Dr. Steele says.

The pressure from all parties continues to rise.

"Donald has always been a good student, but he's started getting bad grades on his tests. I can't figure out what's going on," says Dee, the mother of a twelve-year-old. "I keep asking him 'What are you doing? You must not be studying hard enough, or something.' He insists that he's studying. But if you're studying hard, why aren't you getting good grades?"

Other members of a child's Village may be called in or kick in.

We experienced this firsthand with Idris, who once had a well-meaning teacher who was extremely anxious about controlling his behavior so that (as she saw it) he wouldn't fail. This woman was Latina, a leader in the New York City independent schools community, and she was on a mission to save boys of color—she was very well meaning. But her anxiety about Idris became a nightmare for our family. If Idris scored one point lower than she thought he should, she would be on the phone to us. She spoke over and over about wanting him to "make it." Apparently she believed that the way to counter the negative stereotypes of black males was to be overly vigilant about even normal interactions. But these exchanges made Idris feel anxious, and test-taking became more stressful for him, causing him to experience the very outcome that she had intended to prevent. Idris fell victim to stereotype threat. Eventually we had to ask everybody to take a step back and to stop pressing him about his grades but support him in other ways to alleviate his stress.

In *Whistling Vivaldi: How Stereotypes Affect Us and What We Can Do,* Dr. Steele wrote, "Perhaps the chief discovery of our research is that the protective side of the human character can be aroused by the mere prospect of being negatively stereotyped, and that, once aroused, it steps in . . . to such an extent that less capacity is left over for the work at hand."

TWICE AS GOOD

Everything the experts have told us makes us believe that stereotype threat is a tremendous risk to black boys' socioemotional and academic well-being—particularly when they are integrating or are one of only a few black males in their environment. And our personal experiences have taught us the same thing.

Most concerning, it doesn't occur only in test-taking situations.

"You have to prove yourself as being really smart in one class, and then you move to the next class and have to prove yourself again," says Dr. Steele. "You have to go through your whole life proving yourself, as long as you are in the domain in which the stereotype applies."

According to Dr. Steele, as children struggle to achieve results that reflect their skills and level of preparation, some kids begin to disidentify or disengage in order to protect their self-regard. This may take the form of not wanting to participate or acting up or clowning or other behavior that distances themselves psychologically from the negative feedback they are receiving.

"It gets very onerous and kids resist that," Dr. Steele says. "They look for other areas of life in which they can feel more comfortable. Certainly sports is one of them, and maybe in inner-city situations, gangs may be one of them. Getting away from this weight is something that kids go through, and it's difficult for parents to appreciate because we don't really have the language to talk about it."

Ironically, this behavior as well may act as a Catch-22, confirming negative stereotypes of black boys not being interested in school.

The pressure may be (unintentionally) compounded by some of the mantras that our sons' Village passes along to them that they have to be "twice as good."

"Our parents' admonitions ring in our ears that we are supposed to bear down and overcome these stereotypes, use them to motivate excellence, and so forth," Dr. Steele says. "But we don't understand that the effort to disprove stereotypes over a prolonged period of time is something that almost nobody can do."

And it may surprise you who is at greatest risk: ironically, it's often the strongest students and those who care the most about doing well. Young people who aren't invested in doing well in a particular area aren't fazed by the negative stereotypes, because they don't care whether they prove or disprove them.

"Their parents and all the people around them may not understand. 'What in the world? Why is this happening?' The teachers may be pulling for them, and so on," says Dr. Steele. "But they are experiencing this pressure, it's having a frustrating and ongoing, almost interminable, effect on their performance relative to other kids they're going to school with. And it's painful, and they need to get away from it."

Dr. Aronson says that parents and teachers need to pay particular attention to what our children do after their performance disappoints them.

"How do you respond after you don't do well? Well, a lot of people respond by trying to protect their self-esteem," he says. "One surefire way to do that is to stop caring about the thing you failed at. One way to show that you don't care is to stop trying."

It doesn't mean a child is bad, doesn't care, or is beyond being helped—this is a sign they're defeated. It can happen to anyone.

"The West Coast is experiencing white stereotype threat in quantitative fields because of the strong performance and almost domination of Asian students," says Dr. Steele. "A lot of white males are giving up in math in San Francisco high schools because they think it's an Asian domain."

BETTER, FASTER, STRONGER

We can counter some of the effects of stereotype threat by teaching children what researchers call a *growth mind-set*. In essence, the growth mind-set requires us merely to tell our child the truth about intelligence—that the brain is like a muscle and that hard work helps to make you smarter.

There are more than thirty years of research led by Stanford psychologist Carol S. Dweck about the widely held belief that intellect or talent are the recipes for success, which "leaves people vulnerable to failure, fearful of challenges and unwilling to remedy their shortcomings," Dr. Dweck writes.[10]

During her days teaching elementary and middle school, Dr. Dweck observed that some students gave up when they encountered difficulty whereas other students persisted and continued to learn. In her later research she discovered what separated the two types of learners, which she labeled "helpless" and "mastery-oriented."

The helpless learners believed that intelligence was a fixed trait, a mind-set that Dr. Dweck labeled "fixed." This is the opposite of the growth mind-set.

"Mistakes crack their self-confidence because they attribute errors to a lack of ability, which they feel powerless to change," she wrote. "They avoid challenges because challenges make mistakes more likely and looking smart less so. . . . Such children shun effort in the belief that having to work hard means they are dumb."

The mastery-oriented students believed that intelligence can be developed through education and hard work.

"They want to learn above all else," she writes. "After all, if you believe that you can expand your intellectual skills, you want to do just that. Because slip-ups stem from a lack of effort, not ability, they can be remedied by more effort. Challenges are energizing rather than intimidating; they offer opportunities to learn."

In one study, Dr. Dweck and her colleagues found that at the start of junior high, the math scores of students with a growth mind-set were comparable to those of the students with a fixed mind-set. But the scores of the growth-mind-set students overtook those of students with a fixed mind-set *by the end of the first semester*—and the gap widened over time.

Students with a growth mind-set believed that learning was more important than getting good grades and that if they worked hard enough at something, they could become better at it.

"Following an incremental model that says 'my ability expands with effort' means that if I experience frustration in the domain of the stereotype, I'm just going to have to work harder. It doesn't mean that I don't belong here and had better get out," says Dr. Steele.

"Our job is to get better—not to be perfect, not to be flawless, not to avoid mistakes, not to win every time, but to get better," says Dr. Aronson, who has conducted research in this area.

"I think that the traditional model in the classroom—the fact that you're spoon-fed info, told 'It's done like this' and 'Just tell me the answer,' or you approach things in the factory way—creates a catch or a double-edged sword," says Tim, a middle school teacher. "Because if you don't do it that way, you fall on your face, and there's no opportunity to get up, start again, and do it a different way and win. I'm not about the 'right answer,' I'm about the process. That's why I'm really into project-based learning. In project-based learning we can say, 'This didn't work, so let's try that. Or this avenue wasn't successful, let's try this.' I think that the exploration together allows you to experience some discomfort but then some wins at the same time."

The persistence of the fixed model of intelligence when the scientific community—not to mention the rest of the world—has moved on to the growth model makes us wonder what purpose the fixed model serves in American culture. We wonder if it persists because it protects some people's privilege and keeps others "in their place," so to speak.

When we teach our sons that they have the power to increase their intelligence, every situation becomes a learning experience rather than a test of whether he belongs there or not or whether he's smart or not.

"I'm taking the same test, but now I understand it as a chance to learn. And because my ability in this area can get better if I practice, if I deliberately practice," says Dr. Steele, who uses the phrase "deliberate practice" to signify that you can apply yourself more and develop a better strategy to improve in it.

"Failure now means something quite different," Dr. Aronson says. "It doesn't mean you're irrevocably, irredeemably stuck. It means you might have had a bad day, but it may also mean that you learned something and your job then becomes to figure out what that is. And learning doesn't preclude making mistakes or even feeling stupid from time to time."

"When we first opened the school, our first year they tried to keep us out of the public league in basketball. They said you'll have ninth- and tenth-graders and lose all the time," says Dave Hardy, president and CEO of Boys' Latin High School in Philadelphia. "My answer to that was, so what? They're gonna get better; next year they'll be experienced varsity players. And we won our division and made the playoffs."

This is very different from what many black parents teach our children—that our kids can't afford to make a mistake. Although we'll be honest: It's easy for a black boy to make a life trajectory–altering mistake. That's why we are placing so much emphasis on helping our sons develop their prefrontal cortex. But we think it's worth exploring the idea that parents and other members of the Village need to channel our anxiety about black males' academic performance differently. Instead, let's communicate very high expectations of them, help them be responsible, and hold them accountable. But within that, give them room to explore themselves, test the far boundaries of their ability, and in the process let them fail. At the same time we can talk about failure as part of a learning process that they can recover from rather than being devastating and permanent.

"I always tell our students that if you come through here and don't fail anything, you haven't tried anything hard," says Hardy. "Failure in and of itself isn't a bad thing."

The school boasts highly ranked teams in Latin, mock trial, robotics, and entrepreneurship competitions as well as football, basketball, and soccer. It sends three-quarters of its students to college—twice the rate of boys of all races who attend college citywide. This in a school that has "very few middle-class kids."

"I'm the type that believes that the tougher things are for kids earlier in life, the better off they are because they learn to deal with it," says one father. "They have to learn how to fail. Or to be disappointed."

Along these lines, we also wonder what kinds of progress we could make if we teach our young people that you become good at something not because you're a "natural" but because you practice and work hard to get there—part of the message that propelled the Civil Rights generation but that seems to have gotten lost in mainstream America's hedonistic, quick-fix culture.

Dr. Dweck encourages people to praise children's effort, which reinforces the growth mind-set, as opposed to their talent or giftedness, which supports the fixed mind-set.

Rather than going along to get along when our sons want to quit something that frustrates them, we can encourage them to stick with it but to try harder, develop another strategy, or try a different approach.

After one study of fifth-graders who had just been given a nonverbal IQ test, "we praised some of them for their intelligence: 'Wow. . . . That's a really good score. You must be smart at this.' We commended others for their effort: 'Wow. . . . That's a really good score. You must have worked really hard,'" Dr. Dweck writes.[11]

The children congratulated for their intelligence shied away from challenging assignments more often than children who were applauded for their effort. And when the researchers gave children hard problems, the ones who'd been praised for being smart became discouraged; those praised for their effort didn't lose confidence when faced with hard problems.

We can teach our young people that our job is to provide for them, but their job is to learn. And just as adults sometimes feel frustrated at work, learning often involves not knowing the answer, feeling frustrated, sometimes even failing. All of these situations give our young people the opportunity to learn something new, although the learning may not be what they—or we—had expected.

For example, we could press our sons who have the capacity for it to take honors-level and AP classes, even knowing that the work will be harder and they may risk getting a lower grade—a grade that will be weighted more heavily because it's honors or AP.

Studying expert Stephen Jones, associate dean for student and strategic programs and associate dean in the College of Engineering at Villanova University, notices that black high school students take easier classes than they are capable of. "They say, 'Well, this is gonna be more work.' But they don't understand that the additional work is going to prepare them for higher levels of learning and the colleges they would like to select."

"Sometimes you don't always get the best results. You can study relentlessly and still get an F. But you look at it and you go, it just requires that I work even harder. And it makes you feel good to know that I may have failed, but I worked hard," says Jamir, 16.

"Once you acknowledge that something is hard, teaching your child to enjoy the struggle takes away its most upsetting implication—that it means you're stupid. Then you can learn to sit back, enjoy the struggle, and find some pleasure in it," says Dr. Aronson. He recounts that after one three-hour intervention in which black college students were taught the growth mind-set, their grades went up half a grade point—across the board.

"It's all about teaching them that they can get smarter," Dr. Aronson says.

"Over the past fifteen years, I have played a lot of pickup basketball with kids," says Peter, an eighth grade teacher. "I noticed that kids don't play as hard as they used to because if they try and get beat they look like a 'punk,' whereas if they don't try and get beat, they just look like, 'Oh, I just didn't try.' But it's the kids who are trying really hard and getting beaten anyway and then going on the court again who are winning."

TIME ON TASK

Research also shows that it's a mistake to tell middle school–aged black boys that they're smart—even though we do it to try to boost their self-esteem. When they think they're smart innately, they have a tendency to believe that they no longer have to work for it—and the working for it, rather than the belief that they're naturally smart is what builds their self-worth.

"If we can find an easy way to get an A, we look for it. But when you get it, sometimes you go: I really didn't work for this; I really didn't get here on my own," says Alex, 17. "But when you struggle night after night studying, and you're struggling to do this work and you get that test, and you aced that test, you go: I did this myself. That worked. That hard work, those hours of lost sleep—I did that. It's mine. You claim that grade because you worked for it."

As parents we should emphasize our son's *time on task,* the amount of time he spends actually engaged in learning the activity— say, studying or doing his homework—as opposed to just *seat time,* which could be spent doodling, doing administrative work, getting organized, or monkeying around and avoiding studying. Time on task is the primary driver of performance in most areas of life, whether in music, math, or sports.

> "You get a Tiger Woods or a Mozart because they began shockingly early in their life to do the task and were given a lot of support to do it," Dr. Steele says. "So by the time other kids their age begin to enter the activity, they look like geniuses. In reality their higher level of performance is linked to this earlier time on task in a structured, well-instructed way."

In other words, they are closer to the ten thousand hours of practice that Malcolm Gladwell, in *Outliers: The Story of Success,* correlates with mastery. Joe finds that low-income people in particular are fixated on the notion of the gifted child, not realizing how much "God blessed" and "special" "geniuses"—people such as Dr. Ben Carson—prepared to become great at what they do.

"Oftentimes somebody who's 'not good in math' is just somebody who hasn't been interested in or immersed in it, or had it taught to them as well, so they don't perform as strong as the other students because they don't have a background in it," says Dr. Steele. "If they applied themselves, they could incrementally get better and maybe become very good in math."

This is one reason why it's important to give our sons exposure to a wide variety of activities in life, starting when they are very young.

"You really have to give and expand kids' exposure to different experiences. Then you have to give them a chance to be deeply involved in those experiences," says Dr. Noguera. "It is when they get the attachment to playing music, that's when they start to say 'I'm a musician' or, 'I'm a scientist, because I belong to a science club and those are my friends who are also a part of that club' or 'I'm a chess player' or whatever it is—a deep social involvement—that leads to the expansion of what your possibilities are for identity."

Once a child begins to identify with an activity, when the going gets tough the work means more to them. Whether it's reading, math, dance, or volunteer work, we need to see the hours put into an activity as investments in our sons' future as well as our collective well-being.

WHAT'S MY NAME?

Researchers believe that one way parents may be able to improve our sons' test performance is by teaching him an *achievement-oriented identity*. Every human being has more than one way of identifying themselves. For example, your son may be black, male, your child, someone's brother or sister, a Central High Mountain Lion, a grandchild, an athlete, a musician, an artist, and so on—all at the same time.

Some data suggest that if an African American child's sense of self includes the expectation of high academic performance, they're more likely to achieve.

"If black children see achievement as congruent with their group's identity, they may be motivated to make that identity come true," Dr. Aronson says. "However, if achievement's not congruent with my group's identity, it's like, 'We don't do this.'"

We can build such expectations into our family narrative.

"I went to Morehouse, my brother went to Morehouse, my father went to Morehouse—we're Morehouse men," says Warren. "You come in this house with anything lower than a B, and we're going to have a problem."

"My children's father and I gave our son and daughter African names intentionally. My living room wall has books on it. My house has art from all around the Diaspora. I drag them to every cultural event that comes to town—sometimes kicking and screaming, but I make them come. I want them to know that they come from kings and queens—from excellence—not all this mess they see on television," says Princess.

Having an achievement-oriented identity means that our sons have to spend not only a lot of time on task learning a topic but also time studying their subjects and preparing for tests. Being highly prepared and comfortable with material helps reduce stereotype threat.

"It's important to know how do you take a multiple-choice test? How do you take an essay exam? How do you get most prepared?" says Dr. Jones. "The more knowledge that you have before you take those multiple-choice or essay examinations, the more you're likely to make the right choice."

It is extremely important to study for the PSATs, SATs, and other college-admission tests rather than studying the week before or just showing up cold—not only to avoid stereotype threat but also to compete with the many other children who get years of preparation from their parents, teachers, tutors, and test-prep companies. Many black students begin studying too late or don't study at all, says Dr. Jones, even though many schools now offer their own SAT-prep programs.

"Today 60 to 70 percent of students taking the SAT have gone through private tutoring and classes, and now you're sitting at the exam and you've never done it before. You don't know how the overall test operates, how many hours it takes, what that's going to feel like, how to keep your energy level high. They've had that opportunity and it's an advantage," says Dr. Jones.

Between taking the PSAT, a test-prep class, and doing practice tests at home, Idris had taken the SAT twelve times before he sat down for the actual test. This gave him the chance to get comfortable with the test instructions, the various formats, and the subject matter as well as build his test-taking skills. Compare that to a kid on his basketball team who took it three times, yet his parent insisted he was prepared. The second time the boy's score went down because he took the SAT in the fall after not studying all summer—that is, his score suffered because he had experienced summer slide.

Too many times black students do not take the PSAT until the fall of their junior year and the SAT until the fall of their senior year. That's too late.

"You're competing against students who have already submitted their college applications at that point," says Dr. Jones.

Instead, our children should prepare during tenth grade to take the PSAT, ideally during either the second semester of tenth grade, but no later than the first semester of eleventh grade. Children should take the SAT for the first time ideally during the first semester—but no later than the spring—of their junior year.

"That gives them the ability to take it more than once, if they don't get the results they want," says Dr. Jones, who notes that colleges will take your highest score on each of the math, reading, and written portions of the tests. "If they wait until first semester of their senior year and don't get the results they want, they're going to submit their application late."

Dr. Jones's book *Seven Secrets of How to Study: Parent's Ultimate Education Guide* (www.studyskills2u.weebly.com/books.html) provides an extremely detailed annual checklist that lays out the time-frame students and parents can follow from grades nine through twelve.

WHAT EDUCATORS CAN DO

But parents aren't the only ones who can address stereotype threat. There's a lot that educators at all levels can do.

Dr. Steele emphasizes the role that teachers of diverse students can play in helping their students of color excel by taking an interest in them, their families, and their lives; by earning their trust; and by helping them understand that they see their potential.

It's also important that schools build a critical mass of students of color. That factor alone diminishes the sense that students don't belong. Parents should ask for demographic information before immersing their child in an environment.

"One time I tried to talk to a teacher about what it means to our son that he's the only black boy in his class, just so she could be aware of how that felt to him. Immediately she deflected what I was saying: 'Oh, but we have an Indian student in the class,' " says Amanda, the mother of a third-grader. "How can we problem-solve about the impact of racial dynamics when educators can't even talk about race?"

Educators can also make an environment more inviting by having a diverse staff—and not just in the cafeteria, as one student we spoke with noted about his private school.

"Where I live there are no black teachers," says one parent of a sixteen-year-old son. "I have gone to the table with the superintendent in my district. There are all these schools and no black teachers. Where are all the black teachers? My son in eleventh grade has his first black counselor. The schools say, 'There's such a paucity of black teachers.' Well, this district attracts black doctors and lawyers to live in it. There are more black teachers than there are doctors and lawyers. So where are you looking? They say they can't find any."

Teachers can also invite diverse speakers to cover a wide variety of topics (not just Black History Month) and make sure that the images around the school make all students feel that they belong.

"I want my students to see people like them in all sorts of professions they don't expect," says Amy, who teaches in a predominately black inner-city school. "We invite scientists, mathematicians, astronomers, people from the CIA—all sorts of professionals who look like our students. It really expands their sense of who they can become. I love it when, say, a black airline pilot comes to school and it blows my students' minds. You can see their self-esteem shoot up."

Dr. Aronson emphasizes the importance of building a school identity that makes all students feel as though they belong there.

"It's important to create situations in which students don't feel like they are being rejected by their teachers or their fellow students or by the academy in general," says Dr. Aronson. "The best schools in the world make fitting in and belonging a priority because they recognize that in order to learn, perform, and be motivated, we need to feel that we belong and that we matter."

And in spite of all the negative stereotypes in society, it's incredibly important that teachers have high expectations of black boys.

"If teachers believe kids are genetically inferior or not interested in school for whatever reason or have limited potential, they teach them in a way that makes them live down to those negative expectations," Dr. Aronson says. "If teachers are less warm, if they spend less time with their students, are less forgiving of mistakes, accept lower achievement as normal given the kids' race, research on teacher expectations shows that they tend to have a much more significant effect on black kids than white kids. To a very significant degree, black children tend to become what their teachers expect them to become. If the teacher has a low opinion, it's more likely that a black student than a white student will lower themselves to meet that expectation."

Keeping the Promise

1. **Tell our children the truth about intelligence.** The truth is, our brains really are like a muscle that gets stronger through exercise. We can strengthen our intelligence through work.

2. **Stereotype threat is real, but it can be combated.** Stereotype threat accounts for a surprisingly large share of the test-score gap, but it can be combated—and even reversed.

3. **Let our children fail.** Failure and challenge teach our children resilience and the importance of hard work.

10

MAKE YOUR PRESENCE FELT IN HIS SCHOOL

How to Participate in Our Sons' Formal School and Advocate for Change

I like to go into the classroom because I get to keep an eye on the teacher, to see directly what the teacher's doing, and also to let the teacher know that I care and my son does have a dad—and, actually, a dad who's able to come in.

It also allows me to be there for the other kids. Because a lot of black boys and black girls and white kids don't get to see a black male who comes in wearing business attire and is helping them. A lot of the pictures that you see in the media are of the white female teacher and the white tutor with the black kids.

I see a lot of the boys around town because I coach, and my sons play in various basketball leagues. That allows me to keep an eye on the boys when I see them at the rec center, the mall, or when they're out and about—I can speak into their lives on various topics because they already know me, and I've helped them.

Coming into the classroom also translates directly to my work as an activist. I can speak directly to what's happening: "No, I was in the classroom yesterday. I know exactly what goes on there."

So it's an hour very, very well spent.

At one point one teacher whose classroom I started going into and getting involved in started talking with me about something, and I mentioned that I am an educator.

And she was like, "Oh, I didn't know you were an educator."

So I told her, "Yeah, I'm a professor of education."

Of course she wanted to know where, so she forced me to lay it on her that it's at a pretty prestigious university.

Her reaction was like I had said I'm a Nobel laureate.

It was like, "I had no idea. You?!" It was just so over the top. So that's been a huge disappointment. It doesn't matter if you show up in a service uniform or a suit, the teachers are just not ready.

—*Edward, the father of three sons*

MAKE YOUR VOICE HEARD

We have a tremendous amount of power to achieve our objectives. No matter whether our son attends a prep school (as Idris did), a charter school, or the neighborhood school, black parents can make our voices heard and our presence felt in ways that increase the chances that our boy will get the best education that his school has to offer. One of the most effective ways of taking charge of our child's educational experience is by rolling up our sleeves and getting involved in his school.

In this chapter we'll focus on the essential role that we can play in helping our son get the education he deserves:

- We'll tell you why it's important to become involved in his school as well as ways to do it if you are strapped for time.
- We'll share strategies for interacting in ways that will help build a supportive environment of educators, fellow parents, and extended family caregivers who can help him excel academically, socially, and emotionally and protect him from harm.
- You'll learn about the role that academic tracking plays in determining his chances of going to college as well as what classes he needs to take to end up on the four-year-college-bound track.
- We'll give you the inside scoop about many educators' fear of conflict in general and fear of racial issues in particular. And we hope to encourage you to join the grassroots movement to help our sons obtain educational equity.

Note that unlike in the other chapters, in this chapter we use the real names of most of our parent activists. That's because they've asked us to.

"When you are an advocate, you belong to the people," says Asad Shabazz, a parent activist in Columbus, Ohio. "It's critical when we advocate that we are available to the people."

> **Promise your son that you will increase the odds that he'll succeed academically by visiting his school at least eight times a year, developing relationships with educators that inspire them to invest in his growth and development, forging relationships with other parents in your son's classroom and school, protecting him from forces that could undermine his success, and committing to join the fight to help all black and brown children fulfill their potential.**

ALL HANDS ON DECK

As we speak to parents around the country, they repeatedly tell us that they want their sons to be safe, get a great education, experience a diverse environment, and grow up in a community of co-parents who have his best interests at heart.

"Black parents want their children to be respected and appreciated by their teachers, by parents of other students, and to have community," says Adria Welcher, Ph.D., an assistant professor of sociology at Georgia Gwinnett College, who is studying how black middle-class families make decisions about education. "They want to feel like everybody is co-parenting together, to feel like we're all on the same road and striving for the same goals."

Research shows that children whose parents are involved at school have higher educational aspirations, are more motivated, perform better academically, and behave better than students whose parents aren't involved.[1] Involved parents are better positioned to monitor what's going on, understand school and classroom activities and dynamics, and match their son's preparation at home with what's going on at school. Teachers tend to pay more attention to kids whose parents are highly involved. They are also quicker to identify problems that could interfere with your son's learning.[2]

"Schools get away with a lot of stuff because the parents are absent," says Asad Shabazz. "An absent parent allows teachers and schools to act with impunity. They can do whatever they want because there's an absence of parent leadership. Some of them will say, 'This is a throw-away kid—we don't ever hear from or see their parents.' You want them to say, 'That mother ain't no joke; don't mess with that parent.'"

And let's face it: A child is more likely to behave well when he knows that one of his caregivers will attend his band concert and might knock on his classroom door at any moment.

"One day all of a sudden all of my friends were telling me that my mother was at the school—she just showed up kind of out of the blue," says Jaylen, 14. "I was like, 'Oh, no, what the heck?' I had been goofing off and having kind of a food fight in the lunch room the day before, and I thought that she found out about it. Later on I found out her visit was totally random. But after that I figured that I probably shouldn't do that again."

"Oh, yes, screw up and I *will* show up at school and come into your classroom and embarrass you in front of all of your little friends—believe it," says Andrea. "I tell all of my children that. And you only have to do it once, and it scares the mess out of them!"

Research conducted by Ivory Toldson shows that the parents of the most successful students come to their child's school eight times each year on average.[3] We should strive to meet or exceed that—and many of us can; we may just have to be strategic. Even though black and Hispanic parents are often negatively stereotyped as being uninterested and uninvolved in their children's education, all parent participation, including black parent participation, has increased dramatically over the years. Research shows that we are as likely as Asian and white parents to attend scheduled meetings with a teacher as well as general school or PTO/PTA meetings—all groups come in at roughly 90 percent.[4]

"The standard comment about African American parents is that we're less concerned about our children's education because we don't get involved with the schools," says Michael Miller, a leader of Parents of Children of African Descent (PCAD) in the Berkeley, California, school system. "Initially we came together to dispel that myth."

But an opportunity does exist for black and Hispanic parents to extract more resources from our children's educational environment than we currently do. Studies show that while black and Hispanic parents are very likely to attend scheduled meetings, we're significantly less likely—there's a 20 to 25 percent difference each—than white and Asian parents to attend a school event, volunteer at school, or serve on a school committee, all of which not only send positive messages to our son and his school but also put us in place to get the skinny on what's happening there, learn the temperament of his teachers, find out what's up with his peers, gain access to insider resources, and get the lowdown about how he's performing and behaving. Sixty-five percent of black and Hispanic students, 72 percent of Asian students, and 80 percent of white students had a parent who attended a school event. And 35 percent of black students, 32 percent of Hispanic students, but 54 percent of white students and 46 percent of Asian students had a parent who had volunteered their time.[5]

Of course it can be hard to get to your son's school when you're a single parent, have more than one child (who may be attending different schools), your job offers little flexibility, money's too tight to mention, going to the band recital means paying for childcare, and you may not have transportation. And many black parents may have had negative experiences with schools and teachers when they were students (often, at the same school the boy is attending), so may cringe at the thought of interacting with the institutions—often the exact same people—that treated us poorly when we were younger. Adding insult to injury, we've heard many a story about teachers too busy to respond to parents' emails or calls, who were condescending or excessively defensive, or who let the parents know in so many ways that their involvement wasn't wanted. (Note that we've also heard many stories of black parents marching in rude and sporting a 'tude.) But it may also be true that, similar to other recent entrants to the middle class, even black parents who have more resources may not understand the extent to which schools expect and the degree to which they and their child will benefit from their active engagement in their child's educational experience—or know just how to go about it.

Fortunately, the research also shows that we should be able to pull this off. Sixty percent of students who live with both parents, about

half of students living with single parents or stepparents, and 37 percent of children living with guardians already have caregivers who are
highly involved at their school. (In this study "highly involved" meant
that the parent engaged in three out of the following four activities:
attending a school meeting, attending a regularly scheduled parent-
teacher conference, coming to a school or class event, or volunteering
in the classroom. Parents who demonstrated low involvement participated in only one activity.) We may merely need to do it more often.

THIS IS HOW WE DO IT

Black parents not only want similar things for their children as parents from other backgrounds want for theirs, most of them also behave similarly to accomplish those goals.

"The African American parents in the interviews did not seem to
be doing different things than the white parents. They were reading to
their children, they were talking to their friends about what they
should do," says sociologist Annette Lareau, Ph.D., the author of *Unequal Childhoods: Class, Race, and Family Life,* an in-depth study of
the daily lives of twelve black and white families of different socioeconomic classes. "But the African American middle-class parents had a
palpable anxiety about their children's progress in schools. They were
anxious about how their children would be treated by educators," she
adds. We hope that the information we provide in this chapter helps
you channel that anxiety productively.

Dr. Lareau's research shows that know-how about managing a
child's education and the techniques that parents use to do it often
vary across socioeconomic lines. For instance, low-income and
working-class people tend to view teachers as being more expert in
educating their child than the parents are. Consequently they tend to
defer more to educators and expect them to shoulder more of the responsibility for schooling their child than middle-class parents do.

"Parents who have a college degree could have been a teacher;
they just simply chose not to," Dr. Lareau says. "So they are an equal
with the educator or perhaps even a social superior. That provides a

big advantage with reading and language development. They also can monitor the institution to help prevent little problems from becoming big problems. And they can help customize their child's educational experience—working-class kids get a generic education."

Dr. Lareau calls this customizing and monitoring *concerted cultivation,* which also involves actively fostering and assessing their children's talents, skills, and opinions—often by talking to them, teaching them words, helping kids become verbally proficient, reading, exposing kids to ideas. Low-income and working-class parents often provide their children with the basics and then allow their children's life to unfold more naturally and provide their children with more autonomy—an approach that we note is not so different from the *slow parenting* movement that is the rage in some more affluent circles.

While concerted cultivation has its downsides—overscheduling, psychological stress, and backtalk from kids, among them—it gives children a leg up when they start school, which is extremely language-oriented.

"Middle-class parents also supervise schooling with a sense of entitlement, which they convey to their children," Dr. Lareau says.

As more black parents become middle-class, we have a tremendous opportunity to increase the bang we get for our hard-earned tax or school tuition dollar by supervising our children's education in a hands-on style similar to what Dr. Lareau describes.

CREATING RELATIONAL FIBER

One essential aspect of concerted cultivation is helping your son develop a strong attachment with his teachers. You will recall from our conversation on early parenting that a secure attachment tells our son that he's safe and loved and that his needs will be meet. He needs to feel a similar closeness to his educators.

"Learning is about emotion, feeling connected to people, wanting to please people, wanting to work together with somebody," Dr. Lareau says. "It's all about connection."

As parents we help set the stage for that connection to develop. We can start by taking very simple steps to let our son's teacher know that we care about his education. The activities we describe below are among those activities that we believe black parents need to engage in, at a minimum, to help secure their son's education.

We remember one parent who presented himself to his son's teacher at the beginning of every year. He would start off by saying, "My name is Ralph Smith, and this is my son Ralph the 3rd, and he is here to learn."

"The more the school knows that you're a parent who cares, the more they're going to respond to you about your child and work with you. In most cases this just happens if you're the parent who says, 'Contact me,'" says Aisha Ray of the Erikson Institute. "Say to the teacher in the beginning of the school year, 'Here's my cell phone number. Call me when there's good news, bad news, or whatever news, I want to hear from you. I'm also going to contact you.' Then ask for their cell, and if they don't want to give it out, get their email address or ask them to send a note home regularly. That says to that teacher, this is a child who really has an active, engaged parent. I'm gonna look out for this child. Because usually what happens in many schools—and particularly in public schools—is you only hear from the school when your child is in trouble."

Make sure to update your contact information if anything changes. More than one educator has complained to us about parents who get a new number but forget to tell the school. As one principal put it, "Some parents change their phone numbers like they change their underwear. No one likes to scramble down the alpha list to figure out what number works."

When each school year begins, let his teacher know that you'd like to set up a meeting so that you can share information with her (or him) about your son that will help make her life easier and help her to be more successful. Also, share your vision for your son's life.

"Adults have to and should build the relational fiber that says, 'At some point even though I might disagree with you, I have enough of a relationship with you that you can hear what I'm saying even though it might not be what you want to hear, and I hear what you're saying as well,'" says Ron Walker, executive director of Coalition of Schools Educating Boys of Color (COSEBOC).

When Walker was a school principal he would encourage parents and teachers to meet at the start of each school year. In that meeting he suggested that parents ask, "What should my son know, be able to do and understand by the time he leaves your classroom?" says Walker. "If you have a teacher who says, 'Thank you, glad you asked, here's what they should know,' that builds an opportunity for the teacher and parent to engage around their mutual interest, which is the child. If the teacher looks at you cross-eyed, like, 'Why did you ask that?' you have a concern."

Some schools host information sessions for incoming parents and students to communicate "here's how we do things, here are the expectations, we'd like parents to be involved, and so forth," says one educator. If your school does this, take advantage of it. Educators play a vital role in this process. Teachers and principals can help get the year off to a fruitful start by reaching out to parents.

"Teachers need to be proactive in developing relationships with all parents, especially when there's social distance between them and the parent and kid along race, class, or whatever," says Dr. Gregory. "They need to go the extra yard to be able to dialogue."

Most educators will be happy to know that you care and will welcome your involvement. But if your son's teacher doesn't respond as quickly or positively to your overtures as you'd like, don't necessarily take it personally or throw in the towel—many educators are overwhelmed. Keep trying. Also give the principal your contact information. Say, "I gave Miss Smith my cell phone number, and I'm giving you my cell phone number. If there's any problem, I want to hear about it right away, not at the end of the school year," suggests Dr. Ray.

Then again, not all teachers want to be bothered. If your son's teacher continues not to respond to your overtures, deliberately uses big words that you don't understand, talks down to you, or otherwise plays games to intimidate you or discourage you from being involved, reach out to other parents to find out what they're experiencing, talk to the parent advocate at your school, and let the principal know what you're experiencing. With any luck, this won't happen often.

Assuming that your son's teacher encourages you to become engaged in the classroom, ask how you can help her. If you have the flexibility to take time away from work (or work a shift that allows you to visit during the school day), volunteer to help in the classroom, chaperone a school trip, or otherwise pitch in as though your son's teachers and classmates were members of your extended family.

"For me visiting the classroom does a number of things. It gets me in there just to get my own head around and see what's going on. Because it's easy to criticize from outside, but when you sit in that classroom for an hour you're like, 'God bless the teacher for being able to deal with this stuff.' You have to see it—it's very, very hard," says Mark Joseph, an associate professor and director of the National Initiative on Mixed-Income Communities at Case Western Reserve University. "Number two is to support my sons. At least for now, they like seeing me in there. And three, I can be there for the other black boys in the classroom, whose mothers—and especially, for me, their fathers—may not be able to come. I want them to see me there in my suit and know what's possible for them."

"Every few months just show your face so people know you," says Shabazz. "I know who my advocates are at the school, plus the janitor and the lady in the lunch line know me. So it's hard for anyone to pull a trick on me."

If you aren't able to make it into the classroom, there are still many ways to build relationships—from donating a few classroom supplies to baking cupcakes for class parties or events, for instance.

"All we have to do is stay communicating," says Shabazz. "Send an email saying, 'My son came home with a good report card, and we appreciate the good work that's being done.' It's very simple to be proactive. You don't have to be committed to fifty hours a month."

Your involvement can also protect your son by expanding the size of your Village.

"One of the goals during the teen years is to stay under your parents' radar," says Miller. "If parents are actively engaged, they'll know things that their student probably wishes they didn't know. If you can be involved with folks who see your child during the school day, you're going to find out things about your child that at first you'll have a hard time believing—'I can't believe my child actually said something like that!' But it almost takes you back to the type of communities that many of us grew up in, where my parents could easily get a phone call: 'I saw your son over at such and such and he was acting crazy.' That is something we're sorely missing in many of our communities of color."

"My son was the class clown. Once he had a school play, and I went, but he didn't know I was in the audience," says Ellis, the father of two. "When he came home from school, I asked how his day went. He said, 'Fine.' I said, 'Why did you have to act a clown?' Of course his eyes got big. Then I asked, 'Now, how do you think I should discipline you?' He said, 'I think you should do what granddaddy would do,' thinking that he had outsmarted me. You see, my son only knew my father as being docile and peaceful and having Alzheimer's. But I was like, 'Dude, do you know who that guy really is?' That was the only time I ever gave my son a spanking."

And make a point of coming to parents' night, school conferences, report-card nights, band concerts, school plays, and the like. If you can't make it—it may not be possible every time—be sure to call or send an email so that your son's teacher knows both that you care and that you appreciate what they are doing for your son. Also, ask a friend, an extended-family member, or even another parent to attend in your place and have them introduce themselves to the teacher and principal so that they know that a representative of your family is there.

"When I go to the school in the suburbs that my daughter attends, you can't find a parking space, there are so many parents there," says Stephen Jones, associate dean of students and strategic planning at Villanova University. "But within that population, the number of minority parents are few, even though there should be a lot more present. I think that it definitely has to do with the expectation that the school is going to give their child the best education. That the parent doesn't need the same level of involvement because the school's going to do it."

For kids whose parents are less able to be involved, some schools intentionally help to build an extended-family network of caregivers who can strengthen the family and support the children's growth by representing them at back-to-school nights, science fairs, and other school activities. Groups like Extended Family Network (www .extendedfamilynetwork.org), an organization dedicated to creating extended-family relationships to help people nurture their children, can help.

We think it's also essential for parents of color to develop relationships with the parents of their children's friends. Not only are other parents a rich source of information about what's going on in the school, but other moms and dads can help you piece together information about the experience that kids like yours are having in that classroom or at that school. Other parents can also help fill you in on the social dynamics going on between the kids themselves. They can cover for you when you can't come see your children's performances, for example, or give you a ride so that you can.

Michèle would often see mothers of Dalton students getting together for coffee after dropping their children off. She always wondered what they were talking about and wished she could be a fly on the wall, but as a practical matter couldn't participate because she had to rush off to work. But many different places to exchange information exist— from the playground to the hairdresser or barbershop to basketball practice to waiting out front to pick your kids up from school.

Bobbye, whose son has dyslexia, says that relationships with the parents of other children who were in special education with her son helped her feel optimistic about his future. "One of the gifts of my son's learning difference was the gift of encountering other parents whose children were equally gifted and telling each other, 'I can't wait to see what your son's going to do. I know he's going to do something meaningful and great!'" she recalls. She participated in email distribution lists with local parents of children in special education as well as Facebook groups where she could communicate with parents from other cities, states, and even nations.

If an organization that represents the concerns of black parents exists, join it. If one doesn't exist, consider starting one.

"We started sharing stories about our experiences and that's when parents started coming out with stories. Not just that Jimmy's mad at such and such, but why are black kids getting expelled in the fifth grade?" says Tiffany.

When we began to worry about Idris's experiences at Dalton, we invited the parents of the other black boys to our home. As we swapped stories about what was going on, we discovered that our son wasn't the only one having certain experiences. But we also discovered that black parents don't always want to air their dirty laundry about their son's problems, even with each other. We think that this penchant prevents us from coming together to leverage our wisdom and influence collectively; instead, it allows schools to isolate our children as though we're the only ones dealing with these issues. As we talk to black parents, we often find that they don't disclose what's really going on with their son until we're well into the conversation.

Just as we discussed in Chapter 9, every human being fears being rejected. This makes it hard to discuss difficult topics in front of a roomful of people. Small groups of as small as two can help us to overcome such fears by providing a safe space to engage in more difficult conversations than we may feel comfortable having in large groups. Indeed, small groups can become spawning grounds in which we find our voice and learn to advocate more effectively for our children.

If your schedule permits, participate in the Parent-Teacher Organization or Association (PTO or PTA), or start one if it doesn't exist. The PTA is designed to give parents a say in certain school decision-making processes, so it can be a place where you give voice to some of your concerns. It can also be a rich source of insider information about the best teachers, tutoring, after-school programs, scholarships, and other information that travels along the grapevine that grows among active parents. And as some of the parent advocates we spoke to will explain, approached strategically the PTA can become an ally in helping you address the achievement gap and other issues affecting children of color, even in predominately white settings.

"Talk to the PTA or PTO and see if you can be an offshoot of it," says Edye Deloch-Hughes, of Oak Park, Illinois, the former president of her middle school's black parents' organization, African-American Parents for Purposeful Leadership in Education (APPLE), an organization that at one time had focused on cultural events, but she and other parents resurrected it to help close the achievement gap.

The website of the National Parent-Teacher Association (http:// www.pta.org) provides resources for starting or joining a Parent-Teacher Organization as well as an advocacy tool kit for corresponding with members of Congress, lobbying lawmakers, and working with the media. Several parents we've spoken to discovered that getting involved not only helped their son, it also created opportunities for them, as parents, to get mentored.

"One day I was complaining about the cost of school, the cost of sports, the cost of equipment, and everything, when an older woman overheard me. She told me, 'A lot of people treat their children as though they're liabilities. Watch them yelling at children in the supermarket. But children are assets. And what do you do with an asset? Invest. You have to take care of them, put money into them, put time into them, invest in them,'" says Lillian, the mother of a fourteen-year-old son, of the advice her newfound mentor offered. "I had never thought about it like that."

Don't be surprised if not every parent who's already involved is welcoming of your input. Some organizations can be cliquish, and never forget that many parents are vying for the same limited resources. You may represent competition to them. We've heard stories of black parents getting interrogated about who they are and why they want to be involved and even feeling iced out of school social networks. But don't let other people's discomfort with you or attempts to keep you from accessing the best resources stop you from fighting for the education your child deserves. The most important thing is that you get in where you fit in. You can both inform yourself and participate in the conversation in your community from many different angles. Jump in wherever and with whomever you feel most comfortable.

You can kick your involvement to a whole 'nother level by connecting with your son's school advisory board or community school board. Start attending school board meetings to learn what they do and how you (and your student) can make your voice heard about issues like excessive discipline and policies that lock black children out of gifted and talented programs.

The school board is one of the most important places where policy decisions get made. In some communities local businesspeople and other prominent community members who don't have children in the school system are disproportionately represented on some public school boards. This means that their interests will be represented, not yours.

GreatSchools.org has resources to help you understand how a school board operates. And the National School Board Association represents school boards around the nation. Visit its website (http:// www.nsba.org) to tap into its resources.

Like everything else, upping our involvement is a balancing act. And although we highly encourage you to figure out a strategy to get to his school eight times a year, we also realize that depending on the child and family, it may be far more important to read to your son than to rush off to a school board meeting. (Visit www.American Promise.org to access a list of resources that will help you support the black boy in your life.)

ENGAGING YOUR MUTUAL INTEREST

Whether at the start of the school year or when you want to talk about something you're worried about, when you want to meet with your son's teacher, be sure to follow the protocol. Make an appointment with his teacher directly, through the parent coordinator, or by following the school's appointment-making process; don't just show up at the school. Prepare in advance for your conversation by jotting down a few notes. Remember, every interaction presents an opportunity to build your relationship with the people who, day in and day out, are helping to raise and educate your child. All parties should plan for and expect a positive outcome and allow room for the other person to be a little nervous. A lot is at stake, even for meetings that kick off the school year, before anything has actually happened.

Sometimes parent-teacher meetings can be very emotionally charged.

"Everyone's pointing their fingers at teachers, so it's really hard to engage them in an authentic, constructive partnership," says Dr. Joseph, an expert in community-building.

What's more, "Many teachers say they don't know how to talk to parents," says Anne Gregory, an associate professor at the Graduate School of Applied and Professional Psychology at Rutgers University. "There can be an intimidation factor where teachers are on the defensive."

Some of the highly involved parents we've spoken to suggest that we start by thanking our son's teacher for all her hard work and for the love and concern she shows toward our son.

"Just say, 'I get it that you are getting your butt kicked every single day. Thank you for what you're doing. I want to talk about tweaking some things, but I want to help you, so just thank you," says Dr. Joseph.

"Teachers like parents who praise them. So a teacher's ideal of a helpful parent is a parent who is positive," says Dr. Lareau.

Describe to the teacher the ways that you can see your son growing and changing as a result of the things that she or he has taught him and emphasize your commitment to helping him grow and excel. Ask for her thoughts about how he is doing and how you can partner with each other. Don't be offended if the teacher tells you she thinks that there are areas that you can work on together. Your first step should be to listen and learn. Force yourself to say as little as possible during your initial encounters. Instead take notes and ask neutral questions to make sure you understand. (For example, "Can you give me an example of how that manifests itself?" "When does it tend to happen?") Also offer your perspective in a positive and productive way and agree on how you will collaborate with her in the best interests of your son. Whether or not you agree with her thoughts, tell the teacher that you'll think about what she's said—then go home and actually think about it.

"The best relationships I see are when a parent says, 'I need some help.' Or, 'Here's how I'm handling this at home. How does this look to you, who see my son every day?' As opposed to 'I don't want to hear what you've got to say,'" says Walker.

If after considering and working with the information the teacher has given you, you see things differently, call or meet with her again. But don't rush in and tell her how to do her job. And even if you do have suggestions, you don't have to get them all in at once. You have many opportunities to interact with the teacher, so focus at first on arming yourself with the facts.

"Even if you think the teacher isn't that smart or isn't nice to your child, I'd try a lot—five, six, seven, eight, nine, ten times—to build a relationship that is positive, helpful, builds on your mutual interest, and makes learning fun," says Dr. Lareau. "Keep trying even if things aren't going as smoothly as you like or you think things are unfair. It's not a bad lesson for a child: the world is unfair. The reality is we have to work with an unfair world."

If you continue to hit a brick wall, read your school's parent manual (if one exists, and it should) about how to handle a disagreement. Then follow the process the manual describes and talk to the parent advocate, parent coordinator, or counselor to see if they can shed light on or diffuse the situation.

Once you've exhausted these options, talk to the principal. Also reach out to organizations such as the Black Alliance for Educational Options (www.baeo.org), which offers training for parents on how to interact effectively with teachers and principals and holds an annual symposium intended to empower parents.

But while all this is happening, try not to let your son know that you don't like or respect his teacher (if that's how you feel).

"It's corrosive to the child's relationship with the teacher if the child is aware that his mother or father has negative feelings about the teacher," says Dr. Lareau. "It undermines the child's relationship with the teacher because it sets up a loyalty battle between their love for their parent and their attachment to the teacher."

THE INTIMIDATION FACTOR

Sometimes race, gender, and socioeconomics complicate the already difficult dynamic of parent-teacher interactions.

"When black women come to schools to advocate on behalf of their children, they're often viewed as angry and confrontational. Black men are often perceived as criminal, uninterested, or uninvolved," says Adria Welcher. "So if they attempt to advocate on behalf of their children—whether it's searching for a school, interacting with school officials, administrators, teachers, or whatever—the literature suggests that black parents do not receive the same return on their cultural capital that white middle-class parents do."

We've heard many stories about teachers and administrators denying, condescending to, stonewalling, and otherwise dismissing black and Latino parents. We've also heard stories of black parents going off.

"The tendency is, 'I'm going to come in and cuss you out and get what I need for my child,'" says Miller. "It's not going to be a negotiation, it's going to be a fight. That's what was happening with PCAD when we first started meeting. We literally sat down with VPs, principals, teachers, and counselors, and they were saying that in some cases they're afraid of us, they don't know how to talk to us, they feel physically threatened when they sit down and talk to us. We had to work through that."

We don't condone verbal fights or abuse on the part of black parents or anyone else. And we can't imagine how reading teachers the riot act could possibly ever be helpful. That said, teachers and administrators often don't understand the level of worry that black parents of all backgrounds have that their children—and particularly their sons—will lose out on their chance at becoming educated and will end up in the school-to-prison pipeline instead—a dynamic that many educators unintentionally contribute to, creating a Catch-22 for the parents.

"One parent asked a white principal if he ever worried about his son ending up in prison instead of college," says Miller. "Of course not—he admitted that he had never thought about that. As an African American male I've considered that about myself—and certainly for my son who gets stopped often within a few blocks of our home in Berkeley."

Nor do nonblack teachers understand the level of frustration that black parents have with schools or their personal history within schools, including during their youth.

"Our parents went to some of these same schools with the same attitudes and stereotypes and hated it then, and now they can see that the same thing is happening to their child," says Miller. "The parent has to make a choice, which basically boils down to: Am I going to get in the place that was so unkind to me and fight for my child or pull back and hope my child can make it through relatively unscathed?"

For black men racialized gender issues can also come into play.

"Some fathers see school as a feminizing place because most teachers are female and the father attended school under female teachers," says Bryant Marks, an associate professor of psychology at Morehouse College and director of the Morehouse Male Initiative, which identifies factors that foster black males' positive personal and academic development. Dr. Bryant says that black men's personal experiences both with feeling disrespected in schools and people having had low expectations of them can kick in. And depending on the quality of education they received, some black men worry whether they are articulate enough to express themselves effectively with the teacher or whether they understand the teacher's teaching philosophy, strategies, or even the concepts she's covering in class.

"There's a level of intimidation and the concern for potential embarrassment," Dr. Marks says.

And within black culture, traditionally many men have seen managing a child's education as a woman's role—a norm that no longer benefits our sons.

"The child needs to see that his parents are invested in his education—both of his parents," says Dr. Marks. "Boys especially need to see their fathers."

Schools can address some of these concerns by having teachers, counselors, and administrators reach out to parents. They can also extend specific invitations to fathers to visit the school, host father/child nights at the school, and create orientation events featuring male teachers, administrators, and involved fathers to make schools feel inviting for dads, for example.

Rightly or wrongly, for both sides this history may waft through the air. We would all do well to give the other side the benefit of the doubt. To the extent that it's possible, focus not on differences but on the interest you share in common: your child. When possible build from there.

"Schools will do things to uplift white kids at the expense of your son—and they're bold with it. It starts to affect your kid's self-esteem," says Scott. "My son earned the MVP award for his track team—he was responsible for 70 of his team's 117 points. But they gave the MVP award to a white kid who scored 11 points. I told my son to remember the hurt and the emptiness and to come back next year so that he'll be untouchable. Then I met with the coach and principal so that my son knew I was there to fight for him. Of course, the coach lied, but I told the principal, 'Anything my children earn, I expect them to get it. My son was screwed over and it's not going to happen anymore. Next time I have to have this conversation, I'm not going to be polite or respectful like I'm being now.' The next year guess who won the student leadership award? And guess who made the decision? The principal. My son had performed, and she remembered how badly they had dogged him before. He finally got what he was due."

ON THE RIGHT TRACK

One of the most important reasons to get involved at school is to have the chance to learn about and observe the school's approach to *academic tracking,* the process schools use to separate students into academic levels based on their achievement. You will need to manage this process actively so that other people's biases and low expectations don't cause your son to get steered away either from your vision for his life or from his own goals for himself.

This is important, because some classes prepare students for four-year colleges, some classes prepare them for very competitive four-year colleges, some classes don't prepare them for college at all, and some position young people to attend a trade or technical school, enter the military, go to cosmetology school, participate in administrative careers, and so forth. By asking questions of teachers and administrators—but also by finding out through the relationships you develop with other parents and your sleuthing efforts—you will have to uncover the age at which your son's school or school system starts to track, how tracking works, and how to get your son on the academic track that corresponds to your vision for him. We use the word *uncover* intentionally, since both formal and informal processes of tracking can exist. For example, although tracking may not officially begin until middle school, some of the parents we've spoken to have told us that their schools are separating children academically beginning as early as second grade. We also note that the descriptions "college prep" and "academic" don't necessarily mean that the educational track will prepare your child for a four-year school. Given what we have learned about how few black children get evaluated for—much less placed in—gifted and talented programs, there's a good chance that unless you have already been managing this process, your son's school may already be tracking him away from a four-year college—and certainly, away from a competitive one. The earlier and more aggressively you can intervene, the better. This may involve helping his teachers increase their expectations for him, asking that your son be given additional projects or work, changing his class schedule, having him take summer school classes to catch up, obtaining additional tutoring, educating him on your own, and so on. Not fair, but it's the truth.

If you want your son to be tracked to attend a four-year college, he must take a rigorous curriculum that typically includes higher-level math (calculus, trigonometry, and/or statistics) in addition to science, literature, history, and foreign language classes. It's especially important to ask how your son is being tracked in math. The typical math track to a four-year college includes algebra I, algebra II, geometry, trigonometry, pre-calculus, calculus, and perhaps statistics. To be tracked to a four-year college, your son needs to take algebra during middle school. This means that his elementary school math must position him for middle school algebra. But for that to happen he needs to have entered kindergarten with numeracy and literacy skills strong enough so that when math shifts to more word problems he is poised to excel (see Chapter 3). If you want your son to attend a very competitive four-year college, he will need to take several honors and advanced placement (AP) classes during high school. So the path to college really begins in elementary school or during early childhood—not once he reaches high school, when, for many students and parents, the focus on college begins to kick in.

Research shows that parents' ability to set their child up to attend college often breaks down along socioeconomic lines. Children whose parents attended a four-year college are far more likely to take algebra in middle school than children whose parents didn't go to or graduate from a four-year college.[6] Indeed, in *Challenge the Status Quo*, the report on black males in education Drs. Toldson and Lewis wrote for the Congressional Black Caucus Foundation, they assert that many public school students do not qualify for admission to their state's most selective public universities just because they live in the wrong zip code. Indeed, only 65 percent of schools serving the most African American and Hispanic students offer algebra II, only 40 percent offer physics, and less than 30 percent offer calculus. Not only is this unconscionable and outrageous, according to Drs. Toldson and Lewis it violates Public Reciprocity in Education for Postsecondary Success (PREPS) standards, the fiduciary responsibility that each state has to provide a public secondary education that prepares children for that state's institutions of higher learning. They encourage parents and community activists to alert school superintendents, school board members, and principals to these types of discrepancies. And they advise schools to provide disclosure statements to parents warning them that their child's education won't prepare them to attend their state's four-year college unless the child takes extra classes elsewhere.[7]

We think that opportunities exist for schools and counselors, of course, but also for extended families, black-parent groups, churches, fraternities and sororities, and other organizations to create programming and initiatives to help to educate parents with less knowledge of how tracking and other educational processes work as well as take on the fight to have the classes our children deserve taught in their schools. And what a wonderful topic of conversation at a family reunion. Since many of our families have educators in them, wouldn't it be wonderful if they came together with other college-educated family members to give less educated or informed family members the lowdown on how to position their child for college?

KEEPING A WATCHFUL EYE

One of the most important benefits of being active in school is that it increases your ability to see and confront systemic issues that affect your son and other children, including those that reflect racial bias.

"You need parents who are engaged in the school and holding the school accountable for what's happening to the kid," says urban sociologist Pedro Noguera, a professor of education at New York University.

"So if there are barriers related to tracking or barriers related to teachers who are discouraging kids, it's more likely that those barriers are going to be addressed. It shouldn't be left on the kids to figure out on their own how to do that."

"Boys have to understand that their job is to learn and report back to parents about their experience," says Margaret Beale Spencer, Ph.D., a professor of human development and urban education at the University of Chicago. "Anything that feels uncomfortable, their job is to bring it home and let the parents handle it. It's not a boy's job to take on adult work."

Not every issue can be objectively documented, so it's often best not to make racial accusations that we cannot prove. In most educational environments there are many things that do not work well, so don't necessarily assume that when something doesn't work for your son that it's race related. If you're already involved and connected in the school, you will have a better sense of what's what. But as the Civil Rights Data Collection unequivocally depicts, some issues do break around race. Others involve gender or both race and gender. How should you handle them? Parents take many different approaches. We encourage you to explore the approach that works best with your style.

During her research Dr. Lareau observed that when middle-class black parents had concerns about race, they rarely let their teacher know. Instead, they would increase their involvement.

"They would just pop in to be helpful, volunteer to be helpful, but they would never tell the teacher that they were worried about race," she says. "They would say, 'Thank you very much; my kid is doing very well.' Then at the end of the conversation, they would sort of lightly say, 'Do you think he's being challenged enough? Do you think we can get him tested for the gifted and talented program?' Or they'd ask, 'Can he do a little report, and will you read it and give some feedback on it?' Or ask for suggestions for how to improve his writing. They'd make the teacher think it was their idea."

This is one way of dealing with things. It differs from the path she observed working-class parents take.

"Working-class parents who felt that their son was being discriminated against would be mad, complain, and be hostile," Dr. Lareau says. "The teachers had a hard time hearing them because teachers don't take well to criticism, when you come right down to it. Teachers are very resistant to parents who are critical or angry."

"Don't come in already upset, taking your child's side without getting all the facts, not making sure that your son's homework is done, cursing, threatening the administration," says one teacher. "You won't have any credibility, and people will resent it."

Unfortunately, even though they're responsible for educating a diverse population, most teachers have no more education in how to handle conversations about race—or conversations across race, or socioeconomics for that matter—than we parents do.

"We don't want to hear this because there is so much on us, but I think we've also got an issue with that cross-race conversation," says Dr. Joseph, whose collaborative work in Shaker Heights, Ohio, schools has included helping to engage the community in electing a more reform-minded school board and pushing for a transparent and inclusive search for a new superintendent. He says, "(a) we're tired, and we don't wanna have it again; and b) we're angry and frustrated, and so we're quick to just react and attack. So when the moment for that weird conversation finally comes, we're like, 'Bam, let's do this. I've been waiting for five years.' But that's not gonna do it. I think we need to work on our end as well. We're not getting to the other side of this conversation, so we, too, have got things to learn. We think we've got it figured out, like, 'We've lived this and you can't tell me anything about it.' But we still have stuff to learn. We can't say, 'Okay now I'm gonna tell y'all about yourselves.' That's not gonna be constructive."

But diversity is not a one-way street, and the browning of America shouldn't be taking anyone by surprise. As administrators and teachers become increasingly responsible for educating students of color and other diverse children, they need to acknowledge the pain that is being inflicted on so many children of color, as the data unequivocally reflect. Consistent with this, they also need to take responsibility for learning to engage conversations across difference. Schools of education and teacher training programs should offer it. Teachers and school leaders also need to learn how to unpack difficult issues such as the impact of white privilege, stereotypes, and racial bias. This shouldn't all be placed on the shoulders of parents of color.

PLAYING THE DATA CARD

If you feel like there are explicit problems with racial injustice at your son's school, there's a very good chance that the Office of Civil Rights data (http://ocrdata.ed.gov) can quantify those problems. Search for the data for your school and school district. Although the database is incomplete, for many schools it is possible to see charts and data that depict discipline, restraint, harassment/bullying, G&T placement, algebra I enrollment in seventh or eighth grade, and other factors that impact our children's success and college and career readiness—broken out by race, gender, disability status, and other factors. By using these hard facts, we can progress beyond merely sensing that something isn't right but not being able to prove it—and being accused of playing the "race card" as a result—to knowing that something is wrong, objectively proving it, humanizing the data by telling the story of how these dynamics hurt our son, and collaborating with others to improve the situation.

"Parents need to organize and connect to the principal and make it a school-wide issue," says Dr. Gregory about racial disparities in discipline and other structural and systemic matters.

But it's almost impossible for one parent to confront such problems alone.

"As an individual parent, it's really hard to take that on without organizing and having more power in numbers to talk about it as a systemic issue," says Dr. Gregory. "If we keep addressing these issues on a one-on-one basis, it's not going to get at the larger systemic processes of kids being sorted and their potential not being seen based on race, across the whole school system for every school—all the different traps or doors being closed or open depending upon who you are."

By combining our willingness to get our own houses in order by improving our parenting skills and other factors at home with the Civil Rights Data Collection that is now at our fingertips, parents and educators now have the ability to impact the futures of black and brown children—and particularly boys—in ways that we never have before and that are very likely to achieve meaningful results.

"We can't even imagine the power we have," says Zakiyah Ansari, a parent leader with the New York City Coalition for Educational Justice, a group of parents that began organizing in the Bronx and whose influence now extends across New York City and serves as a model of what's possible, including in low-income and working-class communities of color. "We wield a lot of power, whether we are college-educated or we have a third grade education. The power and the passion we feel for our children is a reality. No one can take our experiences away. So while some people in power will look us in our faces and say, 'It's a coincidence' or 'It's not really happening,' our experiences tell us differently every day. If one of us understands that and we can share that with somebody else, that's how we build power. That's why the organizing piece is so powerful."

But how do we move forward? For a community of people who historically have been discouraged from actively participating in many schools and who are still growing in our involvement and understanding of how the system works, we may not possess the individual know-how about where or how to start. Yet part of the answer can be found in our willingness to leverage our cultural legacy of working together, as embodied in the Kwanzaa principle of *ujima,* which means collective work and responsibility.

To shorten our learning curve about how to get started, we asked Ansari and a few other parent activists to share some secrets of their success.

Focus on developing relationships. In this day of overscheduled lives, texts, and emails, many of us are as guilty as our children are of failing to communicate face-to-face and struggling to build authentic connections. It's important for all of the stakeholders to take time with each other in person and to commit to working together and continuing a dialogue over the long term.

"One of the things we don't do today is build relationships, earnest relationships. We don't value the idea of having relationships or speaking out just for the sake of doing it so you can even practice your ability to do it," says Shabazz. "But we need to work from a place of proactivism instead of reactivism. We are reactionary because the proactive work is not as sexy as reactionary work. There's not a lot of hype around working proactively before something happens. We like big and sexy—'Oh, yeah, they called me a nigger. Oh my God, they did this because I'm a woman, or I'm a man.' But build earnest relationships, and you'll see a lot of things change."

"I developed partnerships with people in the school, teachers, people in the community, businesses," says Deloch-Hughes, who worked with other parents to set up a parent-led tutoring and mentoring program as well as other programming. "One of the colleges had a strong education program. We struck up a deal to have student teachers tutor the kids. The faculty and principal funneled the kids to us. All of the kids passed their classes, and 10 percent made the honor roll."

In Shaker Heights, Ohio, organizers knocked on one thousand doors in one section of the community.

Act strategically. Find out what the needs are at your school and in your school district. Be prepared to explain that addressing the achievement gap isn't just another problem but that it can be part of the solution that helps a school meet its objectives.

"I sat with the principal to get the vision of what she wanted her school to be," says Deloch-Hughes.

"The district was desperate to do something. They had been wringing their hands for years and years," says Michael Miller of the academic performance of the black students in Berkeley's school system. When black parents discovered not only that the entering class of 2004 would be the first to have to pass an exit exam but also that about 30 percent of the roughly nine hundred ninth graders were already failing two core classes, they realized that they had a chance to turn this problem into an opportunity. Over a Christmas break parents envisioned what would eventually be called the Rebound Program, a hands-on academic enrichment program that eventually permitted a group of fifty African American students to start their ninth grade year over, beginning that February and continuing through August of the same year. In August almost all of the students were ready to rejoin their class and enter the tenth grade on schedule.

Meet people where they are. Don't assume that just because you're all fired up that every parent you talk to will be. It's hard work to "fight the power," as Public Enemy once put it. People's commitment and energy levels ebb and flow. Allow for that.

"Everybody's not going to start in the same place. Not every parent is going to go out to a rally or call this person and that person," says Ansari. "But if a person will make a phone call or write a letter or send an email—there are so many different ways to utilize our power. History shows that when we come together as a people, we can move mountains."

"I approached certain parents who had certain skills," says Deloch-Hughes. "One of the fathers had started a tutoring program at his job. Another parent was in PR and event marketing, so she would help with communications. Another parent was a lawyer; we would talk to her about rights. Then some parents just wanted to be chaperones or sell donuts for a fundraiser. I used whatever skills, talents, and gifts that they wished to share."

In time, and as they see results, some people may become more committed and others may even step into leadership.

Forge alliances with other groups and organizations. Think big. Your school district, principal, school security officers, and teachers but also local churches, mosques, synagogues, colleges and universities, businesses, caring community members, allies of other races and ethnicities, and other progressive affinity groups, such as women's organizations or the LGBT community—they may all be interested in playing a role.

"We invited a broad community of folks together for a luncheon at the fire station, where we presented a plan and talked about what we intended to do," says Miller of the push to start the Rebound Program. "We impressed upon them that we can't do this by ourselves. We needed others' help and support. As a result of that and some other meetings, we had the principal, city council, mayor, and three out of the five school board members on board. One school board member was adamantly opposed to it because it was just another program and what sense does it make to funnel money to these people and we really don't know who they are? All valid questions and as a steward of the school community, that's what she should be asking."

Eventually a community of committed teachers, parents, student teachers from the local college at the University of California at Berkeley, and other interested community leaders and members came together to support the students. The City of Berkeley eventually contributed $60,000 in funds and $40,000 in in-kind contributions, such as mentoring by city workers.

"I offered an olive branch to the PTO and other organizations that had been white-oriented and had an adversarial relationship with APPLE in the past," says Deloch-Hughes. "I told them that our success is everyone's success. When black children prosper and do well, the whole school does well."

Deloch-Hughes and other black parents were able to convince the PTO and parents of other races to partner to help improve opportunities for all of their children.

"We put together a symposium over a weekend—'The Hidden Truth: Everything You Want to Know about High School,'" says Deloch-Hughes. "The high school people were like, 'Rah, rah!' but you need to know some deep stuff. Like freshman year you need a strategic plan if you want to get him to go to college. Here are the classes he needs to take, the things you need to do: some community service, some AP classes, and so on. You need to plan it out. You can't just wait until his junior or senior year. We talked to the white kids and parents too, but it's imperative that everyone have that information." A lot of the black kids didn't have it.

Follow the money and connect the dots. Keep your eyes peeled for the relationships that link the money, the policies, and the people.

"Everything is connected," says Ansari, "the budgets, the school-to-prison pipeline, the politics—that was my 'Aha!' The politics are so entrenched in education. That helps me understand that we have to have our own political infrastructure. Once you understand that, you can become strategic."

"When we teach young people about politics, we talk about political development, not just government," says Shabazz, who founded a youth advocacy organization, Young People in Action (www .YoungPeopleInAction.com), that teaches young people the spiritual, social, political, economic, and educational aspects of leadership. "Political development is the politics of influencing the distribution of limited resources when there are competing interests for those resources. Time, energy, money, attention, space, education—all these things are resources; however, they're limited. We have to influence the distribution of those resources from a proactive standpoint, so when something happens you're already in the mix, you're already working. It's not that difficult to do."

Expect to feel discouraged sometimes. Mama said there'd be days like this. Once you begin to become active, the realities you will uncover will disturb you so much that some days you'll want to get back in bed and pull the covers over your head.

"It can be so overwhelming that you just want to stay ignorant," says Ansari. "I've felt that way many times—I wished I didn't know. But eventually it becomes your passion. You live and breathe it."

Take risks. When it comes to issues of race, sometimes it seems expedient to play it safe. Playing it safe may have allowed us to make some progress, but places exist where we are still stuck. And if we keep doing what we've been doing in those areas, how can we free ourselves?

"I was talking to the administration at my son's school and writing to the special education director at the district, but I stopped there," says the mother of a son with ADHD whose family had moved to a neighborhood that they thought had high-quality schools, only to discover that the special educators were on leave and had never been replaced. "I should have filed with the Department of Education. But once they said, 'Sorry for you,' I accepted that because we were relocating. People are afraid of lawsuits. They don't have time, they can't put together the evidence, they think it will help someone five years down the line and their child won't get immediate relief. But telling the story is valuable. If I had to do it over or advise parents, I'd say it doesn't require you to sell your house to file a complaint. It allows you to put your complaint on record, then you decide how far to go with it."

We may be surprised to discover how much respect we garner when we have the courage to speak our truth clearly and compassionately.

"The very school system that I am about to battle just approved a contract for me to teach a leadership program," says Shabazz.

Graduate to the next level. You may start by just trying to make your eight visits to your son's school. But over time set a goal of learning, growing, and moving on to the next level—the same process that you expect of your son. Join the black parents' organization, participate in the PTA, network with parents from other schools who are dealing with similar issues, but keep developing yourself.

"Eventually our organization got involved with a broader grouping of folks. We started a coalition, United in Action (UIA), comprised primarily of African American and Latino organizations, and some city council and school board members, and others," says Miller, whose activism continues even though his children are long out of high school. "We came together initially to identify school board candidates. In 2004 we had two candidates that we supported; one was elected. We now have a school board that consists of all directors supported by UIA. But it's not as easy as it seems. We can support and encourage those directors to have our best interests at heart, but we clearly are unable to make them make the right decisions. It's still a struggle."

UIA also partnered with the city council and school district to set goals to eliminate disparities for black and Latino youth by 2020.

OUTWIT, OUTLAST, OUTPLAY?

But many of the parents we spoke with pointed to an inevitable reality: children grow up, and they and their parents move on. Because of this, some believe that teachers, schools, school systems, teachers unions, and so on that want to can drag their feet, cover up realities, and resist change merely by waiting until we run out of time, money, or energy.

"It is very slow, almost glacial, even if all of us who have the wherewithal to talk put our voices together," one parent told us. "There are people who are not accountable for these things, and it can go on indefinitely. At some point the law takes you to age twenty-one and you're out of it."

But only if we quit or fail to handle our handoffs to the next generation of leadership. The Reverend Dr. Martin Luther King once told us, "The arc of the moral universe is long, and it bends toward justice." By working together we can curve the arc more sharply.

We live in an age in which an online petition demanding justice for a seventeen-year-old black young man murdered with Skittles and a cell phone in his hand can amass 1.5 million signatures from people around the world in less than three weeks.[8] A world in which a revolution in Egypt can be ignited by hidden posts on a dating website and an Arab Spring can be sparked by a video taken from someone's cell phone. With tools like Facebook, Tumblr, Twitter, and Pinterest at our fingertips, just imagine what we can catalyze if we follow in our forebears' footsteps and fight for a cause that's bigger than ourselves so that our grandchildren can become the highly developed human beings that they are capable of being. If our ancestors could work from "can't see in the morning 'til can't see at night," pray for a better day, and survive the bullwhip and other instruments of terror so that we can experience the conveniences that we do, do we not also owe a similar debt to future generations? If our grandparents' generation could fight in the Civil Rights movement, do we not owe it to them to run the next leg of that race: winning access to an equitable education for all children, regardless of their race, gender, or socioeconomic background?

We agree that the fight for an equitable education is the Civil Rights movement of the twenty-first century. But to get there, the adults of today must take some bold steps that include fighting off the seductive and hedonistic pull of American popular culture and demonstrating the future orientation that we learned about in Chapter 7.

It also requires that we commit ourselves to look out for each other's children like the Village used to do, not so far back in the day.

"We have to get back to the 'we' mentality," says Ansari.

"I wrote letters for my son—but not only for him but also for the other two moms who didn't have time to investigate," says Portia, the mother of two sons.

The parent activists whom we quote in this chapter did not all start out as activists. For example, some became engaged when their children required special education services but were being underserved.

"I realized that my son's education experience turned depending on the academic environment of the district," says Jana of her son, who has ADHD. "He was fine in early elementary school when he attended two school systems that had support systems in place. But when our family relocated to "Lake Wobegon, where all the women are strong, the men are good-looking, and the children (worth caring about) are all above average," she knew she would have to roll up her sleeves and fight for her son's education.

Ansari became increasingly involved after she began to volunteer in her older children's middle school and realized that while her children had art, drama, and foreign language, students in other schools didn't.

"There were kids in Brooklyn who had been in inequitably funded programs for decades," she says. "If my kids are going to grow up and marry somebody, the one child that mine decides to marry could be the one that no one stood up for."

Over time, the mother of eight became increasingly committed, progressing from working with her daughters' school's PTA to becoming a powerful voice for change citywide.

"We started getting the research and the data," Ansari recalls. "Now we become powerful because we sit at the table with Department of Education heads or elected officials. They don't know half of what we know. We are not only knowledgeable about our own children, we are knowledgeable about the system."

(To see a documentary describing some of the accomplishments of Ansari and her peers and the process they followed to effect change, search for the video "Parent Power" on YouTube or type this URL into your browser: http://www.youtube.com/watch?v=WszSeRBqHtA.)

Rather than allowing another generation of black and brown children to be deprived of the opportunity to fulfill their potential—and letting the nation miss out on their gifts, talents, and imaginations—we have the power to pave the way for our sons to help solve our planet's problems.

We'd like to suggest to every black parent, as well as members of our son's Village, educators, allies of other races, and others that you can join the building grassroots movement to achieve educational equity. We no longer have to walk from Montgomery to Memphis or have fire hoses turned on us and police dogs attack us—our ability to flex our might lies right at our fingertips on our smartphones. We can wield text messages; our Facebook, Tumblr, Twitter, Pinterest, and Instagram accounts; colorofchange.org, Change.org, MoveOn.org, and other online petition sites; Skype; and tools that haven't even been invented yet to connect with other parents and activists, share strategies, and spread our success stories. We can email our congressional representatives and march on school board meetings as well as Washington, D.C. We can connect with affinity groups of other progressives—from black and Latino organizations to women's groups to our allies in the LGBT communities. All of us can do something to help spread the word and ignite the movement to achieve educational equity.

If you haven't already watched *American Promise*, we invite you to visit our website (www.AmericanPromise.org) to request a screening or find one taking place near you. And join the conversation that we are setting in motion by liking our Facebook page and following us on Twitter at @PromiseFilm. We also encourage you to engage in the features on our website and download our mobile app. The app will help you make micro-changes that will help you be a better parent.

We won't have to face dogs and hoses, but we should expect to encounter resistance in the form of our own fear, other parents who see things differently—some of whom will be black and brown—as well as institutional delays, budget battles, and so forth. We will have to face our own fears that come when we step out of our comfort zones, engage in unfamiliar behaviors, work with people we haven't worked with before, and have conversations about race, gender, and class that it would be easier not to have—if our children and the nation's and planet's future were not in peril.

This, of course, means we must take some risks.

As Erin, the mother of a fifteen-year-old son, told us, "I'm a master teacher, but I'm blacklisted everywhere within my son's school district, and I'm okay with it. It's the length we as parents have to be willing to go. When I got my calling to become an activist, God told me, 'Let me tell you a little of what this entails. You're not in it to receive respect from other persons or to be in a popularity contest. And every now and then this walk will be a little bit uncomfortable.' And I said, 'Here I am. Choose me.' "

This type of courage is contagious and makes us feel extremely optimistic for our sons and our world.

The shaky global economy? It's no match for an overweight butterscotch-brown boy with dreads who has a mathematical equation bouncing around in his brain that will make today's Nobel Prize winners applaud him. World hunger? The mind of a doe-eyed adolescent whose shoes are run over is already pondering ideas to solve it that haven't dawned on any of us. Global warming? An ebony-skinned boy with ashy knees has a cerebellum that is perfectly suited to crafting solutions that will help to cool the planet.

But we adults have to be able to envision their potential.

Can you?

He's out there.

We promise.

EPILOGUE

A lot has happened since we began our odyssey to document our son's educational experience. Between the time Idris and Seun started kindergarten and graduated from twelfth grade, we amassed more than eight hundred hours of footage—so much that it would have taken more than five weeks straight to watch it from beginning to end. At the end of 2012, we finally completed the film—titled *American Promise*—an educational coming-of-age story of two black boys that examines issues of race, class, gender, parenting, and educational opportunity.

We have been amazed by the positive reception that our film has received, starting with an invitation to premiere at Sundance, the World Series of film festivals. What a thrill and an honor! But as you might imagine, after thirteen years of filming—and with our son and family in starring roles!—we were extremely anxious about birthing our "baby" to the public. We worried that no one would come, and that audiences might not laugh when we wanted them to laugh, cry when we wanted them to cry, or empathize with African American boys, since society has vilified them so much.

Yet one night in January 2013 we held our breaths as some of the most intimate moments of our lives unfolded onscreen in front of the audience that had come to the Temple Theater in Park City, Utah. Although they were complete strangers, viewers connected deeply with the film. Afterward the woman sitting next to Joe tearfully asked him for a hug and said it was the best documentary she had ever seen. There's almost nothing more satisfying a filmmaker can hear! During the Q&A afterward Idris and Seun were poised, mature, and eloquent in their responses. After all of our struggles, few things have been more satisfying. The two of us, as well as Tony and Stacey, were beaming from ear to ear.

The reviews, as well, were powerful and moving testimonials to both boys' spirits. The film critic from *Variety* found *American Promise* "riveting." *Hollywood Reporter* called our film "engrossing" and "inspiring," saying that it "shows the strength and potential that minority males possess, and how that may be successfully directed."

To top it all off, we won the Special Jury Prize for achievement in filmmaking, an extremely prestigious honor! (As we write this chapter six months later, accolades continue to roll in. We were invited to participate in the elite New York Film Festival, where we premiered to sold-out audiences and received three standing ovations on opening night.)

At Sundance we also kicked off a grassroots engagement campaign whose goal is to draw the public's attention to the challenges facing black males. We have started out by partnering with Big Brothers/Big Sisters to call for mentors for black boys, who have a harder time finding mentors than any other boys. Our campaign has three goals in mind:

1. to raise national awareness of some of the obstacles that black males face;
2. to provide black boys' parents with tools and information that they can use to support their sons now so that they thrive even as change unfolds;
3. to have a measurable impact on black males' collective academic achievement as our nation embarks upon the new Civil Rights movement: attaining education with equity for all children—a lofty goal that may take decades to achieve.

But while social movements can take generations, we want to help the tipping point happen sooner. So in addition to the film, we have created several dimensions to our engagement campaign: this book, which we hope will frame the challenge, give people tools to use with their sons, students, and family members, and extends the conversation into both classrooms and living rooms; our website (www.American Promise.org), where you will find discussion guides, tools for educators, home party kits for parents, resource lists, as well as a free mobile app designed to help you achieve some of your parenting goals; and traveling installations that will advance the dialogue nationwide.

Over the next year we will take the film and this conversation on the road, hosting community screenings nationwide and partnering with organizations whose mission includes supporting black male academic, social, and emotional growth. Already, we've screened at Harvard's Graduate School of Education and the University of Michigan's School of Education; chapters of Big Brothers/Big Sisters; the National Urban League; the Open Society Foundation's Black Male: Re-Imagined II Conference; General Colin Powell's America's Promise Alliance; the California Endowment; conferences of the Coalition of Schools Educating Boys of Color (COSEBOC) and Great Schools; a gathering of guidance counselors convened by The College Board; and with diversity groups at Google, BMP Parbas, and Banco Popular, among others.

Already such screenings are helping to deepen the dialogue and build relationships with parents, educators, neighbors, and other members of our children's Village. Among the issues that audiences repeatedly raise, some folks express shock and/or amazement that we've exposed so many personal and parenting shortcomings and painful experiences that people tend to keep private. We exposed ourselves intentionally, of course, hoping that by showing our vulnerabilities and talking about real solutions, audiences will connect to us and our children through the language of common experience. One of our goals as filmmakers (and now authors) is to create change using the powers of stories and cameras. By their very nature, stories about real people expose those people to the world, allowing their humanity to touch viewers' hearts. Real people and true stories also bring issue-based films alive. Our willingness to share our sons' challenges reflects our beliefs that moviegoers will connect with them, that over the long term they will be fine, and that we can shield them from most of exposure's downsides.

And the Conventional Wisdom that frames vulnerability as being negative? We no longer buy into that at all. Indeed, we have come to believe in vulnerability's power. Because once we shared our experiences with advisors who could shed light on the issues that Idris was facing, the insight we gained helped us become better parents and positioned us to share what we learned through this book. Exposing ourselves in our film has situated us to connect with thousands of parents, helping us to understand black boys' experiences more deeply and allowing us to enter and help propel forward conversations about potential solutions.

Indeed, airing our dirty laundry helped us to break free. This has been one of our more powerful lessons: that shame kept us stuck. This is an essential message we hope our audiences and readers learn.

By exposing both our imperfections and the boys' vulnerabilities, we hope to spark revelations, create fresh connections, and inspire breakthroughs in a dialogue that for years has been stuck. Already, many black people have told us that they are overjoyed to see real middle-class African Americans—and particularly black boys—on film. We have generated quite a dialogue about parenting as well. The conversations that are happening already are priceless.

And more than a few non-black viewers have told us that, while they don't want to minimize the issues that black boys face, they can see that what happens at black families' dinner tables is strikingly similar to what happens at their own. These are among the most satisfying pieces of feedback we could hope to receive. For we believe that when people see black boys' humanity, they will be able to envision more of their promise instead of merely believing them to be problematic. We hope people will fear black boys less, care about them more, and perhaps even join us in advocating for their future. Together, the Village can catalyze change.

We started our parenting journey with a very lofty vision: great grades, high test scores, acceptance to top colleges, and aspirations that Idris would save the world—math meets Milwaukee, minus the marijuana. And while we did a lot of things right—from holding high expectations of him, to encouraging his critical thinking skills, to being willing to speak openly with him and hear his ideas out—we grew to understand that some of our goals were not appropriate. We started out unknowingly having internalized some very narrow definitions of academic achievement and success—definitions that with hindsight we no longer subscribe to. We knew that for Idris to do well we needed to support his whole being—his mind, emotions, body, and spirit. But we also discovered that we would have to place tremendous attention on his social and emotional wellness, if he stood any chance of fulfilling his potential in a society whose playing field is unlevel. We also learned that the ball was in our court: The school was not going to engage this work.

Indeed, to excel academically Idris needed a lot more than just to study; the academic, social, and emotional were all intertwined. Getting regular exercise, understanding morality, and knowing how to manage interpersonal relationships, trust and care for others, be creative, think critically, and demonstrate self-esteem, for instance, all turned out to be very important. He also needed his entire Village to respect him and for us to stay engaged with all of them, all the time—even when it was tough and we didn't want to. After speaking with scores of experts and educators and thousands of parents, we realize that we had only a partial view of how Idris's childhood was unfolding. Now that he is an adult (and we are much wiser), we are closer to having a 360-degree perspective. It's been very humbling.

We hope that our openness frees you to share your son's struggles—no matter where you live, how much education you have, or your socioeconomic class. We also hope that our film and book inspire parents, educators, policymakers, service providers, and advocates of other races to support children to whom their own children's future is inextricably linked—whether they are classmates, play on the same soccer team, live in the same community, or because we inhabit the same planet whose fragility requires all of us to link hands to confront the challenges that face us.

Please take advantage of the many resources that you will find on our website; follow us on Facebook (AmericanPromise), Twitter (@promisefilm), and YouTube (AmericanPromiseDoc); and participate in your community's conversation about black male achievement.

We hope to see you when we're on the road!

Sincerely,
Joe and Michèle

ACKNOWLEDGMENTS

First we must thank Dr. Alvin Poussaint, who flipped the script after Joe and Michèle interviewed him for the film *American Promise* by validating their viewpoints and suggesting they use their voices to lead. When Joe was a student at Harvard Medical School, Dr. Poussaint—who was knowledgeable not only about psychiatry but also the social dynamics of American society, with a focus upon race and class—often provided analysis whenever important events involved black people. He did not back down from his interpretations of the world and has encouraged us to stand up for ours.

Madeline Morel, thank you for connecting us with Steve Ross, who saw the promise of this book and strongly advocated for us in many different ways. We're grateful for you, Steve.

Christopher Jackson, Cindy Spiegel, Julie Grau, and the team at Spiegel & Grau, thanks for sharing our vision and helping us put our best foot forward editorially. We're grateful also to Annie Chagnot, Laura Vanderveer, to the marketing and promotions team, and all of the others behind the scenes whose hard work makes book publishing seem effortless.

You can't write a book about parents, educators, and children without talking to a lot of them. We're grateful to the many moms and dads, caregivers, teachers, principals, counselors, tutors, and young men of promise who shared their stories with us. We have disguised your identifying characteristics to protect you; however, the power of your words will help to change the world. Tony and Stacey

Summers, and parent activists Asad Shabazz, Edye Deloach-Hughes, Mark Joseph, Michael Miller, and Zakiyah Ansari, thank you for being so public and powerful.

We are tremendously grateful to the amazing community of experts who have dedicated their lives to this work, particularly those who allowed us to interview them and whose expertise has informed our strategies: Adria Welcher, Aisha Ray, Alvin Poussaint, Alyn Waller, Annette Lareau, Bryant Marks, Carol Cheatham, Charles Nelson III, Claude Steele, Dave Hardy, David Grissmer, Diane Hughes, Elizabeth Gunderson, Fleda Mask Jackson, Howard Stevenson, Ivory Toldson, Jelani Mandara, Jermaine Bond, John H. Jackson, Joshua Aronson, Kathleen Walls, Latham Thomas, Lauren Rich, M. Natalie Achong, Margaret Beale Spencer, Michael Holzman, Michelle Gourdine, Nilanjana Dasgupta, Pamela Freeman, Pedro Noguera, Robert Jagers, Robert Sellers, Roland Warren, Ronald Ferguson, Ron Walker, Sara McLanahan, Stephen Jones, Susan Levine, Tabbye Chavous, Ursula Johnson, and Vanessa Cullins. We hope that our book shines light on your brilliant work. Thanks as well to the experts whose research we cited but whom we didn't interview.

April Eugene, you cared that every word in hundreds of hours of transcripts was typed correctly; for that we are grateful. Thanks also to the *American Promise* interns who helped with research: Ayana Enomoto-Hurst, Bernardo Sarmiento, Cem Kurtulus, Henry A. Murphy II, and Xinyi "Leila" Lin. We've never met the virtual assistants at Timesvr.com, but their ability to track down studies, statistics, experts, and resources greatly increased our productivity.

To our funders and partners—particularly Kathy Im, Orlando Bagwell, Rahdi Taylor, Raquiba Labrie, Rashid Shabazz, Shawn Dove, Sheila Leddy, and our many other supporters we have worked with at the Fledgling Fund, the Ford Foundation, Kellogg Foundation, MacArthur Foundation, and the Open Society Foundation's Campaign for Black Male Achievement—thank you for providing us with a ripe environment in which to make our film and pursue this book in the hope that we touch many lives, families, and communities.

In the fifteen years since we started working in this field, we have encountered countless organizations that have blazed the trail for the study of black achievement, including the Achievement Gap Initiative at Harvard University and the Coalition of Schools Educating Boys of Color (COSEBOC), both of which lent their expertise to this book. Thank you for your dedication to the work and for setting such a high standard.

JOE BREWSTER

I'll start by giving thanks to my wife, Michèle. Because it's one thing to attempt to make my way in this world alone; it's another to struggle and sometimes succeed with a partner who is caring, the smartest person I know, and a great mother to our children. Michèle brings that awareness to our relationship and our family. She has lived in Haiti, Canada, the U.S., Africa, and Brazil; she is comfortable with diverse cultures and socioeconomic groups; and is stimulated by differences in people. It's exciting to share life with someone so interesting.

Above all the other major influential forces—education, life experience, and so on—parenting is the great influencer. Thank you, Idris and Miles, for hanging in there while we learned on the job.

We are very grateful to Tony and Stacey Summers and their children, especially Seun, who believed in and have been extremely trusting of us. We are still trying to live up to their belief and trust. Thank you for allowing us to tell our sons' stories.

I must acknowledge my parents, who were part of the very rich life of African American Los Angeles, and who exposed us to concerts, poetry readings, and other art within the context of the church. Because our lives were so full of music, art, and love, when we were young we did not know what we didn't have. Thank you also to my siblings, who have always supported me (and my wanderlust).

I want to thank my teachers and advisors. Miss Vernell Johnson at Normandy Avenue Elementary School in Los Angeles helped shaped my awareness and gave me a different gaze upon the world—a black gaze—and helped position me for the accelerated math track. Thank you to Craig and Felicia Hudson for pushing me to explore my artist brain. Professor William Dement and Dr. Alvin Poussaint both rescued me without judgment on multiple occasions. And thanks to Dr. Shervert Frazier and Dr. Chester Pierce, who taught me the virtue of early morning labor and caffeine-laden moonscapes.

MICHÈLE STEPHENSON

Joe, there are no words to describe the deep love and gratitude I feel for having met you, for your companionship, and for putting up with my insecurities as we have taken this path of life together. You have challenged me to be the best that I can be, and your intelligence, quirky sense of humor, compassion, and directness have fueled my creativity and allowed me to take risks I never thought I would be capable of. You've made me a better human being.

I'd like to thank Idris and Miles for challenging me to face my weaknesses and question so many assumptions about parenting as well as for giving me the opportunity to grow as a mother and a person. Sometimes I'm shocked and oh so proud to witness what bright, inquisitive, and caring human beings you are. Thank you for opening your vulnerability to the world and for allowing us to share your story.

Hilary, we would not be here without you. Joe and I are so deeply grateful for the sequence of events and encounters that led us to you. What serendipity. Your selfless giving spirit permeates throughout the pages of this book. You made the impossible happen in such a graceful way. It's been a beautiful ride and we thank you for all your hard work and for sharing your keen intellect and talent in the making of *Promises Kept*. We are so lucky! Friends forever, now.

At Dalton we experienced some struggles, but a core group of parents and educators supported and protected us. We'd like to thank Andrea DeJesus, Babby Krentz, Barbara Weinreich, Carla Roach, Ellen Stein, Holly Carter, Libby Hickson, Marilyn Coxall-Europe, Myrla Van Slutman, Raul Roach, and William Fisher. At Benjamin Bannecker, thanks to Daryl Rock, Debbie Almontaser, and Mr. Muhammad.

Thinking so much about parenting and education has caused me to reflect upon the lives of my own parents, Andrea Delgado and Edouard Stephenson, who left everything and everyone they knew in Panama and Haiti to immigrate to an unknown world in pursuit of their vision of a better future for their family. My father had a high school degree and my mother, until her forties, had only a sixth-grade education, yet they instilled a sense of education's importance in me. They also lay the foundation that ultimately allowed me to raise two healthy black boys. Papi, I wish you could have witnessed more of the fruits of your sacrifices.

I'd like to acknowledge the influence of my dear friend Richard Iton, who always challenged me intellectually and encouraged me to think outside of the box, before passing away earlier this year. Thank you Deborah Baker for sharing stories about our sons and providing a listening ear during our morning workouts. I fondly recall my fourth-grade teacher, Mrs. Preiss, for her openness and challenging us to think differently. To Mr. Gonyer, my drama teacher, who made high school a safe haven for me, believing and trusting in my dreams. I cannot forget Professors Ralph Premdas and Kellis Parker for their intellectual creativity and encouragement to pursue ideas that were complicated and fascinating. They allowed me to be comfortable in those gray areas of thought, ideas, feelings, and art. Thank you for your mentorship and guidance. And, Cecilia Loving, you helped me survive in those crucial moments. Thank you for being there.

I can't give enough thanks to the entire production team from *American Promise*. Our administrative team especially—Caroline de Fontaine Stratton, Gregory S. Jones, and Lauren Pabst—who made it all possible for us to pursue the making of this book, while you were juggling so many balls in the air. Thank you.

HILARY BEARD

At this point I should no longer be surprised by the amazing projects God brings me, or the process by which they land on my plate. Still, I remain awestruck and grateful! Joe and Michèle, I'm so glad that the oversharing I did in my response to your initial inquiry clued you in that I was the right writer rather than scare you away. I can't imagine working with better co-authors or on a more meaningful project, and the icing on the cake is that I get to call you friends! Thank you for being brilliant, courageous, unselfish, and visionary, and for loving our children so much that you would put your own on the line for the greater good. Idris, Miles, and Seun, your pure spirits, honesty and generosity are sparking a dialogue that will help advance humanity. Thank you for continuing to share yourselves. I'm grateful, Tony and Stacey, for your courage and openness.

Bless you, Retha Powers, for recommending me for this project. Madeline Morel, you are my ace in the hole. Steve Ross, aka Home Team, I admit it: I grumbled when you had us revise our proposal one last time, but I'm grateful that you pushed us, and it's been fun to work with a native Clevelander. Chris Jackson, thanks a million for tightening us up! Your compliments have been priceless.

The more parenting experts I interviewed, the clearer I became about what an amazing job my parents, Charles and Peggy Beard, did. It could not have been easy to break the color barrier at work, in the world, or in our neighborhood—much less to thrust their children onto the front lines of that grand, yet perilous, social experiment called integration. Thanks to their love, we emerged remarkably unscathed. Jonathan and Alison, nothing makes me prouder than being your sister. I admire you, and forever owe you and Jennifer a debt of gratitude, for raising such kind, thoughtful and bright children—who love me, lucky me! Alex, Kailey, Jadon, and Ralph, thank you for keeping me laughing and loving. I pray that this book helps create a world that cherishes you and benefits from your brilliance.

Muchas gracias to the family members and friends who encouraged me as I wrote and conducted an exhaustive amount of research in a compressed time frame: Bonnie and Ray Morgan, Mrs. Eula Cousins, Alphonso and Leticia Rosario, and Stephen Woods; Glenn Ellis, Isaac Ewell, Saleema Curtis, Valerie Harrison; my family at Enon Tabernacle Baptist Church, especially my Home Slice, Pastor Alyn E. Waller, the ministerial staff, the Faith Workers and Prayer

Warriors; Linda Villarosa, the mother of all mentors; Phill Wilson, the visionary of all visionaries; the writers of WordSpace, especially Eileen Flanagan, Lori Tharps, and Tamar Chansky; Bill Harvey, Katy Hawkins, and Malikha Washington for helping me stay healthy under pressure; the members of my Beard, Carson, Lanton, and Montilla/Rosario extended families, who cheered me on; my Philly/Mt. Airy, Cleveland/Shaker Heights, and Princeton friends; and the teachers who have made a tremendous difference in my life: Mary Krogness, Robert Hanson, and Kenny Bingham.

I call the name of Manie Baron, my first agent who, as an editor, saw my potential and gave me the break of which every aspiring writer dreams. Finally, I honor my ancestors, whose dreams for a better future were so mighty and prayers so powerful that even generations later I still draft in their wake.

NOTES

INTRODUCTION

1. Tom Van Riper, "Most Expensive Private High Schools," Forbes.com, December 11, 2006, available at http://www.forbes.com/2006/12/09/private-schools-most-expensive-biz-cx_tvr_1211prep.html, accessed May 2, 2013. For the classroom ratio statistics, see the accompanying slide show "In Pictures: America's Most Expensive Private High Schools."
2. Schott Foundation for Public Education, *The Urgency of Now: The Schott 50 State Report on Public Education and Black Males, 2012,* 39.
3. Ronald F. Ferguson, "What *Doesn't* Meet the Eye: Understanding and Addressing Racial Disparities in High-Achieving Suburban Schools," Wiener Center for Social Policy, John F. Kennedy School of Government, Harvard University, October 21, 2002, 7.
4. Schott Foundation, *Urgency of Now,* 32.
5. The Transformed Civil Rights Data Collection, *Revealing New Truths About Our Nation's Schools,* June 26, 2012, available at http://cecblog.typepad.com/files/crdc-2012-data-summary.pdf, accessed May 2, 2013.
6. "2006 National and State Estimations," Civil Rights Data Collection, ED.gov, available at http://ocrdata.ed.gov/StateNationalEstimations/projections_2006, accessed February 11, 2013.
7. Anne Gregory, Russell J. Skiba, and Pedro A. Noguera, "The Achievement Gap and the Discipline Gap: Two Sides of the Same Coin?" *Educational Researcher* 39, no. 1 (2010): 59–68.
8. Amanda Datnow, *The Gender Politics of Educational Change* (New York: Routledge, 1998), 27–28.
9. "2006 National and State Estimations," Civil Rights Data Collection.
10. Schott Foundation, *Urgency of Now,* 7.
11. Ivory A. Toldson and Chance W. Lewis, *Challenge the Status Quo: Academic Success among School-age African-American Males,* Black Male Achievement Research Collaborative, 12, available at http://www.cbefinc.org/oUploadedFiles/CTSQ.pdf, accessed May 2, 2013.
12. Schott Foundation, *Urgency of Now,* 13.

13. U.S. Census Bureau, 2008 American Community Survey.
14. The Princeton Review, "What's a Good SAT or ACT Score?" available at http://www.princetonreview.com/college/good-sat-score-act-score.aspx, accessed February 8, 2012.
15. Data from the Center on International Education Benchmarking, "Top Performing Countries," available at http://www.ncee.org/programs-affiliates/center-on-international-education-benchmarking/top-performing-countries/, accessed May 2, 2013.
16. "Comparing Countries' and Economies' Performance," figure 1, "Key Findings: What Students Know and Can Do: Student Performance in Reading, Mathematics and Science," Programme for International Student Assessment 2009, Organisation for Economic Co-operation and Development, available at http://www.oecd.org/pisa/46643496.pdf, accessed May 2, 2013.
17. Educational Testing Service, "Differences in the Gender Gap: Comparisons across Racial/Ethnic Groups in Education and Work," 2001, available at http://www.ets.org/Media/Research/pdf/PICGENDER.pdf, accessed May 2, 2013.

CHAPTER 1: CLOSE THE GAP BEFORE IT OPENS

1. Iheoma Iruka, "Opening Discussion: Condition of Young Black Boys in the United States," ETS's Addressing Achievement Gaps Symposium: A Strong Start: Positioning Young Black Boys for Educational Success, 2011, available at http://www.ets.org/s/sponsored_events/achievement_gap/flash/2011_conference/iheoma_u_iruka.html (accessed February 23, 2013).
2. Zero to Three, "FAQ's on the Brain," available at http://www.zerotothree.org/child-development/brain-development/faqs-on-the-brain.html, accessed November 12, 2012.
3. Stacy Beck et al., "The Worldwide Incidence of Preterm Birth: A Systematic Review of Maternal Mortality and Morbidity," *Bulletin of the World Health Organization* 88 (2010): 31–38, available at http://www.who.int/bulletin/volumes/88/1/08-062554/en/, accessed May 2, 2013.
4. Richard E. Nisbett, *Intelligence and How to Get It: Why Schools and Cultures Count* (New York: Norton, 2010), 5.
5. Katrina C. Johnson, "Does Preterm Birth Affect Cognitive Ability?" Maternal Substance Abuse and Child Development Project, Emory University, 2007, available at http://www.psychiatry.emory.edu/PROGRAMS/GADrug/feature_articles.html, accessed May 2, 2013.
6. Brenda Patoine, "The Vulnerable Premature Brain: Rapid Neural Development in the Third Trimester Heightens Brain Risks," Dana Foundation Briefing Paper, May 2010, available at http://www.dana.org/media/detail.aspx?id=27882, accessed May 2, 2013.
7. Patoine, "Vulnerable Premature Brain," 2.
8. Centers for Disease Control and Prevention, "National Prematurity Awareness Month," available at http://www.cdc.gov/features/prematurebirth/, accessed February 23, 2013.
9. Centers for Disease Control and Prevention, "Births: Final Data for 2010," *National Vital Statistics Reports* 61, no. 1 (2012): 13–14.
10. Fleda Mask Jackson, "Race, Stress, and Social Support: Addressing the Crisis in Black Infant Mortality," Joint Center for Political and Economic Studies Health Policy Institute, 2007, available at http://www.jointcenter.org/research

/race-stress-and-social-support-addressing-the-crisis-in-black-infant-mortality, accessed May 2, 2013.

11. Carol Sakala and Maureen P. Corry, "Evidence-Based Maternity Care: What It Is and What It Can Achieve," Childbirth Connection, the Reforming States Group, and the Milbank Memorial Fund, 22, 23, available at http://www .milbank.org/uploads/documents/0809MaternityCare/0809MaternityCare. html, accessed May 2, 2013.

12. Sakala and Corry, "Evidence-Based Maternity Care," 6.

13. Centers for Disease Control and Prevention, "Births: Final Data for 2010," 12.

14. Sakala and Corry, "Evidence-Based Maternity Care," 27.

15. Centers for Disease Control and Prevention, "Preterm Birth," available at http://www.cdc.gov/reproductivehealth/maternalinfanthealth/PretermBirth. htm, accessed February 23, 2013.

16. Joy V. Browne, "New Perspectives on Premature Infants and Their Parents," Zero to Three, November 2003, 8–9, available at http://www.zerotothree.org /child-development/health-nutrition/vol24-2a.pdf, accessed May 2, 2013.

17. "Caring for Your Premature Baby," FamilyDoctor.org, available at http:// familydoctor.org/familydoctor/en/pregnancy-newborns/caring-for-newborns/ infant-care/caring-for-your-premature-baby.printerview.all.html, accessed February 23, 2013.

18. Mia Zola and Laura Lindberg, "Unintended Pregnancy: Incidence and Outcomes Among Young Adult Unmarried Women in the United States, 2001 and 2008," Guttmacher Institute, August 2012.

19. Zola and Lindberg, "Unintended Pregnancy," table 1.

20. Centers for Disease Control and Prevention, "Births: Final Data for 2010," 10.

21. Zola and Lindberg, "Unintended Pregnancy," table 1.

22. Centers for Disease Control and Prevention, "Births: Final Data for 2010," 10.

23. Office of Minority Health, "Infant Mortality and African Americans," available at http://minorityhealth.hhs.gov/templates/content.aspx?ID=3021, accessed May 2, 2013.

24. Fleda Mask Jackson, Diane L. Rowley, and Tracy Curry Owens, "Contextualized Stress, Global Stress, and Depression in Well-Educated Pregnant, African-American Women," *Women's Health Issues* 22, no. 3 (2012): E334; "Depression during and after Pregnancy Fact Sheet," Womenshealth.gov, available at http://womenshealth.gov/publications/our-publications/fact-sheet/ depression-pregnancy.cfm#b, accessed May 2, 2013.

25. Jackson, Rowley, and Owens, "Contextualized Stress," E334.

26. Keith A. Frey et al., "The Clinical Content of Preconception Care: Preconception Care for Men," *American Journal of Obstetrics and Gynecology* 199, no. 6, Supplement B (December 2008): S389–S394.

27. Health Resources and Services Administration, "Women's Preventive Services: Required Health Plan Coverage Guidelines," available at http://www.hrsa .gov/womensguidelines/, accessed February 23, 1013.

28. Centers for Disease Control and Prevention, "STDs in Racial and Ethnic Minorities," available at http://www.cdc.gov/std/stats11/minorities.htm, accessed March 15, 2013.

29. "Facts on Sexually Transmitted Infections in the United States," Gutt-macher Institute, June 2009, available at http://www.guttmacher.org/pubs/FIB_STI _US.html, accessed May 2, 2013.

30. U.S. Department of Justice, "Extent, Nature, and Consequences of Intimate

Partner Violence: Findings from the National Violence Against Women Survey," 26, available at https://www.ncjrs.gov/pdffiles1/nij/181867.pdf, accessed January 30, 2013.

31. Zero to Three, "FAQ's on the Brain."

32. Barbara L. Philipp and Sheina Jean-Marie, "African American Women and Breastfeeding," Joint Center for Political and Economic Studies, Washington, D.C., 7, available at http://www.jointcenter.org/hpi/sites/all/files/IM -Breastfeeding.pdf, accessed May 2, 2013.

33. Philipp and Sheina Jean-Marie, "African American Women and Breastfeeding," 1–2.

34. Michael S. Kramer, M.D., Frances Aboud, et al. "Breastfeeding and Child Cognitive Development: New Evidence from a Large Randomized Trial," *Archives of General Psychiatry* 65, no. 5 (2008): 578.

35. National Center for Chronic Disease Prevention and Health Promotion, "Pediatric Nutrition Surveillance 2010 Report," Centers for Disease Control and Prevention, 4, available at http://www.cdc.gov/pednss/, accessed May 2, 2013.

36. "Racial and Ethnic Differences in Breastfeeding Initiation and Duration by State: National Immunization Survey, United States, 2004–2008," *Morbidity and Mortality Weekly Report,* March 26, 2010, available at http://www.cdc .gov/mmwr/preview/mmwrhtml/mm5911a2.htm, accessed January 29, 2013.

37. Health Resources and Services Administration, "Women's Preventive Services."

38. "Early Exposure to Toxic Substances Damages Brain Architecture," Working Paper no 4, National Scientific Council on the Developing Child, Harvard University.

39. "Lead: Pregnant Women," Centers for Disease Control and Prevention, available at http://www.cdc.gov/nceh/lead/tips/pregnant.htm, accessed May 2, 2013.

40. "Lead poisoning," MedlinePlus.com, available at http://www.nlm.nih.gov/ medlineplus/ency/article/002473.htm, accessed May 2, 2013.

41. National Institute of Environmental Health Sciences, "Lead Poisoning," available at http://kids.niehs.nih.gov/explore/pollute/lead.htm, accessed May 2, 2013.

42. "Lead poisoning," MedlinePlus.com.

43. Emily Willingham, "ADHD, Fish, and Mercury Exposure during Pregnancy— What's the Connection?" Forbes.com, October 8, 2012, available at http:// www.forbes.com/sites/emilywillingham/2012/10/08/mercury-pregnancy-fish -and-adhd/, accessed May 2, 2013.

44. U.S. Department of Agriculture, "Food Safety for Pregnant and Breastfeeding Women," available at http://www.choosemyplate.gov/pregnancybreastfeeding /eating-fish.html, accessed May 2, 2013.

45. Tara Parker-Pope, "Pesticide Exposure in Womb Affects I.Q.," *New York Times,* April 21, 2011, available at http://well.blogs.nytimes.com/2011/04/21/ pesticide-exposure-in-womb-affects-i-q/, accessed May 2, 2013.

46. Environmental Working Group, "EWG's 2013 Shopper's Guide to Pesticide in Produce," available at http://www.ewg.org/foodnews/summary/, accessed May 2, 2013.

47. Annie Murphy Paul, *Origins: How the Nine Months Before Birth Shape the Rest of Our Lives* (New York: Free Press, 2010), 93–100; Leah Zerbe, "Chemicals in Cosmetics, Other Products Affect Unborn Kids," Rodale.com, available at http://www.rodale.com/makeup-chemicals-and-pregnancy, accessed May 2, 2013.

48. "Early Exposure to Toxic Substances Damages Brain Architecture."

49. "Alcohol Use and Binge Drinking among Women of Childbearing Age: United States, 2006–2010," *Morbidity and Mortality Weekly Report,* July 20, 2012, available at http://www.cdc.gov/mmwr/preview/mmwrhtml/mm6128a4.htm#tab1, accessed May 2, 2013.

50. March of Dimes, "Alcohol during Pregnancy," available at http://www.marchofdimes.com/pregnancy/alcohol_indepth.html, accessed May 2, 2013.

51. Substance Abuse and Mental Health Services Administration, "New Report Shows More Than One in Five Pregnant White Women Smoke Cigarettes," May 10, 2012, available at http://www.samhsa.gov/newsroom/advisories/1205093619.aspx, accessed May 2, 2013.

52. Substance Abuse and Mental Health Services Administration, "New Report Shows"; P. M. Dietz et al., "Estimates of Nondisclosure of Cigarette Smoking among Pregnant and Nonpregnant Women of Reproductive Age in the United States," *American Journal of Epidemiology* 173, no. 3 (2011), available at http://aje.oxfordjournals.org/content/173/3/355, accessed May 2, 2013.

CHAPTER 2: BUILD YOUR SON'S BRAIN

1.   Richard E. Nisbett, *Intelligence and How to Get It: Why Schools and Cultures Count* (New York: Norton, 2010), 5.

2.   "What Parents Should Know from Brain Research," panel discussion, Achievement Gap Initiative, Harvard University, June 2011, available at http://www.agi.harvard.edu/video/listvideoall.php, accessed February 19, 2013.

3.   U.S. Census, "Child Poverty in the United States 2009 and 2010: Selected Race Groups and Hispanic Origin," available at http://www.census.gov/prod/2011pubs/acsbr10-05.pdf, accessed October 29, 2012.

4.   "Births to Unmarried Women," Child Trends Data Bank, available at http://www.childtrendsdatabank.org/?q=node/196, accessed February 19, 2013; "Children in Single-Parent Families by Race, 2011," Kids Count Data Center, Annie E. Casey Foundation, available at http://datacenter.kidscount.org/data/acrossstates/Rankings.aspx?ind=107, accessed January 1, 2012.

5.   Alicia Parlapiano, "Unmarried Households Are Increasingly the Norm . . . ," *New York Times,* July 14, 2012, available at http://www.nytimes.com/interactive/2012/07/15/us/unmarried-families-increasingly-the-norm.html?ref=us, accessed May 2, 2013.

6.   "Reading to Young Children," Child Trends Data Bank, available at http://www.childtrendsdatabank.org/?q=node/274, accessed May 2, 2013.

7.   "Family Structure," Child Trends Data Bank, available at http://www.childtrendsdatabank.org/?q=node/231, accessed February 19, 2013.

8.   Parlapiano, "Unmarried Households."

9.   "Family Structure," Child Trends Data Bank.

10. Oscar Barbarin III, "Opening Discussion: Condition of Young Black Boys in the United States," ETS's Addressing Achievement Gaps Symposium: A Strong Start: Positioning Young Black Boys for Educational Success, available at http://www.ets.org/s/sponsored_events/achievement_gap/flash/2011_conference/oscar_a_barbarin_iii.html, accessed February 23, 2013.

11. Robert A. Hummer and Erin R. Hamilton, "Race and Ethnicity in Fragile Families," *Fragile Families* 20, no. 2 (Fall 2010): 118.

12. Sara McLanahan and Audrey N. Beck, "Parental Relationships in Fragile Families," *Fragile Families* 20, no. 2 (Fall 2010).

13. Angela Dungee Greene et al., "Measuring Father Involvement In Young Children's Lives: Recommendations for a Fatherhood Module for the ECLS-B," prepared for the U.S. Department of Education, February 2001, 3–4.
14. McLanahan and Beck, "Parental Relationships," 27.
15. Greene et al., "Measuring Father Involvement," 18.
16. McLanahan and Beck, "Parental Relationships," 22.

CHAPTER 3: BE HIS FIRST TEACHER

1. Oscar Barbarin III, "Opening Discussion: Condition of Young Black Boys in the United States," ETS's Addressing Achievement Gaps Symposium: A Strong Start: Positioning Young Black Boys for Educational Success, available at http://www.ets.org/s/sponsored_events/achievement_gap/flash/2011_conference/oscar_a_barbarin_iii.html, accessed February 23, 2013.
2. "Birth Cohort (ECLS-B)," Institute of Education Sciences, National Center for Education Statistics, available at http://nces.ed.gov/ecls/birth.asp, accessed February 25, 2013.
3. "Fast Facts: Knowledge and Skills of Young Children," Institute of Education Sciences, National Center for Education Statistics, available at http://nces.ed.gov/fastfacts/display.asp?id=90, accessed February 25, 2013.
4. "Children's Reading, Language, Mathematics, Color Knowledge, and Fine Motor Skills at About 4 Years of Age, by Age of Child and Selected Characteristics: 2005–06," *Digest of Education Statistics*, available at http://nces.ed.gov/programs/digest/d11/tables/dt11_121.asp, accessed Feb-ruary 25, 2013.
5. "Fast Facts: Early Literacy Activities," Institute of Education Sciences, National Center for Education Statistics, available at http://nces.ed.gov/fastfacts/display.asp?id=56, accessed February 25, 2013.
6. "Reading to Young Children," Child Trends Data Bank, available at http://www.childtrendsdatabank.org/?q=node/274, accessed May 2, 2013.
7. David Grissmer et al., "Fine Motor Skills and Early Comprehension of the World: Two New School Readiness Indicators," *Developmental Psychology* 46, no. 5 (2010): 1008–1017.
8. Grissmer et al., "Fine Motor Skills."
9. Barbarin III, "Opening Discussion."
10. David Grissmer, "Rethinking the Importance of Early Developmental and Academic Skills in Predicting Achievement Gaps and Children's Outcomes," Achievement Gap Initiative, Harvard University, June 2011, available at http://www.agi.harvard.edu/video/listvideoall.php, accessed February 19, 2013.
11. "Reading Proficiency," Child Trends Databank, available at http://www.childtrendsdatabank.org/?q=node/258, accessed February 25, 2013.
12. Grissmer, "Rethinking the Importance."
13. "Parents' Reports of the School Readiness of Young Children from the National Household of Education Surveys Program of 2007: First Look," Institute of Education Sciences, National Center for Education Statistics, August 2008, table 2, p. 7.
14. "Parents' Reports of the School Readiness," table 3, p. 9.
15. "Parents' Reports of the School Readiness," 31. Low income was defined as a household income of less than $20,000 for a family of four.
16. "Parents' Reports of the School Readiness," table 2, p. 7.

17. "Parents' Reports of the School Readiness," table 5, p. 13.
18. "Parents' Reports of the School Readiness," table 6, p. 15.
19. "Parents' Reports of the School Readiness," 7.
20. "Parents' Reports of the School Readiness," table 1, p. 5.
21. Grissmer et al., "Fine Motor Skills."
22. Grissmer, "Rethinking the Importance."
23. Interview with David Grissmer, August 16, 2012.
24. John Ratey, "The Power of Play," Achievement Gap Initiative, Harvard University, June 2011, available at http://www.agi.harvard.edu/video/listvideoall.php, accessed February 19, 2013.
25. Ratey, "Power of Play."
26. Betty Hart and Todd R. Risley, "The Early Catastrophe: The 30 Million Word Gap by Age 3," *American Educator,* 2003, available at http://www.gsa.gov/graphics/pbs/The_Early_Catastrophe_30_Million_Word_Gap_by_Age_3.pdf, accessed February 19, 2013.
27. Elizabeth A. Gunderson and Susan C. Levine, "Some Types of Parent Number Talk Count More than Others: Relations between Parents' Input and Children's Cardinal-Number Knowledge," *Developmental Science* 14, no. 5 (2011): 1.
28. "Early Childhood Program Enrollment," Child Trends Data Bank, available at http://www.childtrendsdatabank.org/?q=node/280, accessed February 25, 2013.
29. "Early Childhood Program Enrollment."

CHAPTER 4: PUT HIS ARMOR ON

1. Duane E. Thomas et al., "Racial and Emotional Factors Predicting Teachers' Perceptions of Classroom Behavioral Maladjustment for Urban African American Male Youth," *Psychology in the Schools* 46, no. 2 (2009).
2. "AP Poll: U.S. Majority Have Prejudice Against Blacks," *USA Today,* October 27, 2012, available at http://www.usatoday.com/story/news/politics/2012/10/27/poll-black-prejudice-america/1662067/, accessed October 27, 2012.
3. Open Society Institute, "Portrayal and Perception: Two Audits of News Media Reporting on African American Men and Boys," November 1, 2011, available at http://www.opensocietyfoundations.org/reports/portrayal-and-perception-two-audits-news-media-reporting-african-american-men-and-boys, accessed May 2, 2013.
4. Interview with Howard Stevenson, September 26, 2012.
5. Enrique W. Neblett Jr. et al., " 'Say It Loud—I'm Black and I'm Proud': Parents' Messages About Race, Racial Discrimination, and Academic Achievement in African American Boys," *Journal of Negro Education* 78, no. 3 (2009): 247.
6. "Bullying," Child Trends Data Bank, available at http://www.childtrendsdatabank.org/?q=node/370, accessed February 25, 2013.
7. Thomas et al., "Racial and Emotional Factors Predicting Teachers' Perceptions of Classroom Behavioral Maladjustment for Urban African American Male Youth."
8. Ronald F. Ferguson, "Toward Excellence with Equity: Research on the Achievement Gap and Implications for Action," presentation, May, 1, 2009.

9. Roland G. Fryer, "Acting White: The Social Price Paid by the Best and Brightest Minority Students," Education Next, Winter 2006, 56–58, available at http://educationnext.org/actingwhite/, accessed May 2, 2013.
10. Fryer, "Acting White."
11. Fryer, "Acting White."
12. "Resilience in African American Children and Adolescents: A Vision for Optimal Development," Task Force on Resilience and Strength in Black Children and Adolescents, American Psychological Association, 2008, available at http://www.apa.org/pi/cyf/resilience.html, accessed February 26, 2013.

CHAPTER 5: HUG HIM AND TELL HIM
YOU LOVE HIM

1. Jelani Mandara and Carolyn B. Murray, "How African American Families Can Facilitate the Academic Achievement of Their Children: Implications for Family-Based Interventions," in *Strengthening the African American Educational Pipeline: Informing Research, Policy, and Practice*, ed. Jerlando F. L. Jackson (Albany: State University of New York Press, 2007).
2. Marvin Lynn et al., "Examining Teachers' Beliefs About African American Male Students in a Low-Performing High School in an African American School District," *Teachers College Record*, 2010.
3. FAQ from *Breaking Schools' Rules: A Statewide Study on How School Discipline Relates to Students' Success and Juvenile Justice Involvement,* Justice Center, Council of State Governments, available at http://justicecenter.csg.org/resources/juveniles#faq.
4. Jelani Mandara, "An Empirically Derived Parenting Typology" (under review).
5. Mandara and Murray, "How African American Families."
6. Jonathan Kozol, *The Shame of the Nation: The Restoration of Apartheid Schooling in America* (New York: Crown, 2005), 64–65.
7. Ronald Ferguson, Jelani Mandara, and Richard Murnane, "Does Parenting Contribute to Achievement Gaps?" WGBH Forum, 2006, available at www.wgbh.org/lectures/does-parenting-contribute-achievement-gaps.
8. "Does Parenting Contribute to Achievement Gaps?"
9. Mandara, "Empirically Derived Parenting Typology."
10. Mandara, "Empirically Derived Parenting Typology."
11. Mandara, "Empirically Derived Parenting Typology."
12. Interview with Ronald Ferguson, September 30, 2011.
13. Mandara, "Empirically Derived Parenting Typology."
14. Presentation delivered by Ronald Ferguson for Jelani Mandara, based on Jelani Mandara, "An Empirically Derived Parenting Typology," June 29, 2011.
15. "Does Parenting Contribute to Achievement Gaps?"
16. Mandara and Murray, "How African American Families," 154–55.
17. Ferguson presentation for Jelani Mandara.
18. Ferguson presentation for Jelani Mandara.
19. Notably, authoritarian parenting has been used more often to raise black boys than black girls, who have had more room to ask questions and challenge authority.

CHAPTER 6: YOU BROUGHT HIM INTO THIS WORLD, DON'T LET OTHER FOLKS TAKE HIM OUT

1. Karen N. Peart, *Pre-K Students Expelled at More than Three Times the Rate of K–12 Students,* Yale School of Medicine, May 17, 2005.
2. Oscar Barbarin III, "Opening Discussion: Condition of Young Black Boys in the United States," ETS's Addressing Achievement Gaps Symposium: A Strong Start: Positioning Young Black Boys for Educational Success, available at http://www.ets.org/s/sponsored_events/achievement_gap/flash/2011_conference /oscar_a_barbarin_iii.html, accessed February 23, 2013.
3. Walter S. Gilliam, "Prekindergarteners Left Behind: Expulsion Rates in State Prekindergarten Systems," available at http://www.hartfordinfo.org/issues/ wsd/education/NationalPreKExpulsionPaper.pdf, accessed May 2, 2013.
4. Tony Fabelo, "Breaking Schools' Rules: A Statewide Study on How School Discipline Relates to Students' Success and Juvenile Justice Involvement," ix– xiii, 40–45. Justice Center, The Council of State Governments and Public Policy Research Institute, available at http://justicecenter.csg.org/resources/ juveniles/report, accessed May 2, 2013.
5. American Psychological Association Zero Tolerance Task Force, "Are Zero Tolerance Policies Effective in the Schools? An Evidentiary Review and Recommendations," *American Psychologist* 63, no. 9 (2008): 853–62; Anne Gregory, Russell J. Skiba, and Pedro A. Noguera, "The Achievement Gap and the Discipline Gap: Two Sides of the Same Coin?" *Educational Researcher* 39, no. 1 (2010): 59–68.
6. Fabelo, "Breaking Schools' Rules," 45.
7. Fabelo, "Breaking Schools Rules," 41.
8. Fabelo, "Breaking Schools Rules," xi.
9. Fabelo, "Breaking Schools Rules," 68.
10. Daniel J. Losen and Jonathan Gillespie, "Opportunities Suspended: The Disparate Impact of Disciplinary Exclusion from School," Center for Civil Rights Remedies, Civil Rights Project, August 2012.
11. Schott Foundation for Public Education, *The Urgency of Now: The Schott 50 State Report on Public Education and Black Males,* 2012, 31.
12. Fabelo, "Breaking Schools' Rules," 66–68.
13. Daniel J. Losen and Russell Skiba, "Suspended Education: Urban Middle Schools in Crisis," 4–9.
14. Losen and Skiba, "Suspended Education," 10.
15. Losen and Skiba, "Suspended Education," 8.
16. Losen and Skiba, "Suspended Education." Quote accessed November 23, 2012 at http://civilrightsproject.ucla.edu/research/k-12-education/school-discipline/ suspended-education-urban-middle-schools-in-crisis.
17. Losen and Skiba, "Suspended Education," 9.
18. Losen and Skiba, "Suspended Education," 2.
19. Ivory A. Toldson and Chance W. Lewis, *Challenge the Status Quo: Academic Success among School-age African-American Males,* Black Male Achievement Research Collaborative, 31–32, available at http://www.cbcfinc.org/oUpload edFiles/CTSQ.pdf, accessed May 2, 2013.
20. American Psychological Association, "Is Corporal Punishment an Effective Means of Discipline?" June 26, 2002, available at http://www.apa.org/news/ press/releases/2002/06/spanking.aspx, accessed November 25, 2012.
21. "Attitudes Toward Spanking," Child Trends Data Bank, available at https://

docs.google.com/document/d/1TIjtyUpMP04aY8rjosRXVvBLq4fbfXR8Yi
_SqIebvMg/edit, accessed February 25, 2013.

22. Daphne S. Cain, "It's Not Just Black Parents," *New York Times*, August 14,
2011, available at http://www.nytimes.com/roomfordebate/2011/08/14/is
-spanking-a-black-and-white-issue/its-not-just-black-parents, accessed May 2,
2013.

23. "Attitudes Toward Spanking," Child Trends Data Bank.

24. American Psychological Association, "Is Corporal Punishment an Effective
Means of Discipline?"

25. Interview with Ronald Ferguson, September 30, 2011.

26. George W. Holden, "Perspectives on the Effects of Corporal Punishment:
Comment on Gershoff (2002)," *Psychological Bulletin* 128, no. 4 (2002): 590,
accessed November 25, 2012 at http://www.apa.org/pubs/journals/releases/
bul-1284590.pdf.

27. "What Is the Best Way to Discipline My Child?" HealthyChildren.org, available at http://www.healthychildren.org/English/family-life/family-dynamics/
communication-discipline/pages/Disciplining-Your-Child.aspx%, accessed
May 3, 2013.

28. "2006 Projected Values for the Nation," Civil Rights Data Collection, ED.gov,
available at http://ocrdata.ed.gov/StateNationalEstimations/projections_2006,
accessed March 7, 2013.

29. "The Use of Corporal Punishment against Specific Groups," chapter 8 of "A
Violent Education: Corporal Punishment in U.S. Public Schools," Human
Rights Watch, 2008, available at http://www.hrw.org/reports/2008/us0808/8
.htm, accessed March 7, 2013.

CHAPTER 7: PROTECT HIM FROM
TIME BANDITS

1. Ronald F. Ferguson, "What Doesn't Meet the Eye: Understanding and Ad-
dressing Racial Disparities in High-Achieving Suburban Schools," Wiener
Center for Social Policy, John F. Kennedy School of Government, Harvard
University, October 21, 2002.

2. Ferguson, "What Doesn't Meet the Eye."

3. Henry J. Kaiser Family Foundation, *Generation M2: Media in the Lives of 8-
to 18-Year-Olds*, 38, available at http://www.kff.org/entmedia/upload/8010
.pdf, accessed March 18, 2013.

4. Henry J. Kaiser Family Foundation, *Generation M2,* 38.

5. Henry J. Kaiser Family Foundation, *Generation M2,* 38.

6. Henry J. Kaiser Family Foundation, *Generation M2.*

7. "Reading to Young Children," Child Trends Data Bank, available at http://
www.childtrendsdatabank.org/?q=node/274, accessed May 2, 2013.

8. Henry J. Kaiser Family Foundation, *Generation M2,* 12.

9. Oscar Barbarin, Auspicious Starts presentation; Henry J. Kaiser Family Foundation, *Generation M2,* 12.

10. "The African-American Audience: Weekly TV Usage," available at http://
www.nielsenmedia.com/ethnicmeasure/african-american/AAweeklyusage.html,
accessed February 23, 2013.

11. Ferguson, "What Doesn't Meet the Eye."

12. Henry J. Kaiser Family Foundation, *Generation M2,* 32.

13. Karl L. Alexander et al., "Lasting Consequences of the Summer Learning Gap," *American Sociological Review* 72 (2007): 167–80.

CHAPTER 8: EDUCATION TO MATCH HIS NEEDS

1. Jawanza Kuwufu in a radio interview with Sandra Dungee Glenn on WURD-900 AM, October 12, 2012.
2. Dan Kindlon and Michael Thompson, *Raising Cain: Protecting the Emotional Life of Boys* (New York: Ballantine, 1999), 32.
3. "Characteristics of Full-Time Teachers," Institute of Education Sciences, National Center for Education Statistics, available at http://nces.ed.gov/programs/coe/indicator_tsp.asp, accessed December 17, 2012.
4. Ivory A. Toldson and Chance W. Lewis, *Challenge the Status Quo: Academic Success among School-age African-American Males*, Black Male Achievement Research Collaborative, TK, available at http://www.cbcfinc.org/oUploadedFiles/CTSQ.pdf, accessed May 2, 2013.
5. Jawanza Kunjufu, *Understanding Black Male Learning Styles* (African American Images, 2011), xi.
6. "School Health Policies and Programs Study: Physical Education," Centers for Disease Control and Prevention, 2006, at http://www.cdc.gov/healthyyouth/shpps/2006/factsheets/pdf/FS_PhysicalEducation_SHPPS2006.pdf, accessed February 23, 2013.
7. Marvin Lynn et al., "Examining Teachers' Beliefs About African American Male Students in a Low-Performing High School in an African American School District," *Teachers College Record*, 2010, 148.
8. Marvin Lynn et al., "Examining Teachers' Beliefs."
9. "An Empirically Derived Parenting Typology," Working Paper, Program in Human Development and Social Psychology, Northwestern University, 2010.
10. "What Are Learning Disabilities?" National Center for Learning Disabilities, available at http://www.ncld.org/types-learning-disabilities/what-is-ld/what-are-learning-disabilities, accessed May 3, 2013.
11. Interview with Charles Nelson, February 12, 2013.
12. "Learning Disabilities," Child Trends Data Bank, available at http://www.childtrendsdatabank.org/?q=node/255, accessed February 23, 2013.
13. http://parenting.kaboose.com/education-and-learning/learning-disabilities/dyslexia_defined.html; Attention Learning Center. Athletes with ADD or ASD at http://newswatch.nationalgeographic.com/2011/11/01/can-you-be-like-michael-jordan-the-gift-of-the-adhd-phenomenon/ http://www.attentionlearningcenter.com/add-athletes-autism.htm, accessed February 25, 2013; http://www.stutteringhelp.org/tiger-woods-wins-golf-and-stuttering.
14. Toldson and Lewis, *Challenge the Status Quo*, 38.
15. Campaign for Black Men and Boys, "We Dream a World: The 2025 Vision for Black Men and Boys," 9, available at http://www.clasp.org/admin/site/documents/files/2025BMBfulldoc.pdf, accessed May 3, 2013.
16. Michael Holzman, "A Rotting Apple: Educational Redlining in New York City," Schott Foundation for Public Education, 3, available at http://schottfoundation.org/drupal/docs/redlining-full-report.pdf, accessed May 3, 2013.
17. Holzman, "Rotting Apple," 22.
18. Toldson and Lewis, *Challenge the Status Quo*.
19. Toldson and Lewis, *Challenge the Status Quo*, p. 12.
20. Campaign for Black Men and Boys, "We Dream a World," 46.

CHAPTER 9: WORKING HARD WILL MAKE HIM SMARTER

1. Interview with Claude Steele, "Secrets of the SAT," *Frontline,* PBS, at http://www.pbs.org/wgbh/pages/frontline/shows/sats/interviews/steele.html, accessed February 24, 2013.
2. Interview with Claude Steele.
3. For research that discredits notions that intelligence is immutable and that blacks have inferior intelligence, see Richard E. Nisbett, *Intelligence and How to Get It: Why Schools and Cultures Count* (New York: Norton, 2010), chs. 3 and 6.
4. Interview with Claude Steele.
5. Claude Steele, *Whistling Vivaldi: How Stereotypes Affect Us and What We Can Do* (New York: Norton, 2010), 10–11.
6. Steele, *Whistling Vivaldi,* 91–92.
7. Steele, *Whistling Vivaldi,* 91.
8. Kay Deaux, Nida Bikman, et. al. "Becoming American: Stereotype Threat Effects in Afro-Caribbean Immigrant Groups," Social Psychology Quarterly, December 2007, vol. 70, no. 4, pp. 384-404.
9. "High School Longitudinal Study of 2009 (HSLS:09)," Institute of Education Sciences, National Center for Education Statistics, table 2.
10. Carol S. Dweck, "The Secret to Raising Smart Kids," *Scientific American Mind,* Dec. 2007/Jan. 2008, 36.
11. Dweck, "Secret to Raising Smart Kids," 41.

CHAPTER 10: MAKE YOUR PRESENCE FELT
IN HIS SCHOOL

1. Paul E. Barton and Richard J. Coley, "Parsing the Achievement Gap II," Policy Information Report, Educational Testing Service, April 2009, 18–19.
2. Barton and Coley, "Parsing the Achievement Gap II," 18–19.
3. Ivory A. Toldson and Chance W. Lewis, *Challenge the Status Quo: Academic Success among School-age African-American Males,* Black Male Achievement Research Collaborative, 10, available at http://www.cbcfinc.org/oUploaded-Files/CTSQ.pdf, accessed May 2, 2013.
4. Barton and Coley, "Parsing the Achievement Gap II," 18–19.
5. Kathleen Herrold and Kevin O'Donnell, "Parent and Family Involvement in Education, 2006–07 School Year, From the National Household Education Surveys Program of 2007," Institute of Education Sciences, National Center for Education Statistics, available at http://nces.ed.gov/pubs2008/2008050.pdf, accessed March 27, 2013.
6. Laura Horn, Anne-Marie Nuñez, and Larry Bobbitt, "Mapping the Road to College: First Generation Students' Math Track, Planning Strategies, and Context of Support," National Center for Education Statistics, March 2000.
7. Toldson and Lewis, *Challenge the Status Quo,* 7.
8. Madison Gray, "Social Media: The Muscle Behind the Trayvon Martin Movement," March 26, 2012, available at http://newsfeed.time.com/2012/03/26/social-media-the-muscle-behind-the-trayvon-martin-movement/, accessed March 25, 2013.

INDEX

what educators can do, 186
what parents can do, 176–78, 186
what policymakers should do, 187
what the Village can do, 186
Downer, Goulda, 21, 24, 26, 27, 28, 33
drug use (substance abuse), 33–34, 109, 136
parenting style and, 147, 151
strict-authoritative parenting style and, 156–57
Dweck, Carol S., 255–56, 258

Early Childhood Longitudinal Study, Birth Cohort (ECLSB), 60–61
early learning at home, 57–86
activities to foster general knowledge, 72
caregivers and, 85
developing literacy skills, 70–71
early comprehension and, 61, 68, 69
executive function, 74–75
father's role in, 66
fine motor skills, 73–74
number-related interactions, 79–81
parents' education level and, 63–64
parents' role as teacher, guidelines, 84–85
play and, 69, 75–76
precognitive skills and, 69–70, 74
promises to make your son, 59, 86
setting the pattern and tone, 66–68
socioeconomic status and, 63
statistics for, 60–62
Early Steps, xvi
Educational-Industrial Complex, xxi
Educational Testing Service (ETS), xxix
conference on black males (2010), xxviii, xxxiv, 6
demographic information on SATs and, 251
"A Strong Start" conference (2011), 39
Edwards, Willarda V., 22
elementary school
black boys' achievement gap and, 62
bullying in, 104
college-bound curriculum, 288
counteracting "not smart" message, 102
reading scores and, 104
what to say about race and when, 102–4
emotional development, 63, 69
authoritarian parenting and problems with, 138–39

authoritative parenting and, 150, 152, 158
single mothers and, 145–46
talking about race and, 99–100
encouragement, 78–79, 152, 191
Enon Tabernacle Baptist Church, Philadelphia, 53, 119, 144, 180
Erikson Institute, xxxii
executive function, 44–47, 61, 63, 69
activities to foster, 74–75
Extended Family Network, 279

family meals, 203–4
fathers
boys testing of, 185
early learning, role in, 66
health of, 14
health of sperm and baby's health, 21, 24–25
hugging of children by, 131
importance of presence in son's life, 51–54
lifestyle choices of, 20–21, 24
nonresident, degree of involvement in child's life and, 52
parenting skills and, 20
preconception health care, 21–22
preconception planning and, 20–22
prenatal role of, 18–19
relationship with son's mother, quality of, 53–54
reproductive life plan and, 23
risks of noninvolvement in son's life, 143
school involvement and, 286, 295
serve-and-return approach to parenting, 42
three roles of, 53
"tough love" approach by, 148
Ferguson, Ronald, xxiii
on achievement gap, xxvii, 6, 199
on black parenting, 132, 139, 140, 148, 152, 181, 185
on children's media consumption, 201, 202, 203
on developmental differences, 6
on expectations of black boys, 228
on homework and studying, 199, 200
on learning disabilities, 233
research on "acting white," 112
on teachers, most effective, 227–28
fine motor skills, 60, 61, 69, 73–74, 220
Freeman, Pamela, 17

ABOUT THE AUTHORS

JOE BREWSTER, M.D., is a Harvard- and Stanford-trained social psychiatrist and the director of numerous award-winning narrative and documentary films. His first full-length narrative film, *The Keeper,* written during his tenure as prison psychiatrist at the Brooklyn House of Detention, was featured at the Sundance and Toronto film festivals and earned him a Paul Robeson Award from the Actors Equity Association, a Best Feature Film Prize from the Black Filmmaker's Hall of Fame, and a nomination at the Independent Spirit Awards for film in 1997. He is the co-director of *American Promise,* the winner of the Special Jury Prize for Excellence in Documentary Filmmaking at the Sundance Film Festival and the Grand Jury Prize at the Full Frame Documentary Film Festival. His clinical work as a psychiatrist has included treating numerous black boys, both within and outside of institutional settings. He lives in Brooklyn, New York, with his wife and family.

MICHÈLE STEPHENSON is the co-director and co-producer of *American Promise.* For more than fifteen years, the Haitian-Panamanian has used her international background and experience as a human rights attorney to document social justice stories about communities of color and produce visual stories in a variety of media. She has also structured human rights campaigns and trained people from across the globe in video Internet advocacy. Stephenson's work has appeared on PBS, Showtime, MTV, and on other broadcast, cable, and digital outlets. She and her work have received international honors, including the Grand Jury Prize for Best Documentary at the American Black Film Festival and the Henry Hampton Award for Excellence in Film and Digital Media. She is a graduate of Columbia Law School and McGill University.

HILARY BEARD is an award-winning writer, editor, and book collaborator. She is the co-author of three *New York Times* bestsellers: *21 Pounds in 21 Days: The Martha's Vineyard Diet Detox*, with Roni DeLuz and James Hester; *Friends: A Love Story*, with Angela Bassett and Courtney B. Vance; and *Venus and Serena Serving from the Hip*, with tennis's Williams sisters. She won an NAACP Image Award for *Health First: The Black Woman's Wellness Guide*. And *Success Never Smelled So Sweet: How I Followed My Nose and Found My Passion* with Lisa Price, founder of Carol's Daughter, has revived many readers' spirits. A native of Cleveland, Ohio, Hilary lives in Philadelphia, where she is active in her community. She is a graduate of Princeton University.

To learn more about promises kept, watch *American Promise*, premiering on *POV*, the Emmy Award–winning PBS series, on Monday, February 3, 2014. Created and directed by Joe Brewster and Michèle Stephenson. Visit www.pbs.org/pov/americanpromise for local broadcast dates and screenings near you or to purchase the film.

To purchase an Educational Edition of *American Promise* or to host a screening, visit www.rocoeducational.com.